Toward Useful Program

Evaluation in College

Foreign Language Education

**NFLRC Monographs** is a refereed series sponsored by the National Foreign Language Resource Center at the University of Hawai'i under the supervision of the series editor, Richard Schmidt. NFLRC Monographs present the findings of recent work in applied linguistics that is of relevance to language teaching and learning, with a focus on the less commonly-taught languages of Asia and the Pacific.

Second language teaching and learning in the Net Generation
  Raquel Oxford & Jeffrey Oxford (Editors), 2009
  ISBN 978-0-9800459-2-5

Case studies in foreign language placement: Practices and possibilities
  Thom Hudson & Martyn Clark (Editors), 2008
  ISBN 978-0-9800459-0-1

Chinese as a heritage language: Fostering rooted world citizenry
  Agnes Weiyun He & Yun Xiao (Editors), 2008
  ISBN 978-0-8248328-6-5

Perspectives on teaching connected speech to second language speakers
  James Dean Brown & Kimi Kondo-Brown (Editors), 2006
  ISBN 978-0-8248313-6-3

*ordering information at nflrc.hawaii.edu*

# Toward Useful Program Evaluation in College Foreign Language Education

*edited by*
JOHN M. NORRIS
JOHN McE. DAVIS
CASTLE SINICROPE
YUKIKO WATANABE

NATIONAL FOREIGN LANGUAGE RESOURCE CENTER
University of Hawai'i at Mānoa

(cc) 2009 John M. Norris

Some rights reserved. See: http://creativecommons.org/licenses/by-nc-nd/2.5/
Manufactured in the United States of America.

The contents of this publication were developed in part under a grant from the U.S. Department of Education (CFDA 84.229, P229A060002). However, the contents do not necessarily represent the policy of the Department of Education, and one should not assume endorsement by the Federal Government.

ISBN: 978–0–9800459–3–2
Library of Congress Control Number: 2009937981

∞ The paper used in this publication meets the minimum requirements of the American National Standard for Information Sciences–Permanence of Paper for Printed Library Materials.
ANSI Z39.48–1984

*cover photo by John M. Norris | book design by Deborah Masterson*

distributed by
National Foreign Language Resource Center
University of Hawai'i
1859 East-West Road #106
Honolulu HI 96822–2322
nflrc.hawaii.edu

# About the
# National Foreign Language Resource Center

THE NATIONAL FOREIGN LANGUAGE RESOURCE CENTER, located in the College of Languages, Linguistics, & Literature at the University of Hawai'i at Mānoa, has conducted research, developed materials, and trained language professionals since 1990 under a series of grants from the U.S. Department of Education (Language Resource Centers Program). A national advisory board sets the general direction of the resource center. With the goal of improving foreign language instruction in the United States, the center publishes research reports and teaching materials that focus primarily on the languages of Asia and the Pacific. The center also sponsors summer intensive teacher training institutes and other professional development opportunities. For additional information about center programs, contact us.

Richard Schmidt, Director
National Foreign Language Resource Center
University of Hawai'i at Mānoa
1859 East-West Road #106
Honolulu, HI 96822–2322

email: nflrc@hawaii.edu
website: nflrc.hawaii.edu

## NFLRC Advisory Board

Robert Bickner
*University of Wisconsin–Madison*

Mary Hammond
*East-West Center*

Frederick Jackson
*independent language education consultant*

Madeline Spring
*Arizona State University*

Elvira Swender
*American Council on the Teaching of Foreign Languagess*

# Contents

**Foreword: Introduction to the Volume**
    *John M. Norris* . . . . . . . . . . . . . . . . . . . . . . . . . . . . . . . . . . . . 1

1   **Identifying and Responding to Evaluation Needs in College Foreign Language Programs**
    *Yukiko Watanabe, John M. Norris, & Marta González-Lloret* . . . . 5

2   **The Role of Evaluation in Curriculum Development and Growth of the UNM Portuguese Program**
    *Margo Milleret & Agripino S. Silveira*. . . . . . . . . . . . . . . . . . . . . 57

3   **Coming to Our Senses: The Realities of Program Evaluation**
    *Frauke Loewensen & Rafael Gómez*. . . . . . . . . . . . . . . . . . . . . . 83

4   **Using Evaluation to Design Foreign Language Teacher Training in a Literature Program**
    *Alessandro Zannirato & Loreto Sánchez-Serrano* . . . . . . . . . . . . 97

5   **Developing and Implementing an Evaluation of the Foreign Language Requirement at Duke University**
    *Ingeborg C. Walther* . . . . . . . . . . . . . . . . . . . . . . . . . . . . . . . 117

6   **Improving Educational Effectiveness and Promoting Internal and External Information-Sharing Through Student Learning Outcomes Assessment**
    *Antonio Grau Sempere, M. Chris Mohn, & Roger Pieroni* . . . . . 139

7   **Study Abroad and Evaluation: Critical Changes to Enhance Linguistic and Cultural Growth**
    *Violeta Ramsay*. . . . . . . . . . . . . . . . . . . . . . . . . . . . . . . . . . . 163

8   **Curriculum, Learning, and the Identity of Majors: A Case Study of Program Outcomes Evaluation**
      *Peter C. Pfeiffer & Heidi Byrnes* .......................... 183

9   **College Foreign Language Program Evaluation: Current Practice, Future Directions**
      *John McE. Davis, Castle Sinicrope, & Yukiko Watanabe* ...... 209

**About the Contributors** ....................................... 227

*foreword*

## Introduction to the Volume

John M. Norris
*University of Hawai'i at Mānoa*

NFLRC
*monographs*

This volume represents in many ways the culmination of work begun in 2005 under the federally funded project "Identifying and responding to evaluation needs in college foreign language programs," for which I served as the principal investigator. The overarching goal of that project was, first, to illuminate the program evaluation needs of college foreign language (FL) educators in the U.S. and, second, to respond to those needs through the development of resources and strategies that might enhance program evaluation capacity and practices throughout the college FL community. The project, hosted at the University of Hawai'i and dubbed locally the Foreign Language Program Evaluation Project (FLPEP), proceeded through a variety of stages, from needs analysis, to resource development and dissemination, to the shepherding of evaluation case studies in a variety of FL program sites (for details, see the project web site at: http://www.nflrc.hawaii.edu/evaluation). The diverse chapters reported in this volume all represent outcomes of the FLPEP, in one way or another, and I believe they collectively express the kinds of impact that I had hoped the project would achieve.

In chapter one, two FLPEP staff members and I report on the findings from a multi-phase needs analysis, focusing on the impetuses, uses, methods, capacities, and resource demands that college FL educators across the U.S. expressed through our interview and survey research. This chapter set the stage both for ensuing FLPEP activities (including the development of numerous resources and their dissemination through the project web site and other venues) and for the approaches pursued in exemplary case studies of FL program evaluation that we collaborated on in institutions at diverse sites around the country.

The processes, findings, and uses of evaluation in those case studies are reported in chapters two through eight. In each chapter, local FL educators—the owners of evaluation—provide insights into the workings of evaluation within their particular institutional and programmatic circumstances. Each case reflects on unique impetuses for evaluation to ensue, followed by the carefully staged development of questions, methods, and analyses that stood a good chance of meeting the particular intended uses for evaluation by real intended users

Norris, J. M. (2009). Introduction to the volume. In J. M. Norris, J. McE. Davis, C. Sinicrope, & Y. Watanabe (Eds.), *Toward useful program evaluation in college foreign language education* (pp. 1–4). Honolulu: University of Hawai'i, National Foreign Language Resource Center.

in the FL program contexts. The types of evaluation reported here range from the highly formative to much more summative activities, but all of them reveal both (a) the use of evaluation in strategic ways to get important work done, and (b) the more transformative impact of evaluative thinking and action on the ways in which FL programs function. The projects also reflect evaluation that is focused on a variety of FL program elements, including student learning outcomes, student identity and perspectives, student needs, curricular and course effectiveness, the quality of teaching and materials, study abroad experiences, and language teacher development; in addition, these evaluations occurred in Chinese, French, German, Italian, Portuguese, and Spanish language programs.

In the final chapter, three language program evaluators, all of whom worked as FLPEP staff, offer their perspectives on important points to be learned by the FL community from the collected evaluation cases. Perhaps the key point they highlight is that useful evaluation can indeed happen in college FL programs, but also that it requires a very localized, proactive, and intentional effort if it is to lead to positive changes within this particular educational milieu. They also go on to articulate priorities for the future agenda of useful evaluation in FL education, stressing the need for professional development and the incorporation of evaluative thinking and action into the fundamental identities of FL educators. Their recommendations would be well attended to by the FL professional organizations, as we face increasing demands for accountability in conjunction with the generalized 'crisis' of FL education in the U.S. today. Indeed, one important insight that the work reported here reveals is that the value of FL teaching and learning may best be expressed and ensured through proactive program evaluation (rather than reactive stances that are all too common in the liberal arts, humanities, and higher education).

It should be clear that the extensive and intensive work reported in this volume would not have been possible without the very active participation of numerous individuals and organizations, and this fundamental importance of collaboration is also something that we have learned about the nature of useful evaluations themselves. Generous funding for the project was provided through an International Research and Studies Grant under the auspices of Title VI of the U.S. Department of Education, and the institutions hosting evaluation case studies all contributed financially to making those projects possible. The Association of Departments of Foreign Languages played a key role early in the FLPEP work, by hosting a variety of evaluation-related events at their annual summer seminars and by making available their mailing lists for survey purposes. The University of Hawai'i National Foreign Language Resource Center (NFLRC) has played an essential role as collaborator throughout the project, providing graduate assistants to work on the project, hosting the web site, disseminating project resources, and so on. Of particular importance, the NFLRC sponsored the 2007 Summer Institute on *Designing Useful Evaluation Practices in College Foreign Language Programs*, where most of the case studies reported here were initiated. Richard Schmidt (director), David Hiple (associate director), Jim Yoshioka (program coordinator), and Deborah Masterson (publications specialist) all have contributed in crucial ways throughout various portions of the FLPEP.

Staff of the FLPEP deserve special mention, as their unflagging (often extremely intensive) and always positive participation has provided the driving force behind many of the efforts reported here. John Davis, Marta González-Lloret, Hyeri Joo, Castle Sinicrope, and Yukiko Watanabe, all graduate students in the Department of Second Language Studies at the University of Hawai'i during their FLPEP tenure, have served as my key collaborators on all aspects of the FLPEP, and the resulting successes are a tribute to their hard work and creativity. Yukiko Watanabe in particular has been involved in the project from its inception, and she has made countless trips to engage in outreach activities, guide evaluation activities at case sites, and present on project findings; she also served as assistant director for the 2007 Summer Institute (where we were assisted by two other students, Dennis Koyama and Weiwei Yang); and she has invested many hours in analyzing and reporting data for some of the chapters reported in this volume. Three of these staff members also served as co-editors with me for this volume, and their work has made its completion possible.

Lastly, the case study contributors to this volume have accomplished something here that is unique and noteworthy within the college FL community. Not only have they successfully pursued multi-year evaluation projects that proved useful to their programs and institutions in a variety of ways, but they have also turned those experiences into cogent reflections on the benefits and challenges of engaging in program evaluation. Their chapters go a long way toward beginning to fill the gap in "concrete examples of evaluation" expressed by so many of our survey respondents during the needs analysis. Their diligence and thoughtfulness in doing so is to be applauded, and it is my sincere hope that college FL educators around the U.S., and elsewhere, will pay attention to what these educator-evaluators have to say.

In the end, this volume consolidates much of the learning that has occurred over the first stages of work in the FLPEP, and it is an important watershed moment in that project and in the FL program evaluation domain. At the same time, much work remains to be done if we hope to accomplish something of a culture shift within that domain, with evaluation taking up a valued role in FL courses, programs, and professional organizations. In the FLPEP, we will continue to work in this direction, and I invite others to join us in this critical endeavor.

John M. Norris
*Honolulu, September 7, 2009*

# Identifying and Responding to Evaluation Needs in College Foreign Language Programs

Yukiko Watanabe
John M. Norris
Marta González-Lloret
University of Hawai'i at Mānoa

*This chapter reports on the methods and findings of a research project that set out to identify the evaluation needs of foreign language (FL) programs and educators in U.S. colleges and universities. Given a variety of possible impetuses and requirements for evaluation in higher education, ranging from accreditation pressures to shifting notions of sound pedagogy, this project sought to illuminate the actual demands, methods, and uses for program evaluation in the contemporary college FL context. In addition, possible resources for capacity development were investigated in terms of their likelihood in helping college FL educators respond to actual evaluation needs. The project proceeded through multiple phases of inquiry, from open-ended interviews with FL educators to a large-scale web-based survey of college FL programs across the U.S. Though low response rates challenged the generalizability of findings, relatively clear patterns emerged in terms of current pressures and uses for evaluation, the methods deemed most effective, and the components of FL programs most in need of evaluative attention. Results also indicated clear priorities among resources that would help in building evaluation capacity. In conclusion, the paper highlights the ways in which findings from this project provided implications for developing and implementing subsequent strategies to enhance program evaluation capacity among U.S. college FL educators.*

## Introduction and background

Foreign language (FL) programs in U.S. colleges and universities are expected to meet critical national and societal demands for the development of citizens capable of using languages other than English for a range of professional, scholarly, cultural, and other valued purposes. A key component of the effectiveness and value of any educational program is the inclusion of on-going evaluation processes, which enable educators to understand, improve, and ensure the quality of a program's delivery as well as its outcomes (Patton, 1997, 2008). Indeed, in college FL settings, an increasing variety of demands for evaluation has emerged in recent years, while traditional impetuses for evaluation continue to persist. Educators must utilize evaluation for such well-known purposes as program review, faculty assessment and tenure/promotion decisions, and gate-keeping, advancement, and other student-related actions. In addition, a host of new demands for evaluation confront contemporary college FL educators (see overview in Norris, 2006). In higher education, regional accreditation processes now emphasize the role of evaluation within institutions, departments, and programs, calling in particular for the use of student learning outcomes assessment to improve and ensure the quality of instruction. Recent standards of practice from FL professional organizations, such as the American Council on the Teaching of Foreign Languages (ACTFL), and from education in general, such as the National Council on Accreditation of Teacher Education (NCATE), require the incorporation of evaluation methods and tools into teacher training, instructional practice, and program administration. Efforts by the federal government to encourage evidence-driven educational practices have led to an increased role for evaluation in providing trustworthy evidence, while a fundamental shift in perceptions about what constitutes quality education has highlighted the integral and balanced relationship between curriculum, instruction, assessment, and evaluation (Wiggins & McTighe, 2001).

Despite these developments, largely absent within college FL education has been any serious attention to the various roles for program evaluation and the ways in which evaluation might best be put into practice. Indeed, as reported in Norris (2008), very little published research or commentary over the past several decades has addressed the problems of evaluation specific to FL education, especially at the post-secondary level in the United States. Of course, language testing and evaluation experts have addressed similar issues in developing generic guides for assessment, program development, and evaluation (e.g., Brown, 1995; Kiely & Rea-Dickins, 2005; Lynch, 2003), but their models and examples of practice have emerged persistently in relation to *English*-language education or in FL settings outside of the U.S. (see, e.g., collected examples in Norris, 2009). Intermittently, U.S. FL educators have made lucid pleas for attention to distinct evaluation demands, such as Liskin-Gasparro (1995), who highlighted both program-external accountability purposes and program-internal improvement uses, or Phillips (2003), who echoed increasing demands on FL departments to meet accountability expectations through evaluation. However, such attention has been scarce, and fewer still are examples of evaluation practices that have been developed in articulation with an initial specification of the uses to which they will be put within actual college FL programs (though see Norris, 2008).

What is very much needed at this point is a clear understanding of the actual priorities for evaluation that face FL programs in the unique setting of U.S. higher education, as well as an indication of FL educators' capacities to respond through meaningful evaluation practices. As an initial effort in this direction, the Foreign Language Program Evaluation Project (FLPEP) was developed at the University of Hawai'i and funded through a U.S. Department of Education International Research Studies grant between 2005 and 2008 (see overview of the project in Figure 1). From the outset, rather than providing FL educators with generic guidelines for how to do evaluation, the project sought an in-depth understanding of the realities, settings, and constraints for evaluation in FL programs (Phase I: Needs Analysis). Based on these understandings, the project then proceeded to the development, and dissemination of a range of strategies, models, templates, and tools that were tailored to priority needs of real language programs (Phase II: Resource Development).

Along the way, the project also sought to investigate, revise, and improve capacity-building strategies and resources through case studies of their meaningfulness and usefulness in representative college FL programs (Phase III: Field Testing).

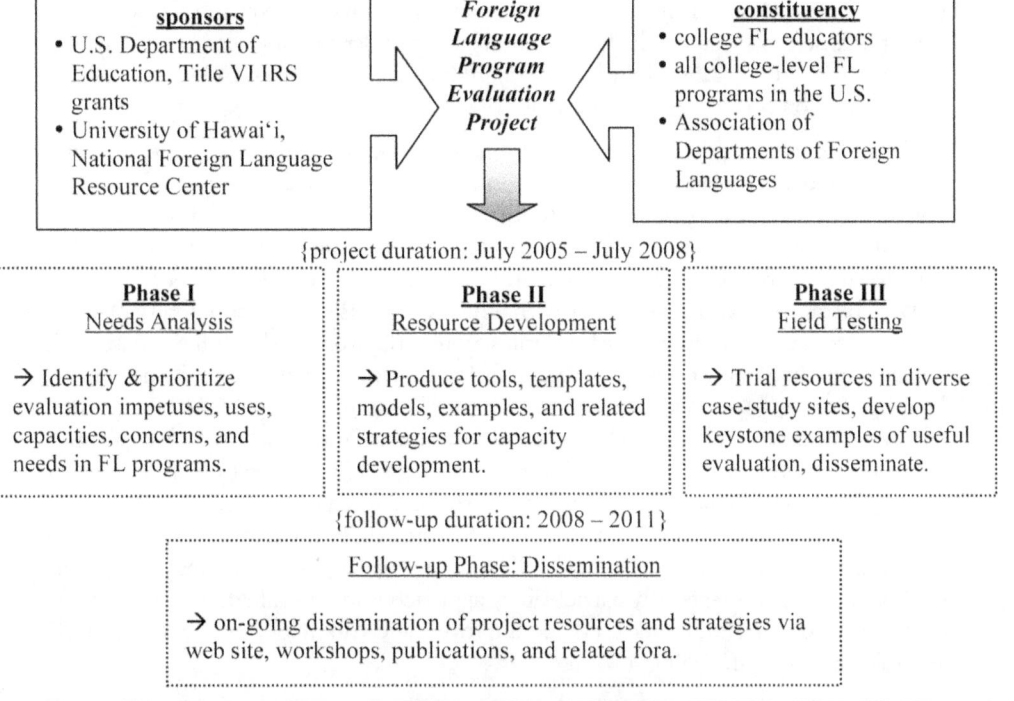

Figure 1: Overview of the foreign language program evaluation project

The present chapter reports on the first phase of the project, needs-analysis, which sought to develop an empirical understanding of: (a) driving forces and pressures for evaluation in U.S. college FL programs; (b) primary uses and methods of program evaluation; (c) current capacities of FL programs to develop and use evaluation models, instruments, and procedures; and (d) capacity development needs and evaluation concerns across different types of FL programs. As background to this needs analysis, we briefly summarize a few key developments in the field of language program evaluation, and we then introduce the basic analytic approach adopted in the study.

## Approaching language program evaluation

Language program evaluation, as a part of educational evaluation more broadly, developed over the second half of the 20th century into a substantial arena of educational research and practice, with professional organizations, disciplinary standards, venues for the exchange of scholarly debate, and so on. Early efforts at language program evaluation in North America were strongly influenced by behavioral psychology and associated experimental epistemologies, such as Tyler (1949), who explored the ways in which educational curricula could be 'validated' on the basis of large-scale quasi-experimentation across programs. Hence, early language program evaluations adopted a heavy focus on the collection of summative information (about learning achievements, usually demonstrated on standardized language proficiency tests) and experimental comparisons of language teaching methods (e.g., Genesee, 1985; Keating, 1963; Scherer & Wertheimer, 1964; Smith, 1970; Swain & Lapkin, 1982). The purpose of evaluation in these early approaches was primarily the building of theoretical understandings about 'good language curricula' rather than other possibilities, such as program improvement or teacher development. However, the reliance on large-scale experimental designs came under severe critique, especially in the watershed work of Beretta during the 1980s, primarily because of (a) the very real impracticality of carrying out a rigorous randomized control-trial design in educational settings, and (b) the fundamental lack of understanding about how or how well programs were functioning, and why that might be the case, when the sole focus was on experimental outcomes (e.g., Beretta, 1986, 1992b).

In the 1980s and early 1990s, language program evaluations began to undergo important changes, though they largely adopted a short-term approach wherein external experts reviewed programs and handed down funding decisions and/or recommendations about needed change on the basis of their expert opinions. Many evaluations were driven by the Overseas Development Association and the British Council (Beretta & Davies, 1985; Beretta, 1990; Coleman, 1992), with a heavy emphasis on accountability of English training programs in former British colonies around the world (Alderson & Scott, 1992). At the same time, some evaluators were realizing the importance of looking beyond language program outcomes or products, and they began to incorporate the collection of diverse kinds of evidence (including qualitative information, such as interviews and open-ended survey data, classroom observations, etc., see Lynch, 1996). Furthermore, some language program evaluators began to extend the lessons emerging out of mainstream educational and organizational evaluation by focusing on evaluation as part of language curriculum development (e.g., Brown, 1995) and by engaging in much longer-term, mutli-methodological, and especially participatory approaches to an evaluation practice that could help program staff understand and improve their work (e.g., Mackay, 1988; Mackay, Wellesley & Bazergan, 1995).

Along these lines, a major conceptual shift also began to emerge during the 1990s, with the rise of utilization-focused and other pragmatic approaches to mainstream program evaluation (Patton, 1978, 1997) beginning to influence a handful of language program evaluators. Thus, Beretta (1992a) outlined perhaps the key future direction for language program evaluation:

> [I]t will be established what *use* will be made of the findings as this will dictate the kinds of questions that are asked, the kinds of designs that are employed, and the kinds of data that are collected. Questions will be prioritized in terms of time, cost, how much will be learnt and how much leverage the findings will have on policy. (p. 20)

Similarly, Alderson (1992) noted that:

> [E]very effort must be expended to ensure that the evaluation that is planned is one that will be acted upon, that the findings reached will be used in the decision-making process. An evaluation that is not used is a waste of time and resources, and all involved in the planning have a responsibility to ensure 'utilization,' as the evaluation jargon calls it. (p. 290)

Over the interim to present day, then, language program evaluation has continued to develop in this pragmatic orientation (Kiely & Rea-Dickins, 2005; Norris, 2006, 2008, 2009), though it has on the whole struggled to find purchase as an undertaking in its own right, as something apart from theory-oriented research endeavors in second language acquisition, language education, or applied linguistics research. What has become apparent is that, in order for the ultimate uses or decisions that derive from evaluation to take the fore (rather than be left as an afterthought), something of a culture shift is required in how language educators understand evaluation. That is, evaluation that is intended to be useful—to play a highly informative role in the various decisions and actions that need to take place within language programs—must issue from a comprehensive initial understanding of what exactly those uses might be. Evaluation so understood is not, cannot be, a tool or test that is imposed from outside of the language education context nor one that is adopted from another language education context; on the contrary, evaluation methods must be designed with maximal articulation and 'situatedness' vis-à-vis the actual language educational milieu, and the specific programs and stakeholders within it. It is in response to this demand that the current project sought a broad-based understanding of the particular context of U.S. college FL education, through needs analysis, as a starting point for developing useful evaluation practices.

## Needs analysis

In order to acquire initial understandings about program evaluation in U.S. college FL education and to inform subsequent efforts at resource development and dissemination, needs analysis proceeded through multiple stages and on the basis of multiple methods and data sources. Needs analysis can take various forms (e.g., existing information, observation, interviews, meetings, focus groups, and questionnaires), and any one procedure has its strengths and weaknesses, leading to the premise that no one procedure is conclusive on its own. Open-ended methods (such as unstructured interviews) are useful to elicit important points and perspectives that the researcher may not have otherwise considered, while closed methods (e.g., structured interviews and questionnaires) will work well in obtaining overall patterns of perceptions or behaviors on pre-determined important points. Brown (2001) and Long (2005) have both emphasized the importance of tapping multiple sources of information through multiple methods, and they have also stressed the need to carefully sequence analytic activities, moving from existing information, to the collection of new knowledge through unstructured techniques, to ultimately testing the validity of patterns across relevant informants with more structured methods.

Following these recommendations, the current needs analysis began with open-ended focus groups and a short survey of FL educators, asking broad questions about evaluation within their programs. A focus group is a "carefully planned series of discussions designed to obtain perceptions on a defined area of interest in a permissive, non-threatening environment" (Krueger & Casey, 2000, p. 5). Focus groups are often used to identify and clarify needs and problems that people from different groups have experienced, seeking consensus as well as divergent opinions. The main purpose of the current focus group was to elicit ideas, views, experiences, and insights from FL educators in a public setting where their comments might encourage ideas from other participants. In addition to the focus group, an open-ended survey was administered to the focus group participants. The purpose of using the short survey in the present study was to provide the focus group attendees with an opportunity to express additional ideas individually that they did not offer in the focus group session, as well as to reiterate and expand on their opinions.

Based on the focus group and short survey findings, we then conducted structured interviews with program chairs and coordinators at several U.S. institutions. A structured interview approach allowed us to collect in-depth data on what seemed to be particularly salient program evaluation categories (as raised in the initial stage), by asking interviewees to elaborate and clarify exactly what they thought about a variety of topics. In turn, based on findings from the interviews, a nation-wide survey was designed to access the perspectives of individuals responsible for evaluation within post-secondary FL programs across the U.S. This structured survey provided a balanced approach to testing our hypotheses about the important themes characterizing FL program evaluation needs, through selected-response items, as well as gathering additional open-ended responses that would help clarify our understandings. Ultimately, we hoped that the combined use of four methods—focus group, short survey, structured interviews, and nation-wide survey—to gather information from informants in a wide variety of relevant FL programs would shed light on the following research questions:

RQ 1: What are the impetuses for program evaluation in the college FL educational context?

RQ 2: What program elements are often evaluated and what elements need more evaluative attention?

RQ 3: What are the common purposes and uses for conducting evaluation? Is there a gap between current evaluation uses and the ways it should be used?

RQ 4: What methodologies for evaluation do college FL educators use?

RQ 5: What are the current and necessary capacities to conduct evaluation in college FL programs?

RQ 6: What resources will help college FL educators to initiate, develop, implement, and use program evaluation?

RQ 7: What are the issues that hinder college FL educators to conduct program evaluation in their context?

For space considerations, the current report focuses on the interviews and the nation-wide survey. Findings from the focus groups and short survey are briefly summarized under the development of the interview study.

## Interview study

Conducted during late 2005 and early 2006, the purpose of the interview study was to gain an initial understanding of the range of practices, needs, and concerns of FL educators in evaluating their programs, and to provide an empirical basis for developing the subsequent large-scale survey of FL educators across U.S. institutions of higher education. We also sought insights into how FL educators talked about evaluation, such that we would be able to communicate with them on mutually comprehensible terms, both in the survey and in related dissemination activities.

## Method

### Participants

Twenty-one FL educators from Hawai'i and several mainland U.S. colleges were recruited via email invitation. Of the 21 participants, 13 were from four-year universities (seven department chairs, four language coordinators, one assessment specialist, and one former program chair), six were from language centers (five directors and one assistant director), one was from a community college, and another was from a two-year college (see Table 1). Note that no efforts were made to conduct representative or randomized sampling of participants, languages, or educational contexts for the interviews; the intent was simply to talk with enough informants in enough depth to acquire an initial understanding of major priorities related to the topic of FL program evaluation, as well as to acquaint ourselves with the related discourse. As such, and given clear patterns that emerged from the interview data, we felt confident that this pool of participants was sufficient for the immediate purposes. Of course, given the non-representative sampling approach, findings from these interviews should not be generalized to the broad domain of U.S. college foreign language programs.

Table 1: Background of interview participants

| ID | program setting | position | language |
|---|---|---|---|
| 1 | 4-year university | chair (department) | German |
| 2 | 4-year university | chair (division) | Spanish |
| 3 | 4-year university | chair (department) | multiple languages |
| 4 | 4-year university | chair (department) | multiple languages |
| 5 | 4-year university | chair (division) | Portuguese |
| 6 | 4-year university | chair | Hawaiian & Indo-Pacific languages |
| 7 | 4-year university | chair | multiple languages |
| 8 | 4-year university | former chair (division) | Spanish |
| 9 | 4-year university | language coordinator | Filipino |
| 10 | 4-year university | language coordinator | Ilokano |
| 11 | 4-year university | language coordinator | Indonesian |
| 12 | 4-year university | language coordinator | Thai |
| 13 | 4-year university | assessment specialist | Japanese |
| 14 | 2-year college | chair (across campuses) | multiple languages |
| 15 | community college | discipline coordinator | multiple languages |
| 16 | language center | director | Middle East languages |
| 17 | language center | director | multiple languages |
| 18 | language center | director | Japanese |
| 19 | language center | director | East Asian languages |
| 20 | language center | director | Chinese |
| 21 | language center | assistant director & president of a professional association | Chinese |

*Interview instrument*

As the starting point for generating meaningful interview questions, a focus group and short open-ended survey (see Appendices A and B) were conducted at a presentation session during the 2005 ACTFL Convention in Baltimore, MD. At this session, we asked audience members to tell us about their understandings of and concerns with program evaluation, both in small focus groups facilitated by colleagues (who took careful notes) and in follow-up written surveys. From the session participants, we learned first of all that they expressed a diversity of understandings about the meaning of terms like "evaluation," "program," and "assessment," and second that they ranged considerably in their perspectives on evaluation, often in conjunction with differences in experiences, program size, language, or institutional context. Accordingly, we decided that the interview should begin by soliciting a definition of evaluation from interviewees, followed by an interviewer-provided and commonly accepted definition of program evaluation, before commencing with thematic questions. In this manner, we would be able to extract a better idea of the ways in which FL educators understood and talked about evaluation, first, as well as then provide a common frame of reference for subsequent questions on the topic. We also decided to identify interviewees from broadly differing educational contexts and languages, such that we would achieve coverage of a relatively comprehensive set of perspectives on evaluation.

Findings from the focus group and short survey led to the development of a set of structured interview questions that elicited respondents' perceptions of: (a) what program evaluation is, (b) the characteristics of their language programs, (c) current and past program evaluation practices in their context (impetus, purpose, methods, and use), (d) the types of program evaluation that are particularly necessary, (e) current status and needs for capacity development to conduct program evaluation, and (f) issues and concerns regarding program evaluation (for the interview protocol, see Appendix C).

The order of questions was structured from general to specific. The first question, "How would you define the term program evaluation?" was prefaced with a warning that it would be a very abstract and general question. This question was asked first to gain a general idea of how respondents talked about program evaluation. The second question "Please describe the language program where you work, and your role within it" helped us identify the type of program and situate respondents in relation to their program. Before moving into more specific questions, interviewers then provided Patton's (1997) definition of program evaluation: "Program evaluation is the systematic collection of information about the activities, characteristics, and outcomes of programs to make judgments about the program, improve program effectiveness, and/or inform decisions about future programming" (p. 23). Following the definition, respondents were asked about the evaluation practices in their language programs. If respondents did not provide detailed information, interviewers prompted additional responses on the impetuses for program evaluation, personnel responsible for making evaluation happen, the purposes for evaluation, the methodologies used, and the utility of evaluation findings. Interviewers also asked if respondents recognized any types of evaluation that should occur but did not in their program. Shifting to capacity development, interviewers then asked about the program's preparedness to engage in evaluation and sought any suggestions for enhancing the same. Finally, to understand the problems/challenges FL educators face, respondents were asked to summarize their main concerns with evaluation.

The structured interview protocol was first piloted on three participants to test the clarity of questions and the extent of responses elicited, and to make any needed adjustments. Minor changes included increased situating, rephrasing, and expanding of the first question (about respondents' evaluation understandings) to elicit more specificity, and the decision to show a note card with the program evaluation definition for face-to-face interviews and the repetition of the definition for telephonic interviews.

### *Procedures*

Interviews were conducted in person or on the telephone by three staff of the FLPEP project, and they lasted between 30 and 45 minutes each. All respondents provided informed consent prior to the interviews. Interviews were audio-tape-recorded, using a handheld digital tape recorder placed between the participants or next to the speaker on a telephone with speaker functions. Data were transcribed and then analyzed by the three interviewers, with each interviewer coding all of the interviews for the same phenomena, such that inter-coder reliability of interpretations could be established. As described in detail below, the three coders sought to extract (a) the ways in which FL educator respondents talked about evaluation, and (b) major themes and qualities associated with FL program evaluation.

*Analysis*

To analyze interview data, we employed a meaning condensation approach, which is a way to systematically abridge interviewees' statements into briefer statements (the natural meaning units) and analyze the central themes that emerge from the data (Kvale, 1996). This kind of thematic analysis allows researchers to find patterns of information across qualitative (in this case interview) data. According to Boyatzis (1998), there are three ways to develop a thematic code: "theory driven, prior data or prior research driven, and inductive (i.e., from the raw data) or data driven" (p. 29). In the current study, a theory-driven approach was utilized, as we had identified nine major themes a priori when creating the interview questions on the basis of our initial background work (ACTFL focus groups, etc.).

The nine major themes were defined as: (a) FL program types, (b) program evaluation impetuses (i.e., causes or demands for evaluation), (c) purposes and uses of program evaluation, (d) current program evaluation foci, (e) methodologies utilized in program evaluation, (f) concerns and issues that surround program evaluation, (g) current operational capacities to conduct evaluation, (h) capacity development needs, and (i) priority evaluation needs. Following Boyatzis' (1998) "structure of useful meaning code" (p. 31), we labeled these themes as *program type, impetus, use, focus, methodology, concern, current capacity, capacity needs,* and *evaluation needs.* Through iterative trials in applying these codes to the transcribed data, the three interviewer-coders clarified the characteristics that constituted each of the themes, and then identified where the themes emerged in each of the interview transcripts (see Appendix D). Coding occurred individually at first, with each interviewer-coder working through each transcript to identify themes wherever they might occur in the data (as is common in interviews, respondents provided insights into a variety of themes throughout the process, not merely in response to a specific question), followed by group coding sessions where coding decisions were shared, discussed, and final values of statements adjudicated.

Average paired inter-coder agreement across all categories was 76%, and disagreements were resolved during group sessions. A final step in coding involved the attribution of a "value" to each of the identified themes within each transcript. Values are meaning labels that represented the particular perspective offered by an interviewee on a given theme (e.g., for the "program type" theme, one value might be "study abroad"). Raters individually attached values to each interview segment that represented a given theme, and later negotiated the final value labels. Sample value labels can be seen for each statement in Appendix D. Once values were finalized, the corpus of values was sorted to analyze the range of issues, concerns, and comments that emerged in each theme.

## Findings: Emerging evaluation themes

Interview findings revealed considerable demands for program evaluation, a wide range of practices being utilized, some existing capacity coupled with substantial constraints on getting evaluation done, a generalized desire to improve evaluation practices, and a variety of suggestions for resources that might help FL educators to conduct useful program evaluations. Findings for each of the nine thematic areas are summarized briefly below. It is also of interest to consider briefly the ways in which informants defined evaluation in response to the first question. Their definitions of program evaluation centered primarily on various foci under evaluation (i.e., what to target), such as curriculum, faculty (tenure and promotion), and program goals and outcomes. Only one interviewee mentioned the uses and purposes of doing program evaluation. This tendency suggests that evaluation is being understood mostly as a way of gathering information about program elements (mostly categorized under faculty teaching, research, and service), without the intended uses of information being considered in explicit ways or at least stipulated within an attempt to define evaluation.

### Program types

Foreign language programs were described according to several parameters by the interviewees. Across the respondents, major characteristics included: (a) institutional setting (public, private), (b) institutional size, (c) institutional type (graduate program, four-year program, two-year program, etc.), (d) language program locus (department, college, specific language section within a department), (e) language program composition (multiple languages, single language, language-family programs), and (f) sub-components of language programs (minor, major, general education requirement, study abroad, special programs). These characteristics helped us to identify the parameters for what might constitute a FL program as well as potentially important factors that mediate evaluation focus, practice, and use.

### Program evaluation impetuses

Interviewees clearly identified four driving forces for program evaluation: the community or public, program external demands, program internal demands, and professionalism. Some interviewees mentioned pressures to demonstrate the value of their programs to portions of the community or public who might have an interest in language courses, requirements, or degrees (parents, local employers, the media). Perhaps most frequently raised, top-down program external impetuses came from federal funding agencies, regional accreditation bodies, and the institutional administration (e.g., dean, provost). From within, impetuses to evaluate stemmed from the interests and/or needs of students, individual faculty members, and department chairs. Finally, several interviewees mentioned the growing expectation within the FL disciplines and professional organizations that evaluation be incorporated into the professional capacities and practices of FL educators.

### Evaluation focus

Interviewees highlighted the following main components or features of their programs that were (or should be) subject to evaluation: (a) program fit in the institution and community; (b) program mission/goals and values; (c) student learning progress and outcomes; (d) curricular articulation across courses and sequences in the program; (e) course syllabi, materials, and textbooks; (f) teaching, administration, and other aspects of job performance; (g) student needs and language learning backgrounds; and (h) specific programs, such as study abroad. Perhaps the most common comment here focused on "effectiveness" of educational efforts, which seemed to cover a general sense of how well all of the above features were contributing to overall program and student success.

### Evaluation use

Interviewees identified three major directions for the uses of program evaluation: internal uses, process uses, and external uses. Internal uses focused on the ways in which programs utilize evaluation findings to develop, articulate, adjust, and improve curriculum, instruction, and student learning; the heavy emphasis in comments here was on formative evaluation at the course or curriculum level. One unique application of evaluation was to use evidence from case studies on student learning during study abroad to motivate new groups of students who might be considering studying abroad. A second major type of use, based largely on positive experiences with program review and other kinds of evaluation, addressed the notion that going through program evaluation required participants to understand the program more profoundly and to appreciate the value of program evaluation itself (i.e., process use, see Patton, 1997). In a third type, evaluation findings were also utilized with audiences or stakeholders external to the program, primarily in the form of demonstrating program value to prospective students, parents, and job recruiters, or to program reviewers, university administrators, and regional accreditors.

*Evaluation methodology*
A variety of tools and procedures was identified for evaluation, including: observations (e.g., peer classroom observation), surveys (e.g., course evaluations, language learning experience surveys, alumni and exit surveys), interviews, faculty and staff planning or policy/practice meetings, assessments (e.g., in-house and standardized tests), classroom data (e.g., student journals, class performance), and document analysis (e.g., placement, enrollment, and GPA information). Primary methodologies in use (or desired) seemed to be program-external assessments and end-of-semester student surveys.

*Evaluation concerns*
Various concerns about program evaluation arose throughout the interviews, including program and institutional constraints (e.g., small scale program, low visibility, communication between programs, no comparable programs), limited resources and funding, difficulty in pursuing evaluation processes (e.g., lack of training, gap between internal needs and external demands), lack of adequate assessment tools, problematic methodologies (e.g., imposed reporting requirements that do not align with program realities), bad experiences with evaluation being misused, misunderstanding and negative perceptions of evaluation by faculty, and personnel constraints (e.g., no interest, no time). A main idea here was that the combination of misunderstandings about and misuses of evaluation led to a major challenge for transforming evaluation into something inherently valuable to FL programs.

*Current evaluation capacity*
A clear discrepancy emerged in the capacity theme, between programs that apparently had capacity in and related positive perceptions of program evaluation, and programs that did not have sufficient capacity and were struggling with evaluation. Perhaps the optimal combination of capacities involved both internal and external personnel and the possibility of seeking additional resources from the institution. Thus, some interviewees reported program-internal evaluation or assessment specialists among the faculty, often in the role of language curriculum coordinators. Others mentioned leadership by dedicated teachers and an active/supportive chair as key capacities for the possibility of a program evaluation culture. In some cases, evaluation guidance was available from people outside the program, such as an instructional or evaluation support center, institution-wide assessment office, or evaluation specialists from other programs on campus (e.g., colleges of education). However, typical responses in this theme either focused on a serious lack of capacity or on the presence of an individual within a program whose responsibility it was to understand and pursue evaluation.

*Capacity development needs*
In order to further develop the ability to engage in useful evaluations, a variety of possibilities emerged. In general, there was an apparent need for infrastructure development to engage in evaluation within programs, but on the basis of guidance and resources offered from outside experts. The need to develop capacity and transform evaluation into a useful endeavor was apparent, but the means for getting there were multi-faceted and disperse.
On the one hand, interviewees suggested awareness raising and training opportunities, for example, workshops at conferences, intensive training institutes, and courses on assessment and evaluation. Less directly tangible efforts were also mentioned, such as increasing

cooperation among faculty, enhancing inter-departmental communication, and motivating faculty and staff to participate. Establishing support centers, such as institution-wide evaluation or assessment offices, and a nation-wide evaluation resource center or federal evaluation support office, was mentioned as a way to create infrastructure for coordinating evaluation practices and providing expertise. Such resource centers were needed, according to interviewees, to disseminate good evaluation models, standards, examples, web-based resources, and what works reports.

On the other hand, a second major area for capacity development emerged from comments on needed student learning and/or proficiency assessment tools that would provide low cost and reliable means for measuring student learning progress and achievement. Similar requests were made for standardized approaches or instruments for assessing students' needs, their longitudinal development in attitudes and dispositions, and diverse features related to language learning (e.g., intercultural competence). In addition to these assessment tools, interviewees thought that interviews, surveys, and focus groups could be utilized to capture stakeholders' perceptions, attitudes, and needs of the program. Many respondents commented on practices that would be useful but were not yet in place in their programs, such as alumni surveys, exit data from completing students, course evaluation forms, student background surveys, and student satisfaction instruments.

### *Priority evaluation needs*

In terms of immediate priorities for program evaluation, interviewees commented on various aspects of their programs, for example, chair evaluation, faculty peer review, student course evaluation, student learning outcomes assessment, program goals setting, curricular articulation, internal standards setting, and even the need to evaluate existing mechanisms for evaluation itself. By and large, priorities mentioned in this theme reflected and reinforced those that had come up in other areas of the interviews.

In sum, these interview findings provided us with a broad basis for understanding aspects of evaluation that seemed to be on the minds of college FL educators. Based on the variety of themes that emerged from their responses, and the values that they attached to these themes, we were then able to develop a second data-gathering approach that would, hopefully, lead to broad-based findings from FL programs across the U.S. Using the discourse about evaluation provided by the FL interviewees also enabled us to communicate with other FL educators, through the survey and in other venues, in much more accurate ways about the realities and perceptions of program evaluation in foreign language programs.

## Survey study

Conducted during the summer and early fall of 2006, the purpose of the survey study was to solicit input on a variety of program evaluation issues from FL educators in tertiary programs across the U.S. In particular, we sought a broad foundation for understanding the kinds of evaluation demands, concerns, capacities, and needs within the diversity of programs that make up the post-secondary foreign language education landscape. These findings were to be used, in turn, to inform further efforts at resource development and dissemination in the service of FL program evaluation.

### Methods

#### *Participants*
Participant identification and recruitment for the survey involved two basic steps. Ultimately, our goal was to come as close as possible to contacting a single representative from each

tertiary FL program in the United States (as it turns out, not a particularly well-defined or accessible population for survey purposes). First, we were granted access to the 2005 membership data base of the Association of Departments of Foreign Languages (ADFL), and we adopted this list as the initial population frame for the survey. A total of 745 members of the ADFL, a professional organization which consists of active chairs, directors, supervisors, coordinators, and others involved in the administration of college FL programs across the U.S., were targeted for participation. Only current members were contacted, with the objective of maintaining a focus in the survey on evaluation issues of immediate priority. Thus, we sought input from those individuals most likely to be involved currently in any program evaluation activities, and we sought to limit input that might not be relevant to current priorities and circumstances. In addition, we targeted only a single respondent from each program context in order to avoid over-representation of any one program in the findings.

Second, in order to reach beyond the relatively self-selected sample of ADFL members—arguably something of a distinctive group who de facto engage quite actively with administrative and programmatic concerns—we identified 1312 additional chairs and directors[1] of all college foreign language programs in the U.S. who could be identified via an exhaustive manual search of public web sites. Any individuals duplicated from the ADFL list were eliminated. Of the 2057 total individuals from the final combined lists who received an invitation to participate, 279 had email addresses with permanent communication failures. For the remaining 1778, it was assumed that the invitation email was delivered successfully, though there was no way of confirming that fact.

An initial email invitation was sent to participants in early June 2006, and follow-up reminder emails were sent again in August and October 2006. Participants were asked in the e-mail to complete a survey about evaluation in their programs or to respond to the researchers with the name and contact information of another individual in the same program who took primary responsibility for evaluation (and these individuals were subsequently contacted with the survey invitation). Survey respondents clicked on a hyperlink in the email message to access the survey web site (hosted on SurveyMonkey, www.surveymonkey.com), and they read and completed an informed consent agreement page before proceeding to survey items. Of the total 1778, 409 individuals logged on to the survey web site, while 336 (19% return rate) entered and completed the survey. Response rates varied slightly from one section of the survey to the next, with 282 (16%) being the lowest number of responses for any one section. Though somewhat disappointing, such levels of response are not uncommon in large-scale survey research (see Brown, 2001), but any interpretations of findings must nevertheless be tempered with the cautionary note that there may well be other unidentified issues and perspectives in the large body of non-respondents.

### Survey instrument

Based on the evaluation themes that emerged from interviews of FL program informants, a survey instrument was developed. Figure 2 displays the eight sections of the survey. Initial questions clarified respondents' FL program contexts, in terms of institutional type and size, languages taught, program locus, and so on. Respondents were then presented with the Patton (1997) definition of program evaluation as used in the interview study, in order to ensure a common understanding of this key construct. The following seven survey sections covered evaluation impetuses, uses, focus, methods,

---

1   Language (section) coordinators were identified if a language program was housed in a non-independent department, such as a Humanities program or Liberal Arts program.

capacity, needed resources, and concerns (items are provided in detail in the results section and the full survey can be seen in Appendix E). The survey items, along with instructions for each section and item type, were posted on a web-based survey to facilitate collection and analysis. Respondents indicated their answers on likert scales, in drop-down menus, and in open-ended comments. The web-based survey was pilot tested with two foreign language program chairs at different institutions for accuracy, relevance, and clarity. We asked the pilot participants to think-aloud about the survey and ask questions at any time for clarification. At the same time, three experts on surveys and language education at the University of Hawai'i provided feedback on the items and survey format. As a result of this pilot-testing stage, the survey was shortened considerably, instructions were clarified, and items were restated to be maximally clear regarding what information was sought. After revisions, the final version of the survey required approximately 30 minutes to complete.

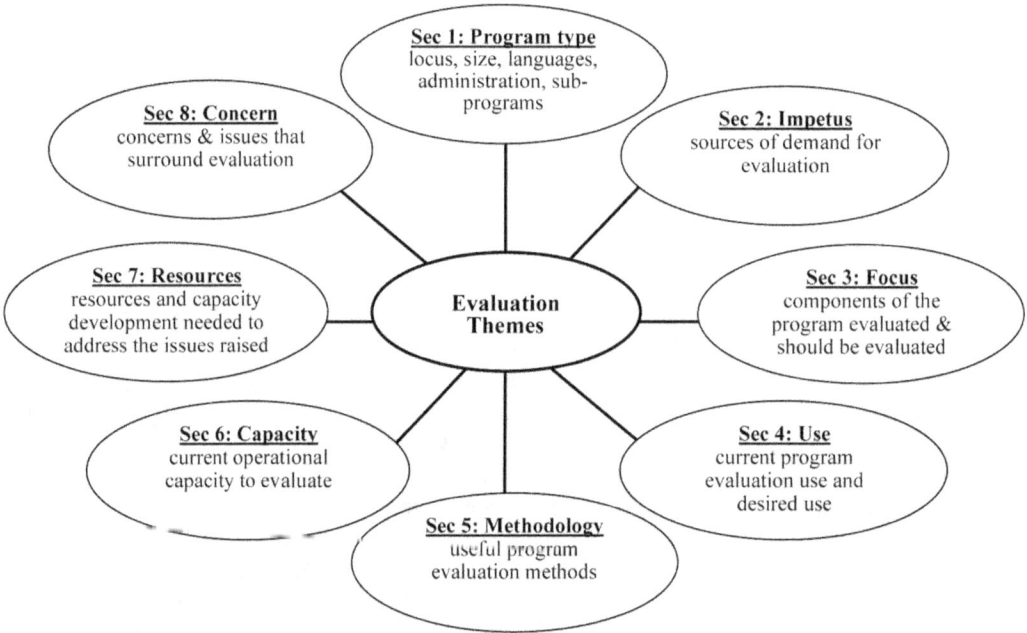

Figure 2: The eight evaluation themes motivating survey sections

*Analysis*

Responses on the four-point Likert-scales were converted to numerical values (not at all=1, a little=2, somewhat=3, a lot=4) for analytical purposes. The proportions of respondents for each scale point, as well as overall mean and standard deviation values were computed for each item, to determine consensus or discrepancy in opinions among respondents as well as to determine the degree of relevance/importance of the item in comparison with other items. For sections on evaluation focus and use, which asked respondents to compare current practices with desired/ideal practices, average differences were calculated for each item. Thus, the rating for current practice was subtracted from the rating for desired practice for each item, and values were then averaged across participants. This approach enabled the identification of conceptual categories for understanding respondents' perspectives on current versus targeted practices: less focus/use, no change, and more focus/use. Finally, open-ended comments were analyzed thematically for major themes and values, much as described in the interview study, and representative quotes were extracted as a way of capturing response patterns in the words of the respondents. Note that full descriptive statistics for responses on all survey items are provided in Appendix F.

## Findings

### Respondent and program profiles

The majority of survey respondents could be characterized as chairs or directors (66%) of a multi-language[2] department, offering undergraduate degrees (majors: 86%; minors: 82%), as well as study abroad programs (81%) and language requirement courses (78%) (see Figures 3–9). The respondents were equally from public or private institutions, though there was considerable variability in institutional size (1000–4999 students: 40%; over 20,000 students: 26%) and with an average per semester student enrollment in the program's language courses ranging from 10 to 6000 (M=670).

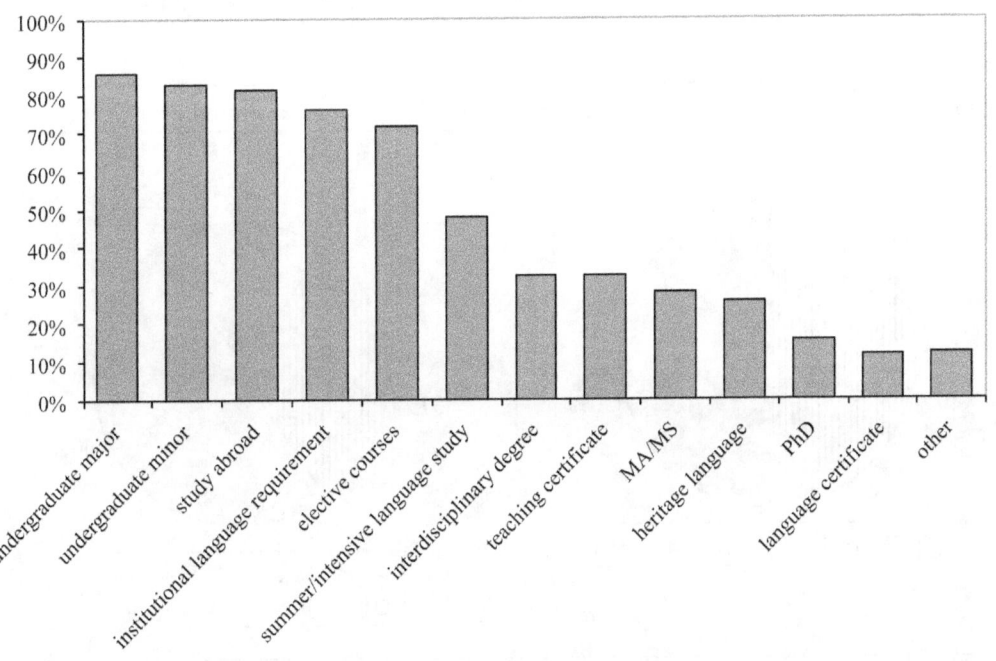

Figure 3: Degrees and other sub-components in respondents' foreign language programs

Respondents identified a total of 94 different languages on offer across the pool of FL programs. Of these, 39 languages were not offered in more than one program (i.e., these were unique language programs in the response pool). The top three most frequent languages offered by the respondents' programs were Spanish, French, and German (represented in 50%–70% of the respondents' programs), with the next most frequent languages being Chinese, Italian, and Japanese (all represented in 35% of the respondents' programs, see Figure 4).

---

2  Most respondents represented departments that ran more than one language program.

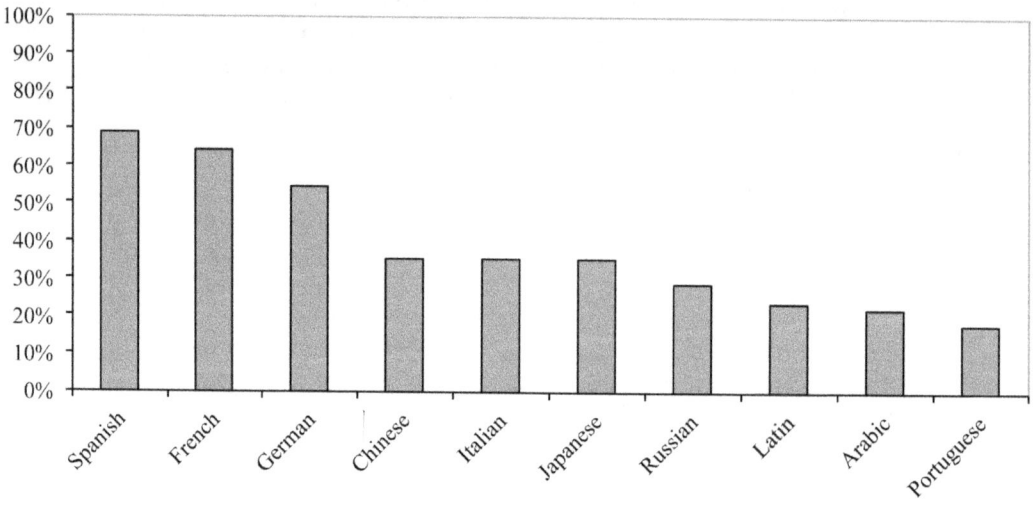

Figure 4: Ten highest frequency languages represented in respondents' programs

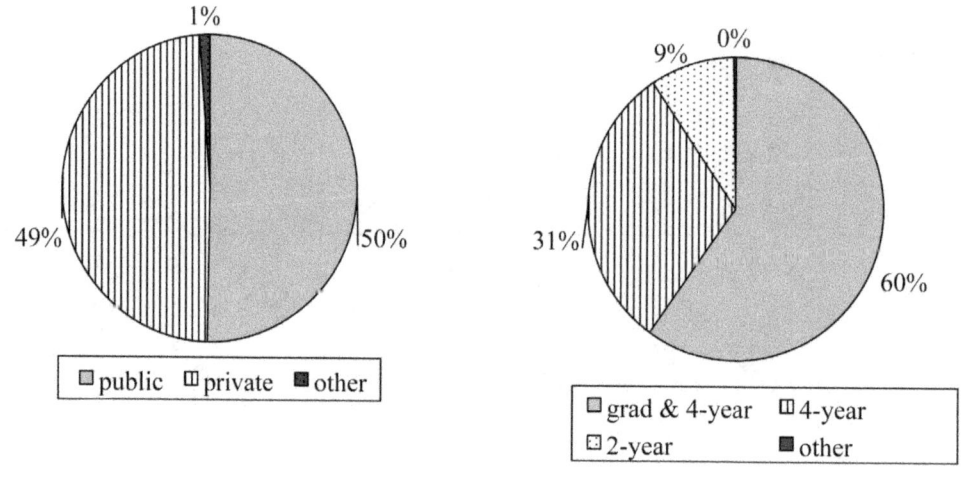

Figure 5: Institutional setting          Figure 6: Institutional type

*Impetuses for program evaluation*

In response to the question, "To what extent do you feel under pressure from the following sources to engage in program evaluation," two primary and distinct types of impetus to evaluate in college FL contexts were revealed: a top-down impetus and an internally-driven impetus. Figure 10 shows results of the 15 items on evaluation impetuses. Not surprisingly, respondents cited management-driven impetuses, such as university administration, accreditation pressures, and the dean of the college/school as primary pressures to engage in program evaluation. However, respondents also identified pressures from trends in the FL field and from the internal desires of program faculty as a whole to engage in program evaluation. By contrast, respondents rated pressures from other possible sources as quite minimal, including tenure and promotion, individual faculty, teacher accreditation, professional organizations, students, employers, external funders, student government, students' parents, and the broader community.

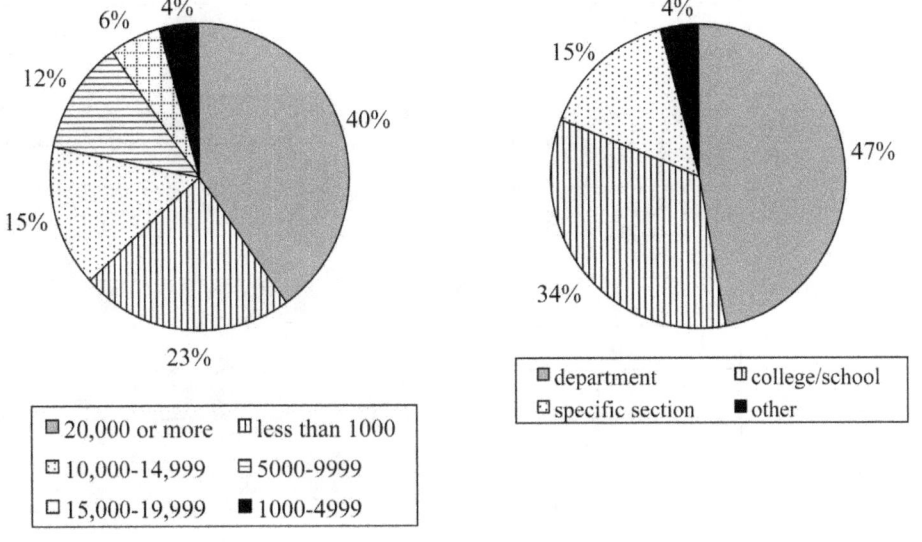

Figure 7: Institutional size

Figure 8: Language program locus

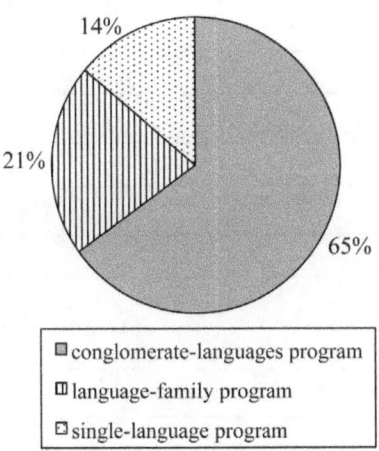

Figure 9: Language program composition

A total of 127 respondents provided open-ended comments regarding impetuses for evaluation. The most frequently cited pressures included the administration of the university requesting evaluation for self-study (e.g., program review) and for accreditation purposes ($N$=35; e.g., "As part of its re-accreditation, the university has required all undergraduate programs to create and implement outcomes-oriented assessment plans."). External pressures also derived from perceived trends in higher education ($N$=4) to conduct evaluation with a "focus on learning outcomes and student centered instruction." Respondents also clarified the nature of a more internally-driven motivation for evaluating FL programs. Nineteen respondents emphasized that educators hold individual and/or group professional ethics that include a responsibility towards students and society to evaluate their program (e.g., "We have a social and moral responsibility towards our students and towards society at large to

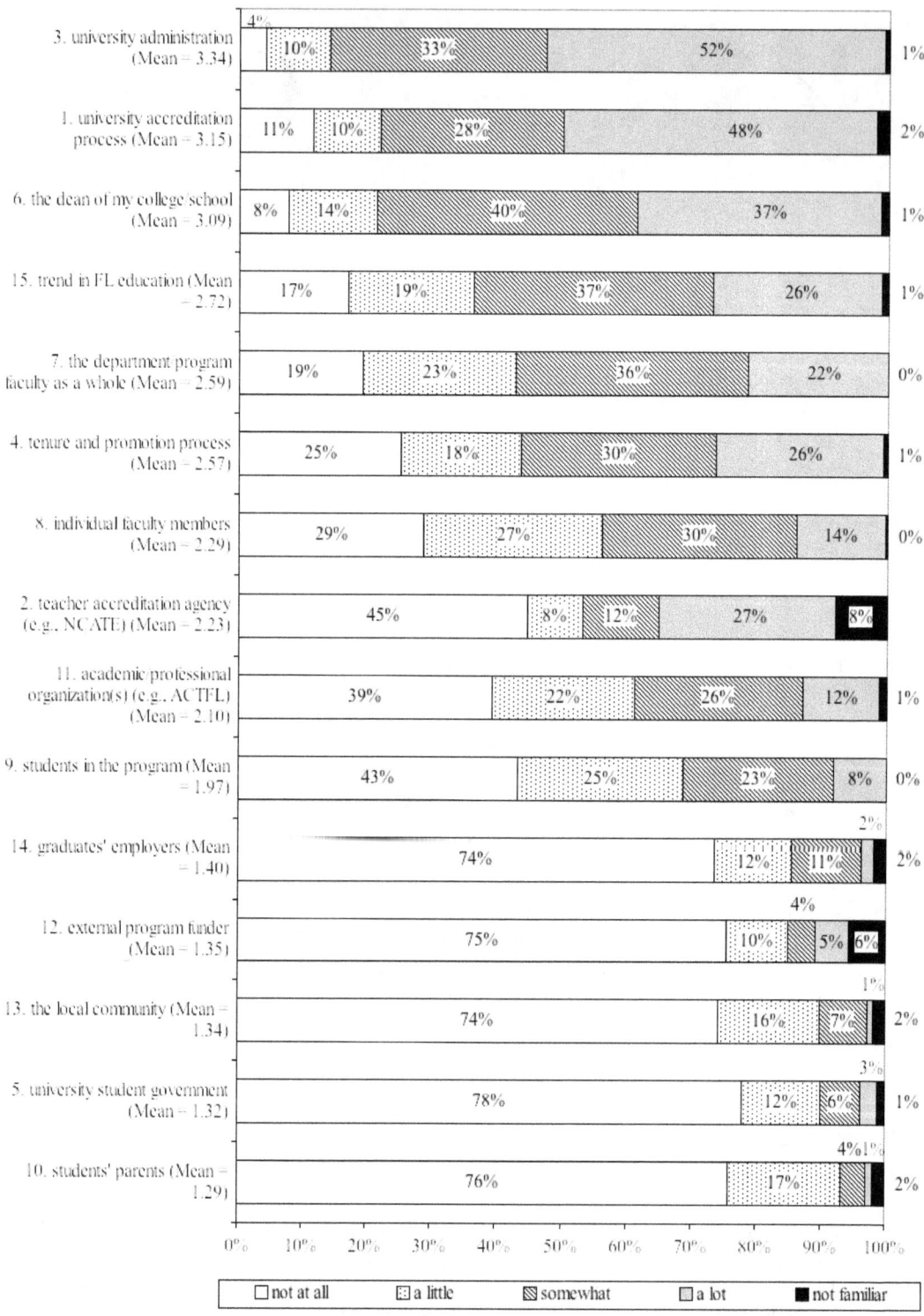

Figure 10: Impetuses for program evaluation

state as clearly as we can what it is that we do for them and why what we do is valuable."). Other program- or language-specific comments addressed particular pressures as well, such as four respondents who commented that changes in student enrollment (both sudden increases and decreases) prompted faculty to initiate evaluation activities. Several felt the need to conduct evaluation as a basis for hiring new faculty (*N*=5), competing with other programs (*N*=2), and communicating and defending the value of language education to colleagues at their institutions (*N*=2). Overall, 77% of the respondents felt at least some or a lot of pressure to engage in program evaluation (see Figure 11).

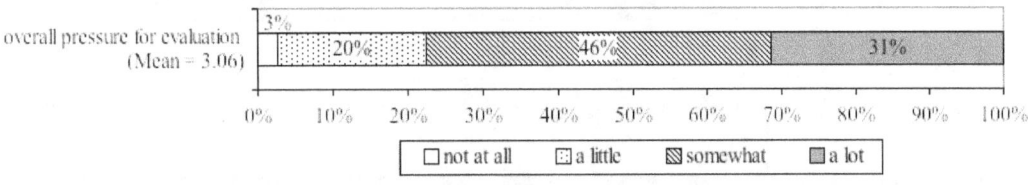

**Figure 11: Overall pressure for conducting program evaluation**

*Program elements under evaluation focus*

For this section of the survey, respondents provided two ratings comparing the extent to which elements of their programs were currently the focus of evaluation versus the extent to which the same elements should be the focus of evaluation. On average, across the ten program elements queried, ratings were higher in the "should be evaluated" than "currently evaluated" categories, indicating that respondents perceived the need for more evaluation to be happening for most aspects of their programs (see Figure 12 for a summary of elements needing less focus, no change, or more focus in evaluation). However, several program elements appeared to be more frequently the focus of evaluation in current practice, with less change required, including: *teaching, curriculum scope and sequence, mission and goals, assessment/testing of students,* and *student learning outcomes* (all had a mean of over 3.00 on the four-point scale for current focus). The three program elements respondents found most in need of more evaluation focus were *teacher development, changes in students' attitudes,* and *learning needs of students*. Note that there was very little in the way of "less focus" called for by respondents for any of the program elements, while even for those items that seemed to have substantial current evaluation going on, a large proportion of respondents suggested that even more focus should be applied.

In addition to the elements listed by the researchers, respondents articulated the following features as currently being evaluated or in need of evaluation in their programs: (a) study abroad (*N*=14; "Overseas programs, their quality, their coordination with the on-campus program."); (b) roles and values of the program in the institution (*N*=10; "The program's role in liberal arts education, which is not quite the same as our mission/goals because it comes from outside the department."); (c) faculty scholarly research for tenure and promotion purposes (*N*=7); (d) technology use in instruction (*N*=5); (d) intra-departmental curricular articulation (*N*=4; "I plan to begin discussion of articulation between levels, especially as it relates to instructional material selection."); (e) inter-departmental program coordination (*N*=4; "department's relationship with other departments on campus"); (f) staffing (*N*=4); (g) learners' cultural learning outcomes and experiences (*N*=2); and (h) learners' post-graduation employment and success (*N*=2).

In rating the degree to which the program as a whole is currently or should be evaluated, 41% of the respondents rated that their programs should be evaluated more than is currently the case. Only 5% of the respondents perceived that programs should be evaluated less (see Figure 13).

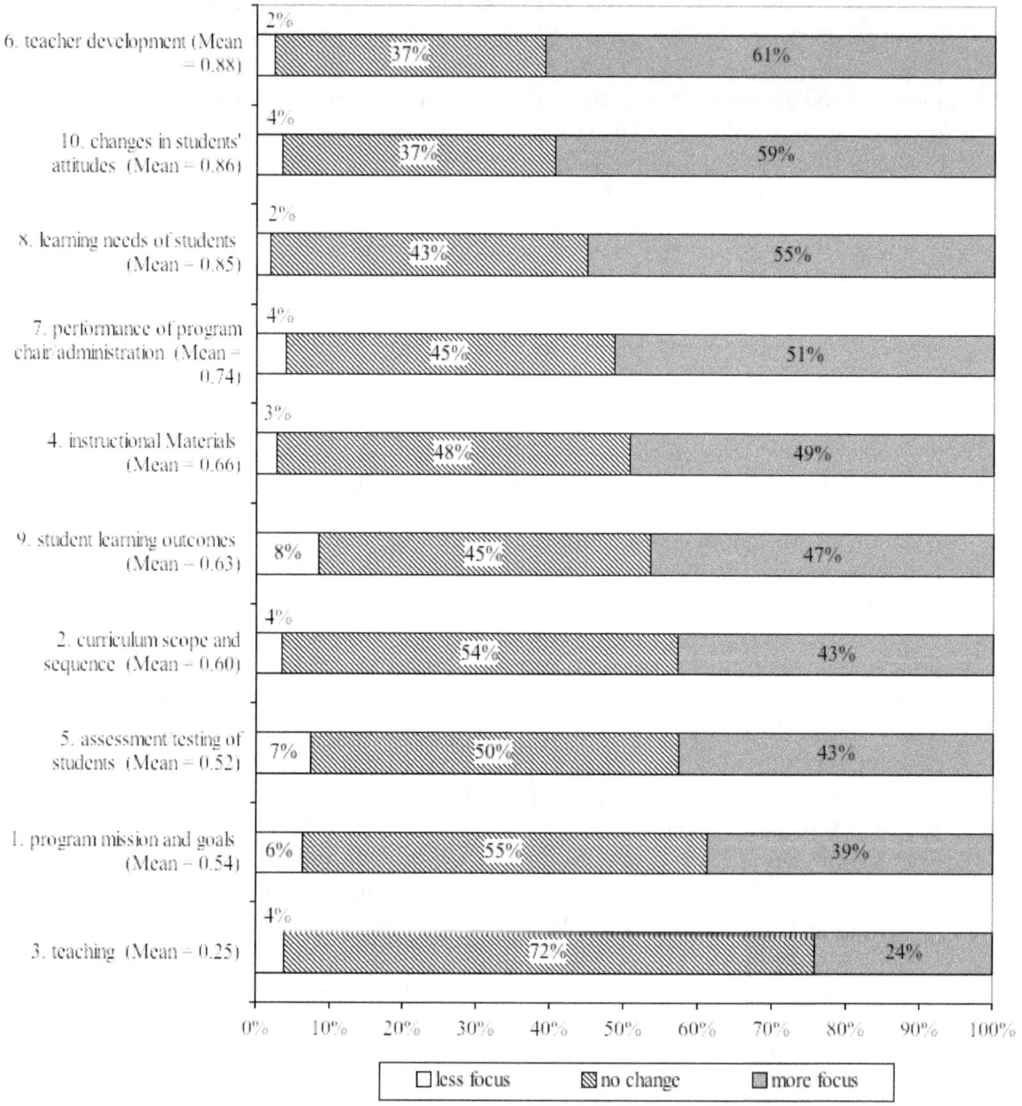

Figure 12: Current versus desired amount of evaluation focus on program elements

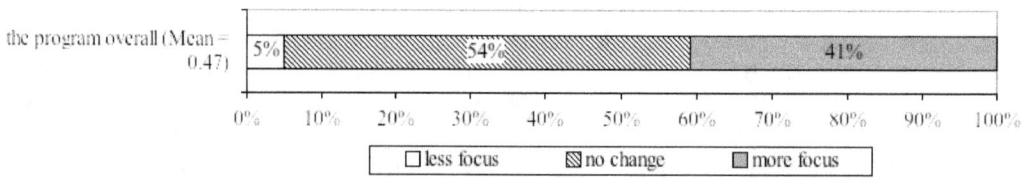

Figure 13: Current versus desired amount of focus on the program overall

## Purposes and uses for program evaluation

In this section, respondents rated the degree of current versus desired levels of evaluation activity associated with a variety of purposes and uses for evaluation (see Figure 14). Though

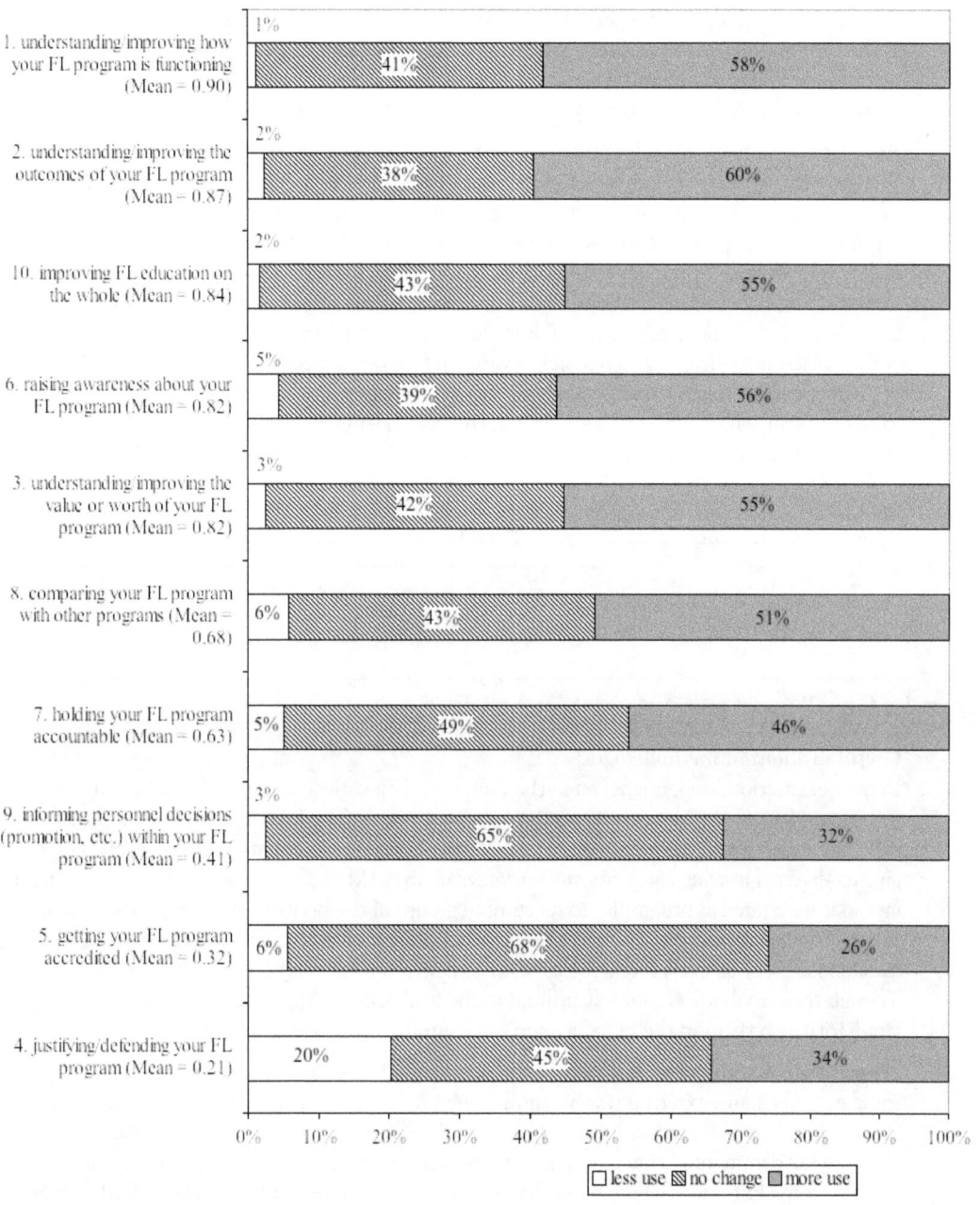

Figure 14: Current versus desired amounts of evaluation for distinct uses

many respondents indicated no need for changes in levels of evaluation activity, on average more programs sought the increased use of evaluation for largely formative purposes, such as *understanding/improving how the FL program is functioning, understating/improving the outcomes of* the FL program, improving FL education on the whole, raising awareness about the FL program, and comparing your program with other FL programs. Evaluation activities that received high ratings for current levels of use, such as evaluating personnel, were rated much lower for desired increases, indicating perhaps sufficient levels of evaluation already in practice. Interestingly, in contrast with the perceived high demand reported above, evaluation for accreditation purposes was perceived as the type of evaluation least in need of additional focus (M=2.09), though opinions here were highly varied (SD=1.21). Similarly, the use of evaluation to justify or defend programs seemed to be a contentious issue, with some 20% of respondents desiring less evaluation for this purpose.

Additional comments regarding the uses for program evaluation were offered by 30 respondents. The most frequent comments targeted the use of evaluation for improving curriculum (N=5; "To assess the undergraduate curriculum and improve it by understanding what your students want."). Although personnel decisions seemed to call for less additional focus in the Likert-scale responses, four respondents mentioned that evaluation could/should be used as a basis for sustaining or obtaining a faculty line. Three respondents also emphasized that it should be used to improve faculty performance ("It is hard in small department to give faculty evaluations of their teaching/colleagueship/research—we're all tenured. It needs to come from outside the department. That might improve our collective performance."). Overall, evaluation was reported to be used somewhat (44%) or a lot (23%) in the respondents' programs. However, for 33%, evaluation findings were reported to be used only a little or not used at all (Figure 15).

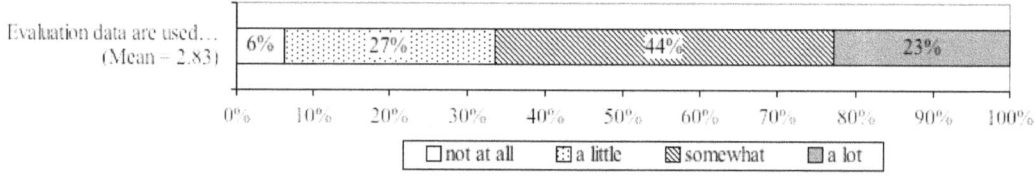

**Figure 15: Overall use of program evaluation findings**

### Useful evaluation methodologies

In the next section, respondents rated the usefulness of a variety of methods, tools, and techniques for meeting evaluation needs in their programs. The five highest rated methods were *program-internal student learning outcomes assessment, semester final exams, classroom observation, program-internal meetings,* and *program document analysis* (M≥3.23; see Figure 16). However, many methods were rated as unfamiliar to substantial groups of respondents, including *focus groups* (41%), *longitudinal tracking of learner development* (31%), *learner introspections/journaling* (27%), *questionnaires* (14%), *interviews* (12%), and *student performance/portfolio assessment* (12%) methods. Though these tools are commonly utilized in the field of evaluation, there is apparently less familiarity with them in the FL education communities of these respondents.

Frequent mention of methodologies in the open-ended comments addressed the use of standardized exams, external reviews, and exit/comprehensive exams. Of note, despite on average low ratings for the usefulness of standardized language proficiency assessment, seven respondents commented that standardized/national exams are needed ("A standard national test will come in handy."). Following their comments, these respondents represented primarily less-commonly-taught languages or institutions that did not have resources to implement currently available standardized tests. On the other hand, a counter argument from one respondent suggested that "Standardized tools do not always reflect our particular needs and situations." The uses and usefulness of standardized assessments would seem to be an area of contention within the field, and the relationship to evaluation purposes in need of clarification.

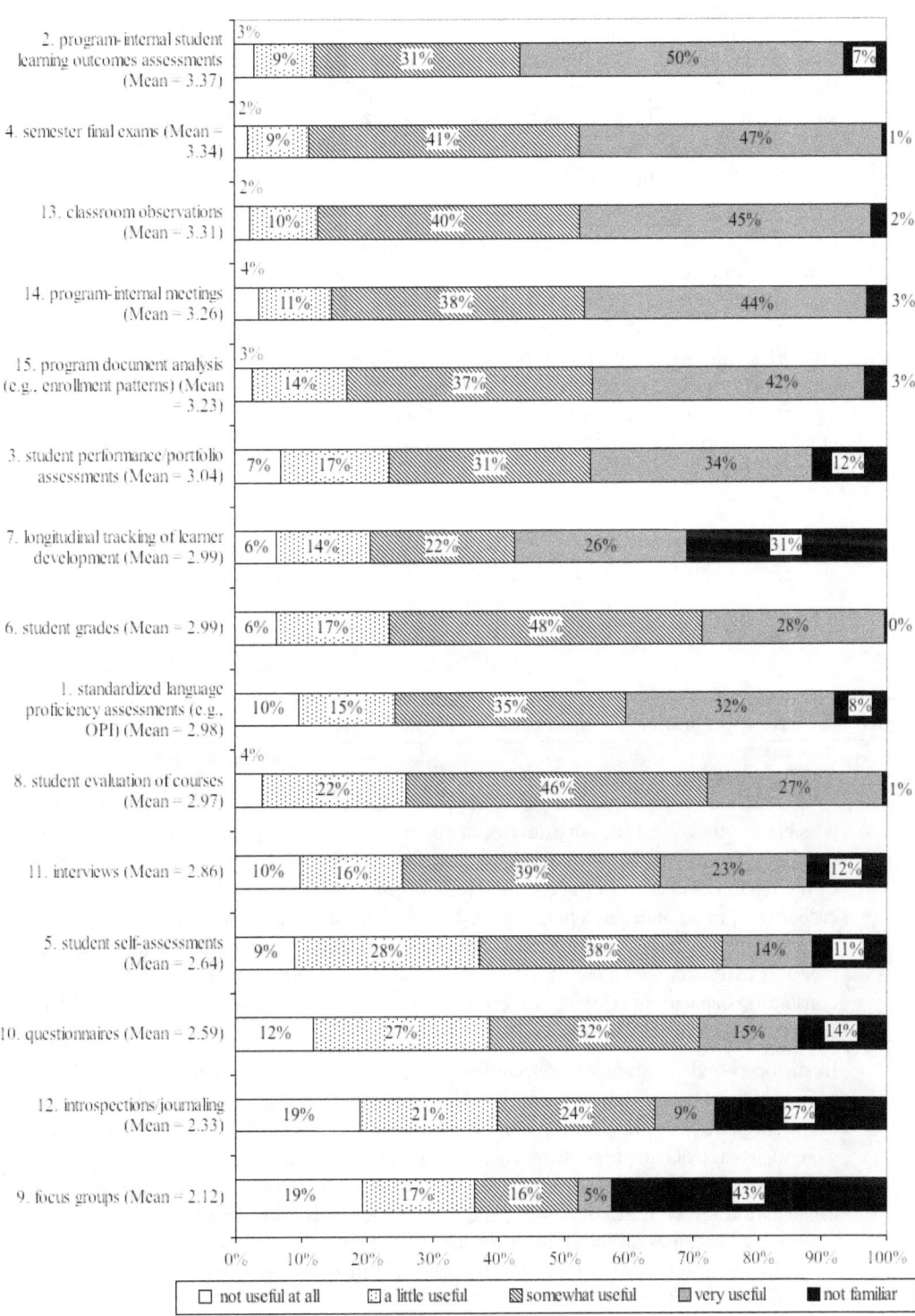

Figure 16: Utility of evaluation methods

Another popular comment addressed the utility of program-external experts' review (*N*=7). Respondents qualified these comments as follows: "competent faculty from other high quality language programs," "the professionals in their field (i.e., the instructors/professors who teach them)," and "external evaluations by both native speakers and those who have learned the language as a L2." These remarks indicated that language and domain knowledge as well as a good understanding of the contexts of FL education are important traits associated with an "expert/qualified/competent" external evaluator.

### Evaluation capacity

Respondents' programs seemed to have some capacity (55%) or a lot of capacity (18%) to engage in program evaluation (see Figure 17), although a considerable proportion also reported none or only a little capacity (27%). In terms of personnel, some programs reported having assessment coordinators (with course release time) or evaluation experts on staff, while other programs reported a need for evaluation expertise and advice. In general, throughout comments made in the survey, resource needs and personnel issues were raised as impediments to conducting effective and useful program evaluations. Further examples of capacity needs and related issues are described in the next two sections.

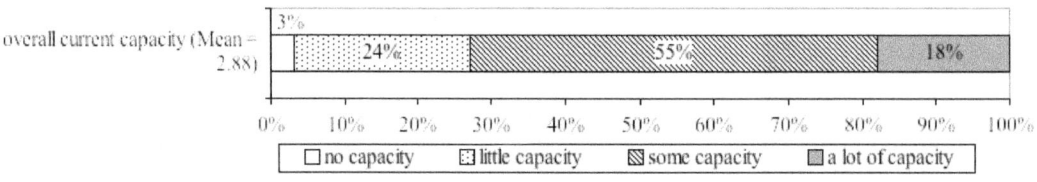

**Figure 17: Current program evaluation capacity in the program**

### Resource needs

In this section of the survey, respondents were asked to rate the usefulness of a variety of possible resources and capacity development strategies related to program evaluation. By far, the highest-demand resource was *concrete examples of FL program evaluation* (M=3.49). Other resources ranked in the top five were *program-internal expertise in FL program evaluation*, *professional development workshops on how to do program evaluation in general*, *systematic approaches for putting evaluation data to use*, and *templates for FL program evaluation processes* (M≥3.20; see Figure 18). Resources that received lower ratings included more time consuming capacity development methods, such as *textbooks, coursework*, and *an online evaluation question and answer service*.

In the open-ended comments, respondents suggested that doing evaluation depends primarily on time, money, and staff (*N*=10; "Concrete ideas that are time-efficient and use what faculty are already doing and department goals as basis."). Other comments were suggestive of the program-specific nature of resource needs coupled with evaluation challenges, as in the following example: "In Slavic, we would benefit by our professional organization (AATSEEL) discussing and working towards a statement of desired and reasonable outcomes on multiple parameters based on degree types. Perhaps other languages have already worked this out, but it has been difficult to engage our colleagues in such a discussion. Any strategies welcome."

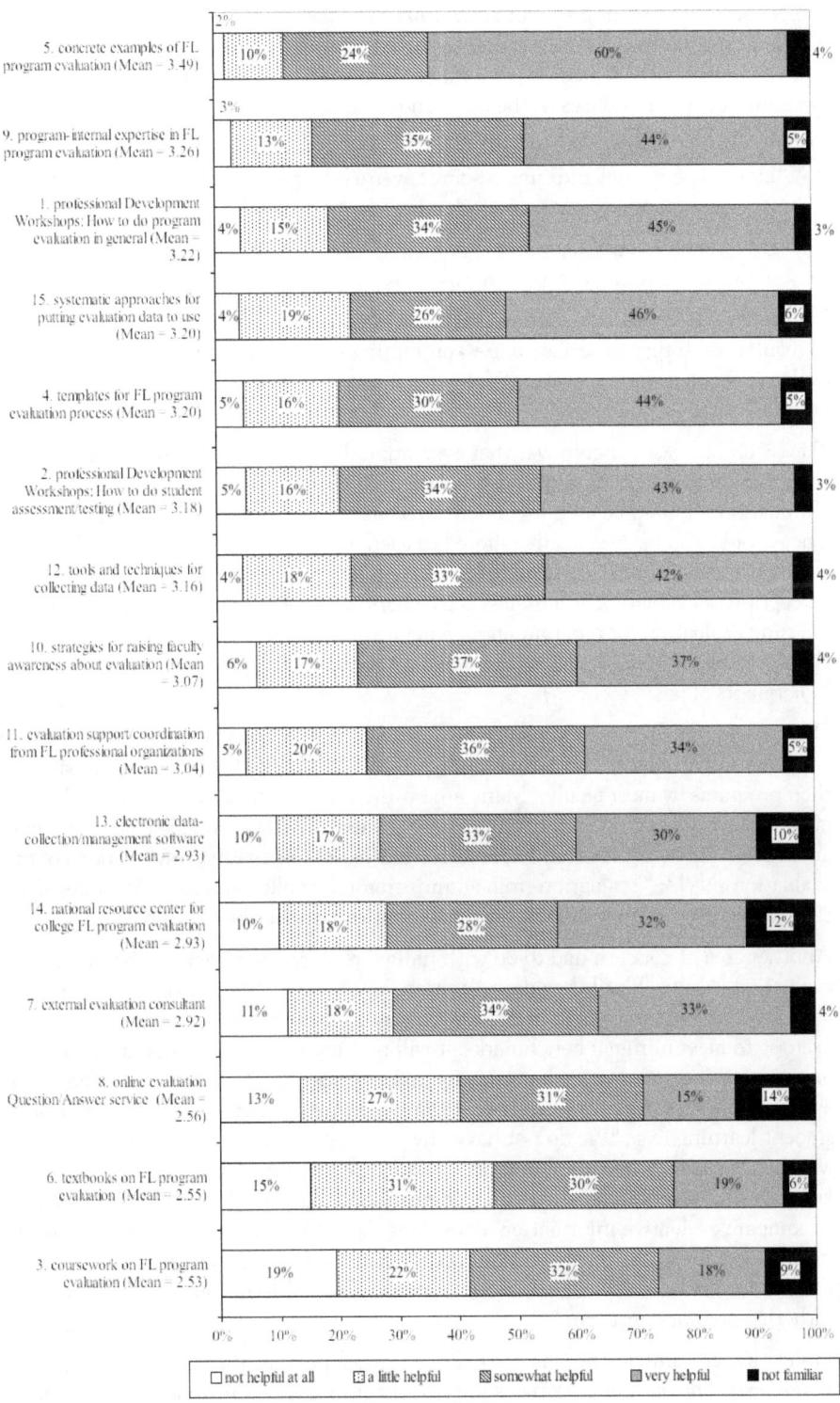

Figure 18: Helpfulness of program evaluation resources

### Issues and concerns in program evaluation practice

The final section of the survey presented an open-ended question asking about respondents' main concerns with evaluation. A total of 198 respondents provided comments, by far the largest number of responses to the open-ended questions. The most frequently mentioned concern had to do with lack of time and overburdened faculty ($N=46$), for example:

> "Limited personnel and time resources versus the personnel and time needed to carry out assessment and program evaluation."

> "Everyone is stretched so thin that most time and effort is spent keeping our heads above water rather than examining what we can and should do better."

In a similar vein, respondents suggested that evaluation is often perceived as an 'add-on' to regular teaching and service duties, prompting several comments on the need to build evaluation into a normal routine of the department instead of doing evaluation only when asked.

The second biggest concern was that evaluation did not make an obvious positive contribution to programs and that evaluation findings were frequently not used ($N=23$; "Evaluation…should be used for concrete results and not just because it is done elsewhere. They should also be specifically tailored to each department."). Some respondents were clearly frustrated that there is no follow-though on evaluation findings and therefore the perception of evaluation as a useless activity and a waste of time. Similarly, a constraint on using evaluation for program improvement came in the form of faculty resistance to change ($N=5$; "There is great resistance to change, because proposed changes are seen as indictments of past practice.").

Other personnel factors were perceived as serious hurdles to evaluation, such as willingness of faculty to participate and achieving buy-in ($N=22$; "Lack of interest in evaluation of their programs by most faculty. Many are hostile even to the idea of needs analysis."), and misunderstanding or no understanding of evaluation ($N=15$). Previous bad experiences and fear of misuse by external forces also contributed to negative connotations of program evaluation ($N=13$; "Evaluation from administrators or colleagues from other departments on campus has often demonstrated how little they know about FL teaching today.").

Another area of concern had to do with limited resources and lack of support/help for evaluation ($N=16$; "Until the administration, often the 'champion' of evaluation and accountability, provides the resources necessary to make evaluation more than just a quick exercise to meet minimal benchmarks, it will not improve."). Respondents indicated that more instruments and procedures specific to FL education ($N=13$) were needed, often in association with ways to appropriately examine particular elements of a program such as student learning (e.g., "We do not have any good assessment mechanisms to determine whether our seniors (majors & minors) are adequately prepared in their respective languages."). Additionally, it was important in some contexts to take into account the desire to compare evaluative information across language programs or with peer or competitor institutions ($N=10$; "Evaluation is not comprehensive (some language areas receive none). Data is not always comparable between language areas. Methods and rubrics of data gathering are not consistent.").

In sum, a spectrum of concerns was expressed, with perhaps the two ends being characterized by opposing attitudes towards the utility and contribution of evaluation within college FL education. On the negative end, the following quote summarizes the perception of evaluation as an activity that is apart from good education:

> "Evaluation is a colossal waste of everyone's time, especially the instructors. More time should be spent on quality instruction and career development or participation in professional conferences and less time on evaluation and assessment. It is a bureaucracy."

At the positive end, other FL professionals perceived evaluation as something essential for the betterment of education:

> "I think that there is a professional ethics that requires us more than anything else to assess and evaluate. As a university (and department) with a social conscience, we must be responsive and have something "real" to say about what we do for our students, even if any single assessment instrument does not capture all of what we do as educators."

## Discussion and implications

Findings from the needs analysis pointed to several important issues and patterns in the nature of program evaluation within U.S. college FL education. However, before proceeding to a summary and the main implications of these findings, it is important to acknowledge several limitations that inevitably constrain this kind of research. First of all, as noted, response rates to the survey were too low to convincingly indicate patterns that might be generalized to the entire population of interest (i.e., college FL programs in the U.S.). That does not mean that findings here are not relevant for a majority of such programs, but it does mean that any particular priorities or rankings may not reflect the specific realities of the FL education community. Nevertheless, some findings are better than none, so we will proceed (though with caution). Second, low response rates also meant that any analyses we originally wished to conduct by way of comparing sub-populations (e.g., priorities expressed in less-commonly taught versus more-commonly taught language programs) were not warranted, the statistical basis being to minimal to support inferential comparisons. Third, responses offered on the survey came from one representative of each program in the target population, and that individual was generally a chair, director, or other administrator within the program. It is therefore quite likely that the views of diverse stakeholders within these programs (e.g., students, non-administrative faculty) might differ considerably from the views expressed here. At the same time, our intent from the outset was to access the perspectives of those individuals within FL programs who are directly responsible for making program evaluation happen, and we believe that targeting administrators offered the best possible means for getting at a representative point of view from each program (though future surveys might be used to get at the opinions of other stakeholders).

With these limitations in mind, we nevertheless believe that findings indicated broad stroke issues that might be used to at least characterize, if not define, the status quo of program evaluation in U.S. college FL education, as summarized here:

**Impetuses:** Generally speaking, FL programs are under quite a lot of pressure to engage in evaluation, and primary impetuses include both external sources (accreditation, university administration) and internal sources (a professional or group ethic to evaluate). These competing impetuses may lead to tensions in the nature of evaluation methods, regarding in particular what kinds of evidence are appropriate for meeting distinct purposes and users.

**Evaluation focus:** While evaluation is already occurring to some extent for certain elements in most programs, in areas such as teacher/faculty performance evaluation (e.g., via student evaluation of courses or peer observation), other program elements are in need of greater evaluative attention, including teacher development itself, students' needs and attitudes, curriculum, and student learning outcomes. On the whole, respondents indicated the need for greater coverage of program elements under evaluation.

**Evaluation use:** On the whole, a substantial increase in evaluation uses seems to be desired, though in clearly specified directions. Respondents indicated the need for more use of evaluation that targeted understanding and improvement, such as internal improvements in program delivery and outcomes, but also awareness-raising in institutions and the FL discipline at large about the value (or potential value) of language education. At the same time, less use of evaluation for purely accreditation-oriented and defensive endeavors is desired. These findings suggest additional dissonance between the kinds of evaluation activities programs are held externally accountable for versus the kinds of uses deemed particularly necessary.

**Methods:** Program-specific and -internal tools are perceived as most useful, including observations, embedded assessments and exams, meetings, and document analyses. Perceived as less useful are tools that might be considered more time-consuming to learn about and/or analyze, including focus groups, student journals and self-assessments, and questionnaires. These findings may also point to a familiarity effect, though, with a larger than expected proportion of respondents indicating a lack of knowledge about some of the latter pool of standard evaluation methods. There also seems to be a considerable diversity in methods considered useful—perhaps due to diverse interpretations for how they are or should be used—for example the tensions noted between positive versus negative perceptions of the information value attributed to standardized proficiency assessments.

**Evaluation capacity:** There is a relatively broad discrepancy across programs in capacity to carry out useful program evaluation, with approximately equal proportions of respondents indicating "a lot of" versus "no" or "little" capacity. Major aspects of capacity include particularly program-internal personnel with good knowledge of evaluation, as well as institutional support in the form of expertise but also time and money.

**Resources:** In terms of resources that would help inform evaluation activities and spur capacity development, FL educators clearly prefer concrete examples, 'how-to' templates, and models of systematic evaluations that lead to actual use. In addition, training that is face-to-face and not time-consuming would seem of interest, while more extensive activities like courses or textbooks are deemed less relevant.

**Concerns:** Major concerns with evaluation in FL programs are those associated with perceptions of the time and other resources called for, faculty resistance versus buy-in, misuse or abuse of evaluation findings by external entities, and a perceived lack of utility.

Based on findings regarding these aspects of evaluation, we drew several immediate implications. First, we were heartened to see that there is a not unsubstantial professional ethic and feeling of responsibility towards program evaluation, suggesting an essential awareness of its potential value for understanding and improving FL education. We believe that building from that internal ethic, both within the FLPEP work as well as through the efforts of professional organizations, is essential for making useful evaluation happen.

Second, the apparent tensions between internal versus external impetuses for evaluation call for careful attention to the educational impact of resulting practices. When external impetuses cause programs to lessen the quality of education being delivered, as was mentioned by several respondents, there is something fundamentally wrong with the system. In the end, though, it will no doubt be up to FL program faculty to counter debilitating external pressures or methods, and a particularly effective way of doing so is likely to be through good internally-driven evaluation that demonstrably leads to improved performance.

Third, across the U.S., college FL programs have diverse evaluation capacities, concerns, and needs—most would like to see the increased use of evaluation but most face time and resource constraints. Certainly, these constraints must be taken seriously, and they will require program faculty as well as evaluation consultants to strategize in making evaluation feasible and manageable (i.e., feasibility must be built in to evaluation planning). At the same time, there would seem to be an important role here for professional organizations to begin addressing evaluation needs and coming up with ways of sharing capacity across the discipline (e.g., through supporting visits by capacity-rich programs to other programs seeking assistance in evaluation).

Fourth, there is a clear need for strategies to leverage institutional and disciplinary awareness and support, as well as faculty engagement, if evaluation is to play a legitimately useful role in college FL programs. Again, the push for support, awareness, and engagement may need to be done from multiple directions: (a) internally, by providing bottom-up evidence of what good evaluation practice should look like; (b) disciplinarily, by informing the professional FL organizations about educators' evaluation ethics as well as capacity needs; and (c) publicly, through articulating and advocating evaluation policies that may actually lead to understanding and improvement versus mere appearance of accountability.

Fifth, it is quite evident that evaluation methods and their dissemination should prioritize efficiency, systematicity, and local utility, though there is also some desire for standardized evaluation instruments. Perhaps equally important, though, it would seem essential to put in place a mechanism for helping FL educators to articulate methodological choices to the purposes and uses for which they are designed. Along these lines, to facilitate better understanding of what such intentional and contextually-bound evaluation looks like, there is an immediate need to disseminate more concrete cases, examples, tools, and use-oriented models that are specific to various types of language programs (distinct languages, program elements, institutional settings).

Finally, in the short-term, evaluation capacity development might best be addressed through program- or topic-specific workshops, direct assistance/outreach where needed, and dissemination of good examples. For the longer-term, however, capacity development likely depends on a more generalized awareness-raising about evaluation (e.g., through publishing, presenting, advocating), knowledge generation (e.g., through research on attributes of evaluation that help or hinder FL educators engage in organizational learning), and discipline-wide attention to professional development in evaluation (e.g., through the inclusion of evaluation strands in FL conferences, or the provision of financial and other resources for evaluation training).

In conclusion, then, we would simply point out that these needs analysis findings and implications have motivated a variety of subsequent research, development, and dissemination activities in the Foreign Language Program Evaluation Project, and they will continue to do so for some time. Of particular interest, the chapters reported in the rest of this volume all feature issues and concerns identified in this needs analysis—but as lived in particular FL program settings—as well as the implementation of strategies for responding to them. We also invite readers to peruse the resources posted on the FLPEP web site (http://www.nflrc.hawaii.edu/evaluation), all of which have been developed on the basis of findings identified in this study. In the end, we do hope that these efforts are helpful, and that the ideas we have highlighted through this needs analysis work will continue to raise awareness within the FL education community, and beyond, about program evaluation and how it might best be put to use in the service of language learning and teaching.

### Acknowledgements

Our thanks go to the Association of Departments of Foreign Languages and the American Council on the Teaching of Foreign Languages for their contributions during portions of this project. We would also like to express our gratitude for sustained support throughout from the National Foreign Language Resource Center at the University of Hawai'i. Most importantly, we appreciate the efforts of those committed foreign language professionals who took the time to respond to the interviews and surveys.

## References

Alderson, J. C. (1992). Guidelines for the evaluation of language education. In J. C. Alderson & A. Beretta (Eds.), *Evaluating second language education* (pp. 274–304). Cambridge, UK: Cambridge University Press.

Alderson, J. C., & Scott, M. (1992). Insiders, outsiders and participatory evaluation. In J. C. Alderson & A. Beretta (Eds.), *Evaluating second language education* (pp. 25–57). Cambridge, UK: Cambridge University Press.

Beretta, A. (1986). A case for field-experimentation in program evaluation. *Language Learning, 36*(3), 295–309.

Beretta, A. (1990). Implementation of the Bangalore Project. *Applied Linguistics, 11*(4), 321–340.

Beretta, A. (1992a). Evaluation of language education: An overview. In J. C. Alderson & A. Beretta (Eds.), *Evaluating second language education* (pp. 15–24). Cambridge: Cambridge University Press.

Beretta, A. (1992b). What can be learned from the Bangalore evaluation. In J. C. Alderson & A. Beretta (Eds.), *Evaluating second language education* (pp. 250–271). Cambridge: Cambridge University Press.

Beretta, A., & Davies, A. (1985). Evaluation of the Bangalore project. *ELT Journal, 39*(2), 121–127.

Boyatzis, R. (1998). *Transforming qualitative information: Thematic analysis and code development*. Thousand Oaks, CA: Sage.

Brown, J. D. (2001). *Using surveys in language programs*. Cambridge, UK: Cambridge University Press.

Brown, J. D. (1995). *The elements of language curriculum: A systematic approach to program development*. Boston: Heinle & Heinle.

Coleman, H. (1992). Moving the goalposts: Project evaluation in practice. In J. C. Alderson & A. Beretta (Eds.), *Evaluating second language education* (pp. 222–246). Cambridge, UK: Cambridge University Press.

Genesee, F. (1983). Bilingual education of majority language children: The immersion experiments in review. *Applied Psycholinguistics, 4*, 1–46.

Keating, R. F. (1963). *A study of the effectiveness of language laboratories*. New York: Institute of Administrative Research, Teachers College.

Kiely, R., & Rea-Dickins, P. (2005). *Program evaluation in language education*. New York: Palgrave Macmillan.

Krueger, R., & Casey, M. A. (2000). *Focus groups: A practical guide for applied research* (3rd ed.). Thousand Oaks, CA: Sage.

Kvale, S. (1996). *Inter Views: An introduction to qualitative research interviewing.* Thousand Oaks, CA: Sage.

Liskin-Gasparro, J. E. (1995). Practical approaches to outcomes assessment: The undergraduate major in foreign languages and literatures. *ADFL Bulletin, 26*(2), 21–27.

Long, M. (2005). *Second language needs analysis.* Cambridge, UK: Cambridge University Press.

Lynch, B. K. (1996). *Language program evaluation: Theory and practice.* Cambridge, UK: Cambridge University Press.

Lynch, B. K. (2003). *Language assessment and programme evaluation.* Edinburgh, UK: Edinburgh University Press.

Mackay, R. (1988). Position paper: Program evaluation and quality control. *TESL Canada Journal, 5*(2), 33–42.

Mackay, R., Wellesley, S., & Bazergan, E. (1995). Participatory evaluation. *ELT Journal, 49*(4), 308–317.

Norris, J. M. (2006). The why (and how) of student learning outcomes assessment in college FL education. *Modern Language Journal, 90*(4), 576–583.

Norris, J. M. (2008). *Validity evaluation in language assessment.* New York: Peter Lang.

Norris, J. M. (Ed.). (2009). Understanding and improving language education through program evaluation [Special issue]. *Language Teaching Research, 13*(1).

Patton, M. Q. (1978). *Utilization-focused evaluation.* Beverly Hills, CA: Sage.

Patton, M. Q. (1997). *Utilization-focused evaluation: The new century text* (3rd ed.). Thousand Oaks, CA: Sage.

Patton, M. Q. (2008). *Utilization-focused evaluation* (4th ed.). Thousand Oaks, CA: Sage.

Phillips, J. K. (2003). Implications of language education policies for language study in schools and universities. *Modern Language Journal, 87,* 579–586.

Scherer, G. A. C., & Wertheimer, M. (1964). *A psycholinguistic experiment in foreign language teaching.* New York: McGraw-Hill.

Smith, P. D. (1970). *A comparison of the cognitive and audio-lingual approaches to foreign language instruction: The Pennsylvania foreign language project.* Philadelphia: The Center for Curriculum Development.

Swain, M., & Lapkin, S. (1982). *Evaluating bilingual education: A Canadian case study.* Clevedon, UK: Multilingual Matters.

Tyler, R. W. (1949). *Basic principles of curriculum and instruction.* Chicago: University of Chicago Press.

Wiggins, G., & McTighe, J. (2001). *Understanding by design* (2nd ed). Alexandria, VA: Association for Supervision and Curriculum Development.

## Appendix A: Focus group protocol

*Responding to program evaluation demands in college foreign language education*
ACTFL 2005, Baltimore

### Facilitator worksheet for small-group discussion

Instructions to facilitator: There will be approximately 25 minutes for group discussion, following our overview presentation of the project. The purpose of the group discussion is to elicit ideas/concerns about program evaluation from the audience members. Your role is to: (a) pose a few basic questions to the group; (b) ensure balanced opportunity to participate among group members; (c) take notes on the main ideas discussed; and (d) provide a brief summary of the discussion when we reconvene at the end of the session.

Discussion prompts: [notes in brackets are further instructions for facilitators]

0. [3–5 minutes; have everyone introduce themselves; take notes on major context features] Please introduce yourself and tell us a bit about your language program context.

1. [8–10 minutes] What types of evaluation occur within your program? [Ask next question as a follow-up, to generate more discussion, time permitting.] What is the impetus for any of these—who asks for evaluations and who is responsible for making them happen?

2. [5–7 minutes] Are there other types of evaluation that should occur but don't?

3. [5–7 minutes] To what extent is your program equipped to engage in program evaluation? How might that capacity be enhanced (e.g., through personnel, training, resources)?

[Note any other main points here.]

## Appendix B: Short open-ended survey

Please take a few minutes at the end of the session to provide your input on program evaluation and this project. Your ideas will help us to refine our methods and enhance the value of project outcomes.

1. Please describe the language program context(s) where you teach, study, or work.
   _____
   _____

2. Please comment on the primary roles played by evaluation in your language program(s). What are your main concerns with the actual or potential uses of evaluation?
   _____
   _____

3. What suggestions do you have for this project? How can the project best meet your needs?
   _____
   _____

Thank you for your participation.

## Appendix C: Structured interview instrument for the Foreign Language Program Evaluation Project

**Preliminaries:**

[SET UP TAPE-RECORDER CLOSE TO INTERVIEWEE]
- Thank you for agreeing to participate.
- I'm going to ask you some general questions, and we will audio-tape-record the interview.
- If there are any questions that you would prefer not to answer, please say so.
- It should take around 30 minutes or so.
- Do you have any questions before we begin?
- I am going to start the tape-recorder now.

**Interview**

[START RECORDING: LET THEM TELL YOU ABOUT EVALUATION, NOT VICE VERSA!]

Q1: First, a very general question. How would you define the term "program evaluation"?

Q2: Please describe the language program where you work, and your role within it.
- department/college
- languages & "programs"
- staff
- students
- role of the interviewee

[I'm going to read to you a definition of program evaluation and ask questions related to that: Evaluation is the systematic collection of information about the activities, characteristics, and outcomes of programs to make judgments about the program, improve program effectiveness, and/or inform decisions about future programming.]

Q3: So, tell me about the kinds of evaluation that occur within your program(s).
- impetus
- responsibility
- purpose
- methods
- use

Q4: Are there types of evaluation that should occur but do not?

Q5: To what extent is your program equipped to engage in evaluation activities?

Q6: In what ways might the capacity to engage in evaluation be enhanced in your program?

Q7: In sum, how would you describe your main concern with program evaluation, if any?

**Closing:**

- Do you have any other comments about program evaluation?
- Is there anyone else from your program that you think we should talk to about evaluation?
- I am going to turn off the tape-recorder now.
- THANK YOU FOR YOUR PARTICIPATION!!!

[SEND FOLLOW-UP THANK YOU EMAIL]

Notes: Avoid answering to the questions raised by the interviewee, such as "What kind of plans do you have for your project?"

## Appendix D: Coding criteria for thematic analysis

| theme labels | meaning of the theme | example statements | attached values |
|---|---|---|---|
| program type | types of foreign language programs at college level | "Study abroad program"<br><br>"Two year freshman and sophomore program." | • study abroad program<br><br>• entry level program |
| focus | Which component of the program is evaluated? | "Are they using their knowledge, are they doing something with it, those kinds of things."<br><br>"We try to identify strengths and weaknesses and then make adjustments in the in the curriculum accordingly" | • learning value<br><br>• curriculum |
| use | What is the use or merit of conducting program evaluation? | "I'd like to see what ways we can improve through an evaluation process."<br><br>"…but now you can sort of demonstrate better the learner results that came out of this" | • program improvement<br><br>• demonstrate value |
| impetus | Where did the demand for program evaluation come from? | "It's definitely asked for by the accrediting agency"<br><br>"We are our own driving force" | • accreditors<br><br>• internal |
| methodology | methodology taken in program evaluation practices | "We collected materials in each of the classes and mentioned those materials that [ended] again what we say that students will be able to do."<br><br>"We would invite someone from outside to evaluate our program" | • stating student learning outcomes<br><br>• external evaluation |
| concern | concerns and issues that surround program evaluation | "Others don't want to hear about it and others don't want to do anything about it."<br><br>"We didn't have manpower to do that." | • resistance<br><br>• no manpower |
| current capacity | current operational capacity to conduct evaluation | "This is the first year of doing that kind of high level test training"<br><br>"The rest of the faculty certainly buy into it. I think that they take assessment and proficiency, and evaluation very seriously" | • test training<br><br>• faculty buy-in |
| capacity needs | capacity development needs that can help solve the issues raised | "That's the major concern. How we can convince the teachers, you know. Why this is good for them."<br><br>"I guess if there were a group with the resources, they could sort of offer on a demand basis." | • strategies<br><br>• expert consultation service |
| evaluation needs | specific evaluation activity that respondents want to do, but not happening yet | "I think we need to kind of bring up what kind of students we have"<br><br>"…will benefit from having a lot more of a systematic collection of information" | • student background<br><br>• systematic data collection |

## Appendix E: Online survey instrument

Thank you for your interest. Please read the following "Consent Form" and then indicate whether you would like to proceed.

CONSENT FORM
1. PURPOSE: The purpose of this survey is to gather information about evaluation in college foreign language programs.
2. PROCEDURES: You will respond to questions about evaluation in your program by selecting or typing answers.
3. DISCOMFORTS and RISKS: There are no known risks involved in completing this survey.
4. BENEFITS: The results of the study are intended to benefit you as a FL program administrator and educator. The results will also benefit FL education on the whole, by identifying features of evaluation in need of development.
5. DURATION: It will take approximately 30 minutes to complete the survey.
6. CONFIDENTIALITY: The survey elicits general information about FL programs and evaluation. The data will be collected on a secure webserver and saved separately from any personally identifiable information such as email addresses. Your responses will be assigned a non-recognizable identification number. Only project personnel will have access to the study data. Findings will disseminated in aggregate form, with no information identifying individuals or individual programs.
7. RIGHT TO ASK QUESTIONS: Contact John Norris (XXX-XXX-XXXX, XXXX@XXXX) with any questions about the survey. If you have questions about your rights as a participant, contact the University of Hawaii Committee on Human Studies (XXX-XXX-XXXX, or email at XXXX@XXXX).
8. COMPENSATION: There is no compensation for completing this survey.
9. VOLUNTARY Participation: You are not required to participate in this study. You can stop your participation at any time.

**✱ Please indicate below whether or not you consent to participate (click blank and select), then click "Next".**

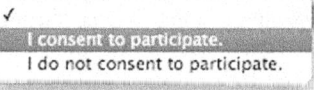

( Next >> )

## General instructions

There are 8 short sections to the survey, each on a separate page. It is recommended that you complete the full survey in a single sitting.

VERY IMPORTANT NOTE: This survey asks questions about your Foreign Language (FL) Program. In responding, please think about the FL program for which you are directly responsible, or in which you primarily participate. For example:

--you may be the chair of a department that consists of multiple languages, in which case you would answer questions with the full department in mind (i.e., provide answers that apply in general to the entire department and all languages)

--you may be the head of a section or department that consists of one language only, so you would answer questions with just your one language program in mind

--you may be...

**In light of the preceding statement, please provide a few words describing your FL program (e.g., "multi-language department").**

**Please provide your email address so that we may track response rates. This information will NOT be associated with your survey responses.**

<< Prev    Next >>

## SECTION 1/8: Program Information

Please answer a few questions about the foreign language program where you work.

**Click on the institutional setting of your program:**

- Private
- Public
- Other (please specify)

[          ]

**College/University Type:**

- 2-year (no bachelor-level degrees granted)
- 4-year (only bachelor-level degrees granted)
- Graduate-degree-granting (bachelor AND masters AND/OR doctoral degrees granted)
- Other (please specify)

[          ]

**Estimated size of your college/university (total number of students):**

- Less than 1000
- 1000-4999
- 5000-9999
- 10,000-14,999
- 15,000-19,999
- 20,000 or more

**What is the maximum number of student enrollments in all of the courses offered by your FL program during any given semester?**

[          ]

**Your FL program is run by:**

- a College or School
- a Department
- a Specific Section in a Department
- Other (please specify)

[          ]

**What is the maximum number of student enrollments in all of the courses offered by your FL program during any given semester?**

[                    ]

**Your FL program is run by:**

○ a College or School    ○ a Department    ○ a Specific Section in a Department

○ Other (please specify)

[                    ]

**Program offerings (click all that apply):**

☐ Institutional language requirement    ☐ PHD
☐ Undergraduate minor    ☐ Study abroad
☐ Undergraduate major    ☐ Summer/intensive language study
☐ Language certificate    ☐ Heritage language
☐ Teaching certificate    ☐ Interdisciplinary degree
☐ MA/MS    ☐ Elective courses
☐ Other (please specify)

[                    ]

**List language(s) offered in your specific program (SEPARATE each language with a COMMA):**

[                    ]

**Provide a few words describing your role in the program (e.g., "Department chair").**

[                    ]

( << Prev )  ( Next >> )

### SECTION 2/8. What is Program Evaluation?

To get a sense of what is meant in this survey by the term "program evaluation", please read this general definition by Michael Quinn Patton, then click "next":

"Evaluation is the systematic collection of information about the activities, characteristics, and outcomes of programs to make judgments about the program, improve program effectiveness, and/or inform decisions about future programming." (p. 23)

Patton, M. Q. (1997). Utilization-focused evaluation: The new century text (3rd ed.). Thousand Oaks, CA: Sage.

## SECTION 3/8. Program Evaluation Impetuses

Now consider evaluation in your college FL program and answer the following questions.

**To what extent do you feel under pressure from the following SOURCES to engage in program evaluation? (15 items)**

| | Not at all | A little | Somewhat | A lot | NOT FAMILIAR |
|---|---|---|---|---|---|
| 1. university accreditation process | ○ | ○ | ○ | ○ | ○ |
| 2. teacher accreditation agency (e.g., NCATE) | ○ | ○ | ○ | ○ | ○ |
| 3. university administration | ○ | ○ | ○ | ○ | ○ |
| 4. tenure and promotion process | ○ | ○ | ○ | ○ | ○ |
| 5. university student government | ○ | ○ | ○ | ○ | ○ |
| 6. the dean of my college/school | ○ | ○ | ○ | ○ | ○ |
| 7. the department/program faculty as a whole | ○ | ○ | ○ | ○ | ○ |
| 8. individual faculty members | ○ | ○ | ○ | ○ | ○ |
| 9. students in the program | ○ | ○ | ○ | ○ | ○ |
| 10. students' parents | ○ | ○ | ○ | ○ | ○ |
| 11. academic/professional organization(s) (e.g., ACTFL) | ○ | ○ | ○ | ○ | ○ |
| 12. external program funder | ○ | ○ | ○ | ○ | ○ |
| 13. the local community | ○ | ○ | ○ | ○ | ○ |
| 14. graduates' employers | ○ | ○ | ○ | ○ | ○ |
| 15. trend in FL education | ○ | ○ | ○ | ○ | ○ |
| OVERALL PRESSURE FOR EVALUATION | ○ | ○ | ○ | ○ | ○ |

**What other specific sources exert pressure for evaluation to happen in your program?**

[                                                    ]

( << Prev )  ( Next >> )

### SECTION 4/8. Program Components Evaluated

For sections 4 and 5 only, we would like to find out about CURRENT versus IDEAL uses for evaluation.

**For the following program COMPONENTS, please indicate the extent to which each (a) is CURRENTLY evaluated in your FL program, and (b) SHOULD BE evaluated in your FL program. (10 items)**

**NOTE: the scale will appear when you click on the blanks in each column.**

|  | a. CURRENTLY EVALUATED | b. SHOULD BE EVALUATED |
|---|---|---|
| 1. Program mission and goals | | |
| 2. Curriculum scope and sequence | | 0–Not at all |
| 3. Teaching | | 1–A little |
| 4. Instructional Materials | | 2–Somewhat |
| 5. Assessment/testing of students | | 3–A lot |
| 6. Teacher development | | NOT RELEVANT |
| 7. Performance of program chair/administration | | |
| 8. Learning needs of students | | |
| 9. Student learning outcomes | | |
| 10. Changes in students' attitudes | | |
| THE PROGRAM OVERALL | | |

**What other specific components are (or should be) evaluated in your program?**

<< Prev    Next >>

## Section 5/8. Program Evaluation Uses

**Exit this survey**

For the following evaluation APPLICATIONS, please indicate the extent to which evaluation (a) is currently used, and (b) should be used. (10 items)

**NOTE: the scale will appear when you click on the blanks in each column.**

| | a. CURRENTLY USED | b. SHOULD BE USED |
|---|---|---|
| 1. Understanding/improving how your FL program is functioning | [ ] | ✓ |
| | | 0-Not at all |
| | | 1-A little |
| 2. Understanding/improving the outcomes of your FL program | [ ] | 2-Somewhat |
| | | 3-A lot |
| | | NOT FAMILIAR |
| 3. Understanding/improving the value or worth of your FL program | [ ] | |
| 4. Justifying/defending your FL program | [ ] | [ ] |
| 5. Getting your FL program accredited | [ ] | [ ] |
| 6. Raising awareness about your FL program | [ ] | [ ] |
| 7. Holding your FL program accountable | [ ] | [ ] |
| 8. Comparing your FL program with other programs | [ ] | [ ] |
| 9. Informing personnel decisions (promotion, etc.) within your FL program | [ ] | [ ] |
| 10. Improving FL education on the whole | [ ] | [ ] |

**What other uses are made (or should be made) of evaluation in your program?**

[                    ]

( Prev )  ( Next )

## SECTION 6/8. Program Evaluation Methods

How useful are the following **METHODS, TOOLS,** and **TECHNIQUES** for meeting evaluation needs in your FL program? (15 items)

|  | Not useful | A little useful | Somewhat useful | Very useful | NOT FAMILIAR |
|---|---|---|---|---|---|
| 1. Standardized language proficiency assessments (e.g., OPI) | ○ | ○ | ○ | ○ | ○ |
| 2. Program-internal student learning outcomes assessments | ○ | ○ | ○ | ○ | ○ |
| 3. Student performance/portfolio assessments | ○ | ○ | ○ | ○ | ○ |
| 4. Semester final exams | ○ | ○ | ○ | ○ | ○ |
| 5. Student self-assessments | ○ | ○ | ○ | ○ | ○ |
| 6. Student grades | ○ | ○ | ○ | ○ | ○ |
| 7. Longitudinal tracking of learner development | ○ | ○ | ○ | ○ | ○ |
| 8. Student evaluation of courses | ○ | ○ | ○ | ○ | ○ |
| 9. Focus groups | ○ | ○ | ○ | ○ | ○ |
| 10. Questionnaires | ○ | ○ | ○ | ○ | ○ |
| 11. Interviews | ○ | ○ | ○ | ○ | ○ |
| 12. Introspections/journaling | ○ | ○ | ○ | ○ | ○ |
| 13. Classroom observations | ○ | ○ | ○ | ○ | ○ |
| 14. Program-internal meetings | ○ | ○ | ○ | ○ | ○ |
| 15. Program document analysis (e.g., enrollment patterns) | ○ | ○ | ○ | ○ | ○ |

**What other evaluation methods are (or should be) used in your program?**

[ ]

**Overall, beyond data collection, to what extent are evaluation data actually USED in your FL program?**

|  | Not at all | A little | Somewhat | A lot |
|---|---|---|---|---|
| Evaluation data are used... | ○ | ○ | ○ | ○ |

( << Prev )  ( Next >> )

## SECTION 7/8. Program Evaluation Capacity--ALMOST FINISHED!

Please indicate which of the following RESOURCES would help you to conduct useful evaluations. (15 items)

| | Not helpful | A little helpful | Somewhat helpful | Very helpful | NOT FAMILIAR |
|---|---|---|---|---|---|
| 1. Professional Development Workshops: How to do program evaluation in general | ○ | ○ | ○ | ○ | ○ |
| 2. Professional Development Workshops: How to do student assessment/testing | ○ | ○ | ○ | ○ | ○ |
| 3. Coursework on FL program evaluation | ○ | ○ | ○ | ○ | ○ |
| 4. Templates for FL program evaluation process | ○ | ○ | ○ | ○ | ○ |
| 5. Concrete examples of FL program evaluation | ○ | ○ | ○ | ○ | ○ |
| 6. Textbooks on FL program evaluation | ○ | ○ | ○ | ○ | ○ |
| 7. External evaluation consultant | ○ | ○ | ○ | ○ | ○ |
| 8. Online evaluation Question/Answer service | ○ | ○ | ○ | ○ | ○ |
| 9. Program-internal expertise in FL program evaluation | ○ | ○ | ○ | ○ | ○ |
| 10. Strategies for raising faculty awareness about evaluation | ○ | ○ | ○ | ○ | ○ |
| 11. Evaluation support/coordination from FL professional organizations | ○ | ○ | ○ | ○ | ○ |
| 12. Tools and techniques for collecting data | ○ | ○ | ○ | ○ | ○ |
| 13. Electronic data-collection/management software | ○ | ○ | ○ | ○ | ○ |
| 14. National resource center for college FL program evaluation | ○ | ○ | ○ | ○ | ○ |
| 15. Systematic approaches for putting evaluation data to use | ○ | ○ | ○ | ○ | ○ |

**What other resources would help your program engage in evaluation?**

[ ]

**On the whole, what is the current capacity (i.e., preparedness, ability) of your FL program to engage in evaluation?**

| | No capacity | A little capacity | Some capacity | A lot of capacity |
|---|---|---|---|---|
| Capacity to engage in program evaluation... | ○ | ○ | ○ | ○ |

( << Prev )  ( Next >> )

## SECTION 8/8. Program Evaluation Concerns and Final Thoughts

**What main concerns do you have, if any, about evaluation in your FL program?**

[ ]

**Add any other comments that would help us to understand your program evaluation needs.**

[ ]

<< Prev    Next >>

## Additional Contacts

**Are there other key individuals in your FL program we should contact for further insights about evaluation there? Please provide name and email address if applicable.**

[ ]

<< Prev    Next >>

## Finished!

Thank you for your crucial input!

Over the next year, we will be developing and disseminating resources in response to the findings from this survey.

When you click on "Done" below, you will be taken to the FL PROGRAM EVALUATION PROJECT WEBSITE, the main location for accessing related information and resources.

<< Prev    Done >>

## Appendix F: Survey results

### Table F1: Evaluation impetuses

| evaluation impetus | N | M | SD | not at all | a little | somewhat | a lot | not familiar |
|---|---|---|---|---|---|---|---|---|
| 1. university accreditation process | 325 | 3.15 | 1.02 | 11% | 10% | 28% | 48% | 2% |
| 2. teacher accreditation agency (e.g., NCATE) | 309 | 2.23 | 1.32 | 45% | 8% | 12% | 27% | 8% |
| 3. university administration | 322 | 3.34 | 0.82 | 4% | 10% | 33% | 52% | 1% |
| 4. tenure and promotion process | 317 | 2.57 | 1.13 | 25% | 18% | 30% | 26% | 1% |
| 5. university student government | 313 | 1.32 | 0.71 | 78% | 12% | 6% | 3% | 1% |
| 6. the dean of my college/school | 318 | 3.09 | 0.91 | 8% | 14% | 40% | 37% | 1% |
| 7. the department/program faculty as a whole | 316 | 2.59 | 1.03 | 19% | 23% | 36% | 22% | 0% |
| 8. individual faculty members | 314 | 2.29 | 1.03 | 29% | 27% | 30% | 14% | 0% |
| 9. students in the program | 315 | 1.97 | 1.00 | 43% | 25% | 23% | 8% | 0% |
| 10. students' parents | 311 | 1.29 | 0.59 | 76% | 17% | 4% | 1% | 2% |
| 11. academic/professional organization(s) (e.g., ACTFL) | 316 | 2.10 | 1.06 | 39% | 22% | 26% | 12% | 1% |
| 12. external program funder | 313 | 1.35 | 0.80 | 75% | 10% | 4% | 5% | 6% |
| 13. the local community | 314 | 1.34 | 0.66 | 74% | 16% | 7% | 1% | 2% |
| 14. graduates' employers | 310 | 1.40 | 0.76 | 74% | 12% | 11% | 2% | 2% |
| 15. trend in FL education | 311 | 2.72 | 1.04 | 17% | 19% | 37% | 26% | 1% |
| overall pressure for evaluation | 312 | 3.06 | 0.78 | 3% | 20% | 46% | 31% | |

## Table F2: Evaluation foci

| evaluation focus | currently evaluated | | | should be evaluated | | | difference between should be evaluated—currently evaluated | | | less use | no change | more use |
|---|---|---|---|---|---|---|---|---|---|---|---|---|
| | N | M | SD | N | M | SD | N | M | SD | | | |
| 1. program mission and goals | 303 | 3.15 | 0.95 | 259 | 3.59 | 0.61 | 253 | 0.54 | 1.01 | 6% | 55% | 39% |
| 2. curriculum scope and sequence | 307 | 3.18 | 0.93 | 260 | 3.69 | 0.60 | 257 | 0.60 | 0.93 | 4% | 54% | 43% |
| 3. teaching | 310 | 3.57 | 0.68 | 257 | 3.78 | 0.54 | 256 | 0.25 | 0.68 | 4% | 72% | 24% |
| 4. instructional materials | 306 | 2.79 | 0.96 | 258 | 3.33 | 0.75 | 254 | 0.66 | 0.87 | 3% | 48% | 49% |
| 5. assessment/ testing of students | 309 | 3.06 | 0.95 | 259 | 3.47 | 0.68 | 258 | 0.52 | 0.91 | 7% | 50% | 43% |
| 6. teacher development | 296 | 2.49 | 0.96 | 256 | 3.29 | 0.74 | 251 | 0.88 | 0.93 | 2% | 37% | 61% |
| 7. performance of program chair/ administration | 302 | 2.48 | 1.03 | 255 | 3.11 | 0.80 | 251 | 0.74 | 0.96 | 4% | 45% | 51% |
| 8. learning needs of students | 305 | 2.75 | 1.01 | 264 | 3.50 | 0.68 | 258 | 0.85 | 0.97 | 2% | 43% | 55% |
| 9. student learning outcomes | 305 | 3.05 | 0.93 | 266 | 3.57 | 0.62 | 260 | 0.63 | 1.02 | 8% | 45% | 47% |
| 10. changes in students' attitudes | 298 | 2.05 | 0.92 | 263 | 2.87 | 0.85 | 254 | 0.86 | 0.96 | 4% | 37% | 59% |
| the program overall | 305 | 3.14 | 0.70 | 258 | 3.52 | 0.56 | 257 | 0.47 | 0.77 | 5% | 54% | 41% |

## Table F3: Evaluation uses

| evaluation use | currently used | | | should be used | | | difference between should be used— currently used | | | less use | no change | more use |
|---|---|---|---|---|---|---|---|---|---|---|---|---|
| | N | M | SD | N | M | SD | N | M | SD | | | |
| 1. understanding/ improving how your FL program is functioning | 290 | 2.79 | 1.02 | 250 | 3.56 | 0.61 | 246 | 0.90 | 0.97 | 1% | 41% | 58% |
| 2. understanding/ improving the outcomes of your FL program | 291 | 2.81 | 0.96 | 250 | 3.56 | 0.64 | 247 | 0.87 | 0.93 | 2% | 38% | 60% |
| 3. understanding/ improving the value or worth of your FL program | 283 | 2.64 | 1.05 | 246 | 3.34 | 0.82 | 239 | 0.82 | 0.99 | 3% | 42% | 55% |
| 4. justifying/ defending your FL program | 288 | 2.72 | 1.06 | 247 | 2.85 | 1.03 | 242 | 0.21 | 1.15 | 20% | 45% | 34% |
| 5. getting your FL program accredited | 252 | 2.09 | 1.21 | 204 | 2.40 | 1.23 | 196 | 0.32 | 0.78 | 6% | 68% | 26% |
| 6. raising awareness about your FL program | 287 | 2.50 | 1.05 | 248 | 3.25 | 0.86 | 244 | 0.82 | 1.03 | 5% | 39% | 56% |
| 7. holding your FL program accountable | 284 | 2.67 | 1.03 | 240 | 3.23 | 0.86 | 237 | 0.63 | 0.97 | 5% | 49% | 46% |
| 8. comparing your FL program with other programs | 286 | 2.23 | 0.97 | 252 | 2.83 | 0.88 | 244 | 0.68 | 1.01 | 6% | 43% | 51% |
| 9. informing personnel decisions (promotion, etc.) within your FL program | 275 | 2.71 | 1.10 | 234 | 3.06 | 0.99 | 228 | 0.41 | 0.79 | 3% | 65% | 32% |
| 10. improving FL education on the whole | 287 | 2.72 | 0.99 | 245 | 3.44 | 0.76 | 240 | 0.84 | 0.96 | 2% | 43% | 55% |

## Table F4: Overall evaluation use

| evaluation use | N | M | SD | not at all | a little | somewhat | a lot |
|---|---|---|---|---|---|---|---|
| evaluation data are used... | 285 | 2.83 | 0.85 | 6% | 27% | 44% | 23% |

## Table F5: Evaluation methods

| evaluation method | N | M | SD | not useful at all | a little useful | somewhat useful | very useful | not familiar |
|---|---|---|---|---|---|---|---|---|
| 1. standardized language proficiency assessments (e.g., OPI) | 287 | 2.98 | 0.97 | 10% | 15% | 35% | 32% | 8% |
| 2. program-internal student learning outcomes assessments | 287 | 3.37 | 0.79 | 3% | 9% | 31% | 50% | 7% |
| 3. student performance/portfolio assessments | 284 | 3.04 | 0.95 | 7% | 17% | 31% | 34% | 12% |
| semester final exams | 291 | 3.34 | 0.73 | 2% | 9% | 41% | 47% | 1% |
| 3. student self-assessments | 288 | 2.64 | 0.87 | 9% | 28% | 38% | 14% | 11% |
| 4. student grades | 286 | 2.99 | 0.84 | 6% | 17% | 48% | 28% | 0% |
| 5. longitudinal tracking of learner development | 287 | 2.99 | 0.98 | 6% | 14% | 22% | 26% | 31% |
| 6. student evaluation of courses | 291 | 2.97 | 0.81 | 4% | 22% | 46% | 27% | 1% |
| 7. focus groups | 286 | 2.12 | 0.98 | 19% | 17% | 16% | 5% | 43% |
| 8. questionnaires | 287 | 2.59 | 0.93 | 12% | 27% | 32% | 15% | 14% |
| 9. interviews | 285 | 2.86 | 0.93 | 10% | 16% | 39% | 23% | 12% |
| 10. introspections/journaling | 286 | 2.33 | 1.00 | 19% | 21% | 24% | 9% | 27% |
| 11. classroom observations | 291 | 3.31 | 0.76 | 2% | 10% | 40% | 45% | 2% |
| 12. program-internal meetings | 289 | 3.26 | 0.81 | 4% | 11% | 38% | 44% | 3% |
| 15. program document analysis (e.g., enrollment patterns) | 290 | 3.23 | 0.81 | 3% | 14% | 37% | 42% | 3% |

Table F6: Current overall capacity to conduct program evaluation

|  | N | M | SD | no capacity | little capacity | some capacity | a lot of capacity |
|---|---|---|---|---|---|---|---|
| overall current capacity | 283 | 2.88 | 0.73 | 3% | 24% | 55% | 18% |

Table F7: Resource needs for conducting program evaluation

| capacity building needs | N | M | SD | not helpful at all | a little helpful | somewhat helpful | very helpful | not familiar |
|---|---|---|---|---|---|---|---|---|
| 1. professional development workshops: how to do program evaluation in general | 286 | 3.22 | 0.86 | 4% | 15% | 34% | 45% | 3% |
| 2. professional development workshops: how to do student assessment/testing | 283 | 3.18 | 0.88 | 5% | 16% | 34% | 43% | 3% |
| 3. coursework on FL program evaluation | 282 | 2.53 | 1.03 | 19% | 22% | 32% | 18% | 9% |
| 4. templates for FL program evaluation process | 283 | 3.20 | 0.89 | 5% | 16% | 30% | 44% | 5% |
| 5. concrete examples of FL program evaluation | 284 | 3.49 | 0.75 | 2% | 10% | 24% | 60% | 4% |
| 6. textbooks on FL program evaluation | 281 | 2.55 | 0.98 | 15% | 31% | 30% | 19% | 6% |
| 7. external evaluation consultant | 283 | 2.92 | 1.00 | 11% | 18% | 34% | 33% | 4% |
| 8. online evaluation question/answer service | 284 | 2.56 | 0.96 | 13% | 27% | 31% | 15% | 14% |

*continued...*

## Table F7: Resource needs for conducting program evaluation (cont.)

| capacity building needs | N | M | SD | not helpful at all | a little helpful | somewhat helpful | very helpful | not familiar |
|---|---|---|---|---|---|---|---|---|
| 9. program-internal expertise in FL program evaluation | 282 | 3.26 | 0.81 | 3% | 13% | 35% | 44% | 5% |
| 10. strategies for raising faculty awareness about evaluation | 279 | 3.07 | 0.91 | 6% | 17% | 37% | 37% | 4% |
| 11. evaluation support/ coordination from FL professional organizations | 283 | 3.04 | 0.87 | 5% | 20% | 36% | 34% | 5% |
| 12. tools and techniques for collecting data | 283 | 3.16 | 0.88 | 4% | 18% | 33% | 42% | 4% |
| 13. electronic data-collection/ management software | 282 | 2.93 | 0.98 | 10% | 17% | 33% | 30% | 10% |
| 14. national resource center for college FL program evaluation | 282 | 2.93 | 1.01 | 10% | 18% | 28% | 32% | 12% |
| 15. systematic approaches for putting evaluation data to use | 280 | 3.20 | 0.90 | 4% | 19% | 26% | 46% | 6% |

# The Role of Evaluation in Curriculum Development and Growth of the UNM Portuguese Program

Margo Milleret
Agripino S. Silveira
University of New Mexico, Albuquerque

*This paper describes the use of evaluation to enhance the Portuguese curriculum and course offerings at the University of New Mexico, and to increase enrollment in this 'less commonly taught' language program. After the creation of new experimental courses to meet the needs of a large proportion of Spanish-speaking students, evaluation was used to identify whether students had enrolled in the appropriate courses (based on their Spanish skill level) and to collect feedback that would help improve course delivery. The findings were also helpful in promoting awareness about the new classes and in improving course content. The Portuguese program has gained invaluable information from the evaluation process and plans to sustain the use of evaluation for similar purposes in the future.*

## Program background, context, and evaluation impetus

It has been a long-term goal of the Portuguese program faculty at the University of New Mexico to re-design the undergraduate curriculum for the purpose of updating course offerings, but also to attract more students and increase enrollments. Traditionally, Latin American studies in general has been a strength and focus of research at the university, and prior to the loss of positions and funding in the 1980s, Portuguese made a healthy contribution to this area of study at both the undergraduate and graduate levels. The current faculty felt that Portuguese should attempt to re-establish its role as a critical part of the Latin American studies area. However, as the program had not been evaluated in many years—a common phenomenon among the less commonly taught languages—it was not entirely clear what courses would meet students' needs. In addition, feedback from students on end of semester course evaluations had suggested for some time that there were problems of articulation in existing course sequences, especially for two distinct populations of students: Spanish versus non-Spanish speakers. Further, it was unclear how many Spanish

---

Milleret, M., & Silveira, A. S. (2009). The role of evaluation in curriculum development and growth of the UNM Portuguese program. In J. M. Norris, J. McE. Davis, C. Sinicrope, & Y. Watanabe (Eds.), *Toward useful program evaluation in college foreign language education* (pp. 57–82). Honolulu: University of Hawai'i, National Foreign Language Resource Center.

speakers enrolled in Portuguese classes and the impact their different skill levels had on instruction.

The challenge of serving the needs of both Spanish and non-Spanish speakers had been a concern for some years in the Portuguese program. The similarity of the two Romance languages appears to give Spanish speakers an advantage in recognition of many shared lexical items and in the application of learning strategies. Non-Spanish speakers recognized these advantages among their fellow students and expressed frustration with their own difficulties, especially in making the transition from intermediate language classes to advanced content courses. Yet, the program had no specific plan to serve the needs of second versus third language learners. The challenge with developing a plan was that the enrollment numbers seemed to favor, and continue to favor, the third-language learners (i.e., Spanish speakers), making it difficult to guarantee classes designed for both groups.

In 2006, at the outset of the project described here, the Portuguese program enrolled approximately 100 students each semester in classes of language and culture at the beginning and intermediate language levels, and in courses on popular music, film, theater, and literature at the advanced levels. The advanced-level content classes combine undergraduate and graduate students, due largely to the fact that many graduate-only courses could not be offered without greater numbers of graduate students to take them, and without greater numbers of undergraduate students to warrant the support of more graduate teaching assistants (something of a vicious circle). As of 2006, there were two faculty members and three graduate teaching assistants who delivered all the courses in the Portuguese program.

Beginning in the period of 2004–06, the discovery of the role of evaluation in program development, following in particular work by Brown (1995), set the course for evaluating, redesigning, and growing the Portuguese program. An initial needs analysis was undertaken at this time in order to get a better fix on the kinds and numbers of students enrolling in the various Portuguese courses available, as well as on the potential changes that might lead to better articulated courses and increased enrollments across the program. Upon completion of the needs analysis, the faculty elected to address the needs of undergraduate students first by creating experimental beginning language courses. Thus, the findings had demonstrated that the Portuguese program needed two types of new beginning language classes for Spanish and non-Spanish speakers. For non-Spanish speakers there was a need for courses that met in a three-day-a-week format, since the existing five-day-a-week intensive format was deemed intimidating to English-only speakers. For Spanish-speakers, by contrast, there was a need for an intensive language course designed to use their language skills and cognate knowledge to move more quickly through the material. It was believed that these new courses would bring students to the study of Portuguese earlier in their college careers and thus provide them with the opportunity to develop their skills over a longer time, enrolling greater numbers in more courses along the way.

In particular, the first actions taken based on the findings of the needs analysis were the creation of three new undergraduate experimental classes. First, the Portuguese faculty developed a two-semester sequence in a three-day-a-week format for true beginners who did not speak Spanish (PORT 101–102). By the end of spring 2007, we had received approval for the two-semester beginning course sequence and secured funding for two years for a part-time instructor to teach the classes. Second, we redesigned one section of Port 275, the existing beginning five-day-a-week intensive language class, as a special section for Spanish speakers (PORT 275–S). Further, in order to recruit students for all three experimental courses we developed new promotional materials and circulated these in Spanish classes, as well as to freshmen orientation advisors and advisors in the College of Arts and Sciences.

The evaluation reported here began at this point. Given that the Portuguese faculty had designed and implemented new courses on the basis of findings from the previous needs analysis, we wanted to know about the impact and effectiveness of our various programmatic changes. First, we wanted to know if students were enrolling in courses appropriate to their Spanish-language background. Again, the aim had been to better tailor pedagogy to students with particular Spanish-background profiles, and it was thus important to know if students were being directed into the right courses in the first place. We also sought a sense of how effectively our promotional campaign was functioning, particularly the degree to which it helped students (and advisors) select the appropriate Portuguese course. Similarly, we were curious if there was any effect from the promotional campaign on enrollment generally, and on freshman enrollment in particular, as the faculty had designed courses with the aim of enticing students to start Portuguese study earlier in their college careers. Finally, we wanted to know how effectively the new classes were functioning— as reflected in levels of student satisfaction— focusing on class activities, assessments, appropriateness of learning outcomes and teacher performance. By asking these questions, we hoped to obtain a better sense of whether the curricular changes we had instigated after the needs analysis were actually responding to students' identified needs. Subsequently, we could build the program from the bottom up and establish an ongoing evaluative process that would carry on past our introductory language classes and into the upper division and graduate-level courses.

An evaluation project designed to address these issues began in fall of 2007 when two of the three experimental classes were first offered. The PORT 101 course for true beginners and the PORT 275–S for native and advanced Spanish speakers were listed at attractive times in the course schedule at 10am and 1pm respectively. The administration stipulated that if the PORT 101 course had sufficient enrollment in the fall of 2007, then the second course in the sequence, PORT 102, would be offered in the spring of 2008. Thus, by spring 2008 all three experimental courses would be in the course schedule offerings.

## Primary intended users, uses, and evaluation questions

Given the concerns sketched above, the evaluation project was designed to answer three questions about the experimental courses:

1. Did students get the information they needed from our promotional campaign to help them enroll in the correct class for their language background?
2. What did students expect to learn in their classes, and did the classes meet their expectations?
3. What types of classroom activities and assessments were most helpful to students?

Findings from the evaluation project would be used mainly by the Portuguese faculty, that is, the individuals responsible for making changes to the new courses and related recruitment activities based on project findings. The Portuguese faculty agreed to put evaluation findings to the following use: information about promotional materials (evaluation question one) would be used to know if the advertising campaign was working effectively in attracting students and placing them in the right courses, and if not, to inform decisions about changes. Further, information about student enrollment, class status/year, and Spanish-language background (question one) would help the faculty track the Spanish and non-Spanish speakers in the program and learn about their numbers, choices, and reasons for the courses they selected. Information about student expectations (question two) would help faculty understand what students in beginning classes wanted to learn, especially the differences in expectations between those enrolled in three-day-a-week classes as opposed to those enrolled in five-day-a-week intensive classes. Findings about helpful class activities and assessments (question three) would assist us in improving the new courses in response to students' needs and articulate the new classes into our existing curriculum.

From a broader institutional perspective, there were additional intended users of evaluation findings as well. The Portuguese program had established a good reputation with the higher administration in Arts and Sciences thanks to its previous evaluation projects. The original needs analysis that led to the current project was supported with monies for the evaluator by the now former dean. When the results pointed to a need for new courses, the data from the needs analysis provided convincing arguments that led to financial support from the associate dean to pay for part-time instructors for the PORT 101 and 102 classes. The project reported here was also of interest to the associate dean, who acknowledged that the work being done in evaluation provided important feedback for funding decisions. In addition, the associate dean noted that if there were further growth in the Portuguese program that could be documented by data, he would support that growth with additional hires. Finally, the deans have repeatedly noted that the data collection and analysis conducted by the Portuguese program serve as an example of what all departments interested in student learning should be doing in terms of evaluation.

## Evaluation design and methods

### Initial instrumentation for data collection

In the fall of 2007, the Portuguese faculty formed a two person evaluation team of a faculty member and research assistant to work with the three graduate assistant instructors in charge of the (newly minted) beginning Portuguese classes. In order to generate needed information, as well as determine appropriate data collection methods, the evaluation team identified a number of indicators (i.e., sources of information) that would help tell us what we needed to know about our project foci. For all three evaluation questions, students were the key informants, and we sought their perceptions and opinions about course experiences, student expectations, language background, effectiveness of class activities, and the degree to which promotional literature was placing students correctly.

Student information was targeted using two main data collection methods: surveys and focus group interviews. With the guidance of evaluation consultants from the Foreign Language Program Evaluation Project we developed two paper-based surveys for the beginning and the end of the semester, and focus group questions for collection of information at the mid-semester point. Data gathered from the beginning-of-semester surveys were intended to illuminate our project foci, but also to make adjustments to (a) questions developed for the end-of-semester paper survey and (b) questions used with the focus groups. For example, we learned that we needed to elicit more specific responses on surveys about where students were getting information about the new Portuguese courses. Originally we included *advisor* as a possible selection, but the term was too general since there are advisors in the Spanish program, in Arts and Sciences, and at freshman orientation. If we wanted to get the right information about our courses to the right people, we needed to know who those specific people were. So, we asked the question about advisors again for the mid-semester focus groups and on the end-of-semester paper survey where we solicited more specific details. Similar adjustments were made in other aspects of the focus group and final survey.

The beginning-of-semester survey was administered by the research assistant/evaluator during class time in the first week of classes in fall 2007 to the two new beginning Portuguese classes (PORT 101, 275–S) and, for purposes of comparison, to the existing intensive beginning Portuguese class (PORT 275; this was the standard course containing a mixture of both Spanish and non-Spanish speaking students). The focus group meetings were conducted at mid-semester in October of 2007. These sessions were administered by two external evaluation consultants from the Foreign Language Program Evaluation Project during class time with students from all three classes. The end-of-semester paper survey was turned in by the students following the end of classes, for extra credit, in fall of 2007. There were three classes with approximately 20 students each that participated in all aspects of the fall evaluation ($N=60$). The two paper surveys were administered again in spring of 2008 with four beginning Portuguese classes participating (PORT 101, 102, 275–S, and 275) and with a total of $N=118$ students.

A summary of the three instruments is provided here, and the instruments are appended. The beginning-of-semester survey asked about student status at UNM, language learning background, how they found out about the course, its convenience, their reasons for choosing the course, their reasons for studying Portuguese, and their expectations for the course (see Appendix A). The mid-semester focus groups were designed to elicit more details about how students found out about the new courses, the techniques and materials that were helping them learn, the activities and assessments that the instructors used that were effective, the impact of Spanish on their learning, and any suggestions for change in the class (see Appendix B). Finally, end-of-semester surveys asked about students' language skills, their experiences in the course, what they learned (from the list of course objectives), and their suggestions for course improvements, including questions about alternative textbooks, and additional courses (see Appendix C).

## Interim findings and actions: Fall 2007–spring 2008

The evaluation instruments administered in fall of 2007 provided data that helped us understand the way the program was changing and informed immediate actions. First, from the beginning-of-semester survey we learned that the percentages of Spanish speakers in our program were growing in comparison with the 2006 needs analysis. Earlier numbers showed 84% of the students were native or second-language speakers of Spanish. By fall 2007, the number had risen to 90%. This finding meant that we had Spanish speakers enrolled in all of our classes, not just the ones that we had designed for them. Thus, despite the fact that we were interested in meeting the needs of those learners who are English monolinguals, our courses persistently contained a substantial audience of Spanish-speakers who are learning Portuguese as a third language.

Second, feedback from the fall 2007 mid-semester focus groups and end-of-semester surveys also helped the instructors revise their classes. The mid-semester focus groups gave the instructors an opportunity to improve the students' experience in the classroom before the semester ended. The end-of-semester survey provided instructors with data about the degree to which students felt they were meeting course objectives (see Table 6) and the effectiveness of assessment methods already in place in each of the courses (e.g., weekly quizzes, mid-term exam, and final exam). Thus, the instructors had information to help them reformulate their syllabi for spring 2008. Since several of the courses were new to the instructors, the feedback gave them concrete information about student needs and the appropriateness of the course objectives for the new course format. There was also a clearer sense of how each of the courses needed to respond to student learning, especially the differences between a three-day-a-week format and a five-day-a-week format, and the differences between a class designed for Spanish speakers and one that was not. The evaluation findings also pointed out the need for better descriptions of the new classes, and better dissemination of those descriptions, so that students and their advisors could identify the right courses for students' language background and language learning needs. (e.g., "Should have moved to 275–S. Stayed because I didn't know how difficult it would be, but now I wish I was in that class," said a student from PORT 275 during the focus group. Another student from PORT 275–S said, "I didn't know that this is for Spanish speakers but happened to register.")

Finally, we had an unanticipated opportunity to put the survey data to use at the end of fall 2007, when the second class of the beginning sequence, PORT 102, appeared for the first time in the course offerings for spring of 2008. Prior to the semester, we encountered unexpected low enrollments in that class. The end-of-semester survey revealed that most of the students in the PORT 101 course had good reasons for not continuing their study in PORT 102 during spring 2008, despite their eventual intentions to do so. However, the administration made it clear that we had to fill the class in order to guarantee further funding for an instructor of the beginning Portuguese sequence. We turned to the data from the evaluation for the solution to our low enrollment problem. The end-of-semester survey showed an interest in yet another type of course, a beginning (i.e., less intensive) three-day-a-week class designed for Spanish speakers. This information led us to re-design the PORT 102 as another entry point for Spanish speakers beginning the study of Portuguese. We were already offering an experimental intensive course for Spanish speakers (PORT 275–S), but we knew from the evaluation findings that many students did not want to attend class five days a week. After the quick re-design, we conducted an advertising campaign via e-mail bulletins and on the department's web site. By January 2008, we had 12 students enrolled in the newly re-designed 102 class, sufficient for it to continue.

Clearly, on an immediate basis, we were able to solve certain problems that appeared in the new course development process with the data garnered from evaluation: (a) the low enrollment problem in PORT 102 and its solution were provided by findings from the evaluation; (b) syllabi were revised and continue to be revised based on data gathered about whether or not the courses were reaching their objectives and utilizing meaningful assessments; and (c) the instructors were complemented on their strengths and guided on their weaknesses thanks to feedback from the evaluation. In addition, beyond these immediate uses for evaluation data, larger-scale and longer-term analyses and uses were undertaken, as described in the following section.

## Long-term findings, interpretations, uses

The findings reported here are based on data collected in the fall of 2007 and spring of 2008 from 190 beginning and end-of-semester surveys and 54 students who participated in the focus groups in the Fall of 2007. The distribution of the data is summarized in Table 1. The participants were given the survey by the research assistant/evaluator and responded anonymously. In the following sections we present the data taken from these different data-collection instruments concerning the three purposes prefaced in the previous section: (a) to verify whether our information campaign had guided students to the right class for their language background; (b) to learn about the students' expectations for the courses; and (c) to collect feedback that would help us improve and standardize course delivery for the future, especially the development of learning objectives and assessments appropriate to each course.

Table 1: Distribution of participants across the different data-collection instruments

|  | beginning-of-semester | | end-of-semester | | focus group | total |
|---|---|---|---|---|---|---|
|  | fall 2007 | spring 2008 | fall 2007 | spring 2008 | fall 2007 | |
| PORT 101 | 23 | 22 | 17 | 0 | 18 | 80 |
| PORT 102 | 0 | 12 | 0 | 8 | 0 | 20 |
| PORT 275 | 18 | 15 | 19 | 0 | 18 | 70 |
| PORT 275–S | 17 | 23 | 16 | 0 | 18 | 74 |
| total responses | 58 | 72 | 52 | 8 | 54 | 244 |

### Beginning-of-semester survey

In this section we discuss the results from surveys given at the beginning of the semester for fall 2007 and spring 2008. After collecting the surveys from all courses, the information was tabulated in Microsoft Excel. The results were summarized in tables before being released to teaching assistants and department administrators. The earlier needs analysis had indicated that the Portuguese program consisted mostly of upper-class students; that is, juniors and seniors. Therefore, with the creation of PORT 101, it was expected that more freshman students would be attracted to the program. What is more, the same expectations pertained to the reworked PORT 102 for Spanish-speakers. Table 2 below shows the distribution of students in the beginning Portuguese courses according to their enrollment status.

Table 2: Distribution of students according to their status in fall 2007 and spring 2008[1]

|  | N | M | SD | PORT 101 | PORT 102 | PORT 275 | PORT 275–S |
|---|---|---|---|---|---|---|---|
| freshman | 37 | 9.25 | 8.85 | 22 | 5 | 8 | 2 |
| sophomore | 16 | 4.00 | 3.46 | 7 | 1 | 7 | 1 |
| junior | 23 | 5.75 | 3.40 | 9 | 1 | 6 | 7 |
| senior | 33 | 8.25 | 7.59 | 4 | 2 | 8 | 19 |
| graduate | 18 | 4.50 | 3.11 | 3 | 2 | 4 | 9 |

Findings indicated that, in the current iteration of courses, freshman students have become as numerous as seniors and juniors overall in the Portuguese program, especially in the classes in which we expected to find them. This finding suggests changes inaugurated after the needs analysis were effective and should be sustained in that attracting freshman students is important for the growth of the Portuguese program. Students who enter our program early in their college careers have an opportunity to achieve higher skill levels in Portuguese and greater understanding of content, taking more courses along the way. Such students also have the opportunity to choose to become majors and minors. In turn,

---

1  The two periods have been combined here because they showed similar patterns in the distribution of students. In other words, there were no large differences from one semester to the other. When significant differences emerge we will show them separately for ease of comparison.

increasing the number of majors and minors would allow Portuguese to assume a greater visibility on the UNM campus.

Another important piece of information that we attained from our surveys was how students found out about our courses. As can be seen in Table 3, the majority of students found out about Portuguese courses through the university catalog, with their advisor being the second most informative source. Third most frequently noted sources were information taken from the Spanish and Portuguese department website and a friend taking Portuguese.

Table 3: Ways in which students found out about the Portuguese courses

|  | N | M | SD | PORT 101 | PORT 275 | PORT 275–S | PORT 102 |
|---|---|---|---|---|---|---|---|
| university course catalog | 45 | 11.25 | 7.50 | 21 | 12 | 9 | 3 |
| website | 17 | 4.25 | 4.03 | 10 | 4 | 1 | 2 |
| poster | 0 | 0.00 | 0.00 | 0 | 0 | 0 | 0 |
| my advisor | 29 | 7.25 | 5.06 | 3 | 10 | 13 | 3 |
| freshman orientation | 7 | 1.75 | 2.87 | 6 | 0 | 0 | 1 |
| announcement in Span. course | 5 | 1.25 | 1.89 | 0 | 1 | 4 | 0 |
| a friend taking Spanish | 2 | 0.50 | 1.00 | 2 | 0 | 0 | 0 |
| a friend taking Portuguese | 17 | 4.25 | 3.40 | 3 | 4 | 9 | 1 |

Even though it seems that the freshman orientation flier inserted in the folders given to incoming students does not fare as one of the most effective ways of advertising our classes, it did contribute its share of bringing us some students. Thus, we would consider the flier to be worth continuing at this point. This form of advertisement was employed to attract freshmen entering UNM in the fall of 2007, and it was revised and expanded to provide more complete course descriptions for all potential students enrolling in Portuguese for the spring of 2008. Findings also showed that in both semesters the number of freshman in our program remained closely the same (19 students in the fall of 2007, and 18 students in the spring of 2008), which points to the effectiveness of this form of advertisement. Two new forms of advertisement that were employed in preparation for fall 2008 were consultations with advisors, and the placement of paper announcements about PORT 101 and PORT 102 in the language learning center. During summer orientation 2008, freshmen students who were taking placement exams in the language laboratory for Spanish, French, and German also saw fliers at their computer desks that invited them to consider enrolling in Portuguese classes, especially since the classes did not require a placement test and would fulfill the core curriculum language requirement.

We also wanted to know whether students were able to enroll in the classes that accommodated their linguistic background. Table 4 illustrates the findings for students' self-ratings of their proficiency in Spanish (students indicated their proficiency by selecting one of the following options: beginner, intermediate, advanced, near-native, and native). The beginning-of-semester survey verified that the placement of students had been relatively successful, with the more proficient students enrolling in the Spanish-focused classes, while the less proficient Spanish speakers were found in the classes that were designed for non-Spanish speakers (see Table 4). Although many students did not receive the new materials used for advertising the courses, the instructors provided them with additional details about the course on the first day. Some students were able to change sections in order to attend a course better suited to their background.

Table 4: Student self-ratings of Spanish proficiency

|  | N | M | SD | PORT 101 | PORT 102 | PORT 275 | PORT 275–S |
|---|---|---|---|---|---|---|---|
| beginner | 9 | 2.25 | 2.63 | 6 | 0 | 1 | 2 |
| intermediate | 18 | 4.50 | 4.04 | 10 | 2 | 5 | 1 |
| advanced | 24 | 6.00 | 3.46 | 3 | 3 | 9 | 9 |
| near-native | 19 | 4.75 | 1.89 | 6 | 2 | 5 | 6 |
| native | 45 | 11.25 | 6.85 | 9 | 5 | 10 | 21 |

The findings indicated that almost 80% of our Spanish-speaking students have a self-assessed proficiency between "advanced" and "native" in Spanish. This factor is of major importance for the methodologies and pedagogy adopted in our program, due to the close typological relationship between Spanish and Portuguese. Although they are different languages, they have derived from the same dialect of Vulgar Latin and therefore share similar structures at all linguistic levels. Studies in the learning of third languages (L3) suggest that one of the most influential factors in determining what structures will be transferred to the target language is the typological similarity between the languages involved (Carvalho & Silva, 2006). Observing that the majority of students who enroll in our Portuguese classes speak Spanish, and that this language may have an impact on the way their Portuguese language skills develop, allows us to predict the kinds of problems and advantages that our students will encounter.

Though the majority of the students enrolled in the Portuguese program spoke Spanish at one of the levels illustrated in Table 4, they appear in most cases to have selected classes that were appropriate to their knowledge of Spanish. Most students who were near-native or native speakers of Spanish tended to enroll in the five-day-a-week intensive Portuguese courses such as PORT 275 or 275 for Spanish speakers. The inverse is also true for the three-day-a-week PORT 101 and 102, in that students with a lower proficiency in Spanish enrolled in these courses. However, it is also apparent that PORT 101 and 102 appealed to highly proficient Spanish-speakers as well as beginners. At the time of this evaluation, approximately one third of the students in these courses considered themselves native speakers of Spanish. Although this factor may not pose a problem for those students taking PORT 102, since it was re-designed for Spanish speakers, students enrolled in PORT 101 may face certain challenges, as the class is designed for true beginners who do not speak Spanish.

Recall that a second aim for the evaluation was to obtain data regarding students' expectations when entering Portuguese courses (see Appendix A, question 5). In order to design courses that will attend to the needs of students, it was necessary to obtain information about what those students expected to learn at the end of each of these courses. Firstly, students remarked that they anticipated being able to master basic grammatical structures in Portuguese. This finding was most salient in the responses provided by the participants taking PORT 101 and PORT 102, where almost 90% addressed something along these lines. This is not to say that the participants enrolled in the other two courses, PORT 275 and PORT 275-S, did not express their wish to learn these structures. On the contrary, since these students already knew that their courses would be more intensive in nature, it would seem that they assumed this basic knowledge of the language would be learned. In their responses, students in the intensive beginning courses expected to learn not only the basic structure of the language, but also gain an ability to converse and write at a basic level. It is not surprising, then, that the students enrolling in intensive language courses had much higher expectations for the course and themselves than those entering at the true beginning level.

Another important finding regarding student expectations was related to students' reasons for learning Portuguese. We expected that students enrolled in PORT 101 and PORT 102 were taking these classes in order to fulfill their core curriculum requirement of three hours of a foreign language. Even though this expectation was not borne out in the data as the primary justification, it was still the second most frequent reason for enrolling in PORT 101. Findings from the earlier needs analysis had suggested that students in the Portuguese program enrolled in courses for pleasure, because they had contact with friends or family from Brazil, or because they had concrete plans to travel and/or work in a Portuguese-speaking country. The findings of the current evaluation (Table 5) echoed those from the needs analysis, to some extent, with "pleasure" being the top response. Some participants also stated that they were interested in learning Portuguese in order to be able to spend some time in a Portuguese-speaking country, while others asserted their interest in learning the language was because of the cultural richness and/or heritage affinity they associated with it.

Table 5: Reasons for taking Portuguese

|  | N | M | SD | PORT 101 | PORT 102 | PORT 275 | PORT 275–S |
|---|---|---|---|---|---|---|---|
| to fulfill a requirement | 66 | 16.50 | 10.08 | 27 | 3 | 16 | 20 |
| for pleasure | 102 | 25.50 | 12.71 | 40 | 9 | 26 | 27 |
| for my major | 1 | 0.25 | 6.58 | 0 | 1 | 0 | 0 |
| to work/live abroad | 48 | 12.00 | 8.69 | 11 | 4 | 13 | 20 |
| to relate to my cultural heritage | 53 | 13.25 | 0.96 | 25 | 4 | 12 | 12 |
| for current work | 7 | 1.75 | 0.50 | 3 | 1 | 1 | 2 |

Interestingly, the students' reasons for taking Portuguese correlated with their expectations in taking Portuguese. Participants who took Portuguese to major in the field expected to gain as much command as possible of the language. For these learners, advancing their knowledge of the language seemed to be paramount for their success as future Portuguese majors. Incidentally, the Spanish native speakers showed a desire not only to learn the basic structures of the language, but also to advance faster within the program based on the knowledge they were bringing to the course (32/45 or 71%). This finding, however, was more pronounced within the group of participants who were taking PORT 275 (18/21 or 86%) for Spanish speakers, reflecting a preconception about what they anticipated to get out of that class, or an appreciation for a special class created for them.

On the other hand, several participants who claimed to have enrolled in PORT 101 and 102 with the desire to fulfill their core curriculum requirements still expressed the intention of learning the language, but at a slower pace. As stated earlier, findings from the needs analysis had pointed to the intimidating nature of the intensive classes in Portuguese, which tended to repel freshmen and sophomores. The new three-hour, three-credit courses seemed to provide students with the possibility of learning the language as well as fulfilling their university requirements, without the pressures exerted by an accelerated format.

## Focus groups

The data collected in the focus groups consisted of answers provided by 54 participants from three classes in the fall of 2007. An outside team of language evaluators conducted the focus groups to assure participant anonymity, thereby facilitating their willingness to contribute to the discussions. Each Portuguese course offered that semester (101, 275, 275–S) was interviewed separately on the same day at different times. Each class was asked the same set of questions (see Appendix B); responses were recorded and also noted by the facilitator. The primary use of focus group findings was immediate, as reviewed above, as details were provided at the mid-semester point to the instructors, who were then able to make adjustments in a variety of course delivery features. In addition, though, several findings led to larger-scale actions, and these are summarized here.

Since the university does not have a placement exam capable of evaluating the skills of both Spanish and non-Spanish speakers entering the Portuguese program, students and their advisors decided upon which course to enroll in. Again, after we developed the new courses, we wanted to know whether students had enrolled in the right course for their background. Overall, findings from the focus groups showed that most students thought they were placed in the correct Portuguese course, and students were generally satisfied with their placement. Importantly, though, some mentioned that it would have been better to have received more information about the class prior to registering so they could have made a more educated choice as to what class to take.

The disparity in placement was mostly observed in the PORT 275 which was initially created to attend to those students who do not speak Spanish. The most important issue raised by the students with regards to their placement in this particular course was the extent to which the course differs from its counterpart, PORT 275–S, in terms of content and pace. Some of the students who were Spanish speakers felt that the pace of the course was too slow, while other students felt that the pace was too fast and determined by the Spanish speakers. In short, there were serious discrepancies observed in this particular course and that were in need of attention.

At the time of this writing, such discrepancies are still observed in this course. However, students are aware of them due to better advertising and education before registering for the course. The instructors, as well, are better equipped to deal with the issues that arise from such a heterogeneous group of learners, having become more aware of these issues through the evaluation findings. Pedagogical materials of many sorts have become available for our instructors to use with their students, especially given that the make-up of the program is still mostly Spanish speakers. Clearly, we cannot ignore that these learners will be present in all courses, and we have an obligation to aid them in their learning.

It is worth noting, however, that issues regarding appropriate placement of students according to their knowledge of Spanish arose primarily in the PORT 275 course. This phenomenon was largely due to the nature of the program, at the time, in that only PORT 275 (for supposedly non-Spanish speakers) and PORT 275–S were offered, thus leaving students without a "third" possibility. In short, those who were not confident enough of their Spanish entered PORT 275 together with those with very little to no Spanish whatsoever, creating a quite varied group of learners.

After careful consideration of these findings, we have improved the ways in which the Portuguese courses are advertised, including information on their content, their intended audience, and the next course in the sequence. We now distribute a flier to all students already enrolled in our courses so they know what classes will be available in subsequent semesters; we also hope that they use the information from this flier to inform their friends about Portuguese classes. Recall from Table 3 that "a friend taking Portuguese" was the third most effective advertisement tool we have in our program. Thus, we have made the commitment to keep our students well informed about our classes so they can also give more accurate information to their friends.

Another question posed in the focus groups was the appropriateness of the textbook and the way it was being used in the classroom. We had just adopted a new textbook for all of the fall 2007 classes, and we wanted to make sure students were satisfied with the new class materials. Overall, students agreed that the textbook and class materials were well chosen and very helpful in their learning. Some students commented that the book was "good, with a lot of pictures and examples" while others commented that it was good because it had "many speaking exercises." Accordingly, we decided to continue working with the text.

In a third area of concern, we requested that the focus groups address the instructors' performance and the activities they use in class. The students stated that they were largely satisfied with the quality of the instructors and with the quality of the activities the instructors brought to class. Students expressed that their teachers were "very helpful and understanding" and the way teachers conducted their classes was "very dynamic." Moreover, the instructors' practice of giving students feedback on their pronunciation and oral skills was praised as being one of their best traits. At the same time, some students did express concern with scheduling of class expectations, such as homework and quizzes. This concern was dealt with through immediate adjustments in how some instructors made students aware of the class expectations and schedule.

The findings of the focus groups were important for two reasons. On the one hand, they gave us a mid-semester feedback on the way courses and instruction were progressing, and on the efficacy of some of the course changes that had been implemented, and they led to immediate adjustments during the semester. On the other hand, they served as a guide for the end-of-semester survey. To illustrate this point, up to this moment we had not yet addressed the important question of the impact of students' knowledge of Spanish and its relationship to their ability to learn Portuguese. In the end-of-semester of semester survey, as will be discussed in the following section, we addressed this question as well as others that had not yet been raised in preceding data collection.

### End-of-semester survey

A third aim in conducting this evaluation was to collect feedback that would help us improve and standardize course delivery, especially the development of learning objectives and assessments appropriate to each course. The set of questions developed to acquire this information attempted to link the students' learning expectations with the learning that actually took place in the classroom by the end of the semester of instruction. These questions were based on an initial version of the learning outcomes established for these classes, which were printed in instructors' respective syllabi. For each learning outcome, in the end-of-semester survey, students were asked to indicate on a scale of one ("not at all") to five ("very well") the degree to which they could perform a given outcome. Key questions are illustrated in Table 6 below.

The most striking finding from Table 6 is that most students' answers are clustered in the middle range of the evaluation scale. The implication raised by such findings points to a reanalysis of the learning outcomes for each individual course, taking into account not only the population of students that are attending these classes, but also other factors such as their expectations for the course, their proficiency in Spanish, and their reasons for entering the program. For example, most of the students who participated in the research said that they would have liked to study and understand Brazilian culture in more detail[2]. Nonetheless, this focus is not explicitly stated in our learning outcomes, at least not for the beginning language courses.

Table 6: Self-rated achievement of key learning outcomes in the end-of-semester survey[3]

| To what extent can you… | | N | M | SD |
|---|---|---|---|---|
| understand your classmates when you talk about university life, friends, entertaining, and family? | PORT 101 | 17 | 3.00 | 1.00 |
| | PORT 102 | 8 | 3.25 | 0.71 |
| | PORT 275 | 19 | 3.21 | 0.71 |
| | PORT 275-S | 16 | 3.25 | 0.71 |
| understand reading assignments about the cultures of the Portuguese-speaking world? | PORT 101 | 17 | 2.88 | 0.70 |
| | PORT 102 | 8 | 3.50 | 0.53 |
| | PORT 275 | 19 | 3.42 | 0.51 |
| | PORT 275-S | 16 | 3.50 | 0.54 |
| ask and answer questions in Portuguese? | PORT 101 | 17 | 2.64 | 0.61 |
| | PORT 102 | 8 | 2.75 | 0.71 |
| | PORT 275 | 19 | 2.95 | 0.62 |
| | PORT 275-S | 16 | 2.75 | 0.71 |
| describe places, people, and events in speaking? | PORT 101 | 17 | 2.71 | 0.59 |
| | PORT 102 | 8 | 2.50 | 0.53 |
| | PORT 275 | 19 | 2.84 | 0.69 |
| | PORT 275-S | 16 | 2.50 | 0.54 |
| describe places, people, and events in writing? | PORT 101 | 17 | 3.00 | 0.71 |
| | PORT 102 | 7 | 3.14 | 0.69 |
| | PORT 275 | 19 | 3.11 | 0.66 |
| | PORT 275-S | 16 | 3.25 | 0.71 |
| use your grammatical knowledge to communicate in Portuguese? | PORT 101 | 12 | 2.17 | 0.58 |
| | PORT 102 | 4 | 1.75 | 0.50 |
| | PORT 275 | 8 | 2.75 | 1.04 |
| | PORT 275-S | 16 | 2.38 | 0.74 |

Another interpretation that can be made from the results above is that, despite the fact that all the courses are entry-level, each individual course serves a slightly different public. Although these courses are different and attend to different populations of students, they

---

2  The two periods have been combined here because they showed similar patterns in the distribution of students. In other words, there were no large differences from one semester to the other. When significant differences emerge we will show them separately for ease of comparison.

3  As can be seen, the N sizes listed here differ from those presented earlier in this section. This is due to the fact that this portion of the survey was only conducted in the Spring of 2008, not in the initial Fall survey. Moreover, each of these courses had other learning outcomes that have not been presented here for the sake of comparison. Thus, the outcomes presented here reflect only those that were the same across the different groups.

all follow a similar pedagogy applied to the same textbook. Thus, we concluded that each of these courses ought to have its own set of learning outcomes and that future surveys should evaluate how well those outcomes are realized.

Another finding that was obtained from the comparison presented in Table 6 is that students who undertake the more intensive courses, such as PORT 275–S, seem to have more confidence in what they have learned. We speculated that students rated themselves higher because intensive courses such as Port 275–S offer daily class meetings and cover a greater amount of course material. Moreover, these learners are exposed to daily interactions with the instructor as well as their peers so that structures are more easily assimilated. Such frequent and constant contact with the language allows the learners to internalize structures more effectively, thus increasing their awareness of such knowledge (c.f. Ellis 2002a, 2002b for a discussion of the way frequency affects linguistic representation).

A second objective of the end-of-semester survey was to obtain information on the way that learners perceived the influence of their Spanish on their learning of Portuguese. According to Table 7, the more proficient in Spanish the learner is, the more likely he or she is to observe the influence of Spanish on the learning of Portuguese. The inverse is also true, that is, that the less proficient the learner is, the less likely he or she is to notice the influence of Spanish on the acquisition of Portuguese. This finding corroborates claims in the literature on the learning of Portuguese as a third language (Carvalho & Silva, 2006).

**Table 7: The degree of Spanish knowledge contribution to learning of Portuguese**

|  | N | M | SD | not at all | a little | some-what | a lot |
|---|---|---|---|---|---|---|---|
| (no Spanish knowledge) | (5) | (1.00) | (0.00) | (5) | | | |
| beginning | 1 | 3.00 | — | | | 1 | |
| intermediate | 12 | 2.92 | 1.00 | 1 | 3 | 4 | 4 |
| advanced | 9 | 3.78 | 0.67 | | 1 | | 8 |
| near-native | 8 | 3.63 | 0.74 | | 1 | 1 | 6 |
| native | 16 | 3.88 | 0.34 | | | 2 | 14 |
| total | 46 (51) | 3.49 | 0.86 | 1 (5) | 5 | 8 | 32 |

These findings obtained in Table 7 also correspond with those borne out in the previous needs analysis whereby many of the learners voiced their concern regarding the interference, or transfer (see Odlin, 1989 for a discussion of the terminology), from Spanish into Portuguese, in that the learning of the latter was facilitated but also hindered by the knowledge of the former. In the end-of-semester survey, similarly, some learners declared that even though the knowledge of Spanish could be very confusing when learning Portuguese, they felt that it was also very helpful. Moreover, others commented that because the grammar and the vocabulary of the two languages are in fact very similar,[4] the learning of

---

4    This primarily due to what Odlin (2002) calls the "psychotypology effect" whereby two languages share similarities in their structure to the extent that one may be predictable in terms of the other. In a study of the acquisition of the subjunctive in Portuguese by speakers of Spanish as either a second language or bilinguals showed that the "psychotypology effect" is indeed statistically more prone to affect transfer than any other factor such as age, order of acquisition, or length of acquisition (see Carvalho & Silva, 2006). Jensen (1999) also found that speakers of Spanish, without any training in Portuguese, are able to comprehend about 50% of what is being said. In addition, Henriques (2000)

these two areas was less problematic. In short, learners ratified the preconceived notion that the knowledge of Spanish indeed supports a faster and more effective learning of Portuguese (Carvalho and Silva, 2006), although it remains important to keep in mind that it presents challenges as well.

Lastly, the results of the survey also pointed to the need for a more standardized form of assessments for all courses and levels, for the purpose of helping both instructors and students target particular learning outcomes. Accordingly, the program has adopted a system of rubrics (that include an item on language transfer) to help students monitor their learning of the language and to increase their awareness of the influence of Spanish. It was observed that in all courses students pointed to correction of language transfer in oral and written work, specifically compositions, as a good form of assessment that helped them learn.

## Summary

In sum, these findings and the actions they led to demonstrate the benefits of conducting evaluations such as the one described here. In the current case, first, it was vital to know and understand the learners' language background. Understanding the skill-level of our Spanish speakers and their presence in our program led to the development and re-design of new courses. Second, examining the learners' expectations of their learning and comparing those results to the course learning outcomes helped instructors and the department as a whole to develop more realistic learning outcomes tailored to specific course content and learner's language skills. Third, advertising the new courses was almost as important as creating the courses, since without this information, students and their advisors would not be able to find the right courses. On the whole, evaluation provided data that tracked each of these steps in relation to the curriculum development process and kept instructors and faculty focused on course content and classroom methodology. The findings helped further clarify the needs of the learners, but they also suggested methods that helped to facilitate their learning.

## Reflection on evaluation processes and impact

Evaluation is time-consuming and requires constant monitoring, revision, and some level of expertise in useful methods and procedures. The needs analysis completed in 2004–06 required two years to conduct because of missteps and delays of financial support from the institution. However, the findings helped the program embark on its journey of growth and curriculum development. The evaluation project described above, under the guidance of the language evaluation consultants, was more strategically limited in scope, involved more feedback given in a timely manner, and reconfirmed as well as built upon many of the initial findings from the needs analysis. Now, in 2009, our Portuguese program knows more about its beginning language courses and students than ever before. The evaluation process has provided us with details that will help us continue to grow. In addition, the data collected helped convince administrators to support our growth, both in terms of the curriculum changes and in the awarding of funds to pay instructors. As mentioned earlier, the administrators of the Arts & Sciences immediately valued the data collected by supporting our requests for additional classes and instructors. We were also told on several occasions that our data collection demonstrated good monitoring of student learning, something the university as a whole is striving to achieve. As a result, the Portuguese program has built a reputation as one that can justify its needs because it monitors the content and delivery of

---

states that about 94% of academic texts in Portuguese is accessible to Spanish speakers without any training in Portuguese. Finally, Green (1988) demonstrates that there is an 85% correspondence between the lexicon of the two languages. These findings, then, suggest that the similarities between the two languages is indeed a factor to be taken into account in our program.

its courses, and takes seriously the needs of its students. After four years of study, a major revision of the Portuguese curriculum based on findings from the evaluation project was recently submitted for approval.

The impact of evaluation on the growth of the Portuguese program has included greater numbers of students but also higher quality courses. The new courses and the promotional efforts did increase enrollments in fall 2007 and spring 2008. Rather than our average enrollment of 100, we are now at approximately 160 students per semester. The course content, particularly the student learning outcomes and effectiveness of assessments, has been standardized in response to student and instructor feedback. A greater number of courses are now available to students, and students are more satisfied with the classroom experience. We know more about our students' language backgrounds and their goals. The teaching assistants are able to use this information in meaningful ways, and they feel rewarded for their efforts when they learn of the students' comments.

Nonetheless, there are several thorny issues that have not yet been resolved. First, we have not been able to provide enough course options to place Spanish-speakers in classes designed for them only, while at the same time meeting the needs of non-Spanish speakers. Native speakers continue to enroll in the PORT 101 class rather than the PORT 102 class that was designed for them. We have distributed information and explained the differences between the two classes, but our enrollment figures in PORT 102 remain low. It may be that it is counterintuitive for beginners of a language to take a course at the 102 level. Further investigation is needed to help us understand this phenomenon.

Beyond providing new course options for Spanish speakers, there is an additional concern with meeting their specific needs. Clearly, Spanish-speakers are the majority of students in the program. Their language backgrounds make it easier for them to progress through the curriculum. However, we also need to find ways to help Spanish speakers with one of the major issues identified in the evaluation, that of language transfer. For example, they need help to become better monitors of their written and spoken language, so that their development is not fossilized into "Portunhol"—Spanish with a Portuguese accent. Building from our evaluation efforts, this concern with language transfer was investigated in fall 2008 with a new paper survey that inquired about how students and their instructors monitored language transfer from Spanish into Portuguese. The findings from this new iteration in evaluation will help us better understand student behavior and develop materials to respond to Spanish-speaking students accordingly.

Related to this concern about students monitoring their own language transfer from Spanish to Portuguese is the need to train the graduate teaching assistants in the best way to meet the needs of Spanish-speakers, while not ignoring the needs of the much smaller group of English-only speakers. In fall 2008, additional materials were introduced which compare/contrast the two languages. These comparative materials are especially important since they supplement the textbook we have adopted. In addition, instructors developed new approaches to working with the heterogeneous populations in our classes. They are learning pedagogies with which to teach two different bodies of students simultaneously. Faculty also are engaged in working with teaching assistants and students so that all of them will be aware of the resources that help limit language transfer and at the same time make the most of Spanish-language and language-learning skills.

It also has become apparent that we need to recruit more graduate teaching assistants to teach our new beginning language classes. Just as anticipated, the growth in enrollments at the beginning course levels necessitated a similar growth in instructors. We now have five teaching assistants working in our program, instead of the original three at the outset of the current evaluation. However, recruiting more undergraduates to enroll in Portuguese classes has proven much easier than finding qualified students for the M.A. program. In order to pursue the second finding from the 2006 needs analysis—the development of new classes for graduate students—we will turn again to evaluation.

In conclusion, the evaluation project has generated energy and excitement among students and faculty in the Portuguese program. How did this happen? The evaluation process builds a feeling of ownership for both teaching assistants and students, because they realize their input is valued and is acted upon. Their answers are thoughtful and they take seriously the responsibility to provide good suggestions. Evaluation has led to change and improvements that all the participants can see as they move through the Portuguese program. If all goes well, new courses will be appearing in the course catalog for fall 2009. By conducting evaluations on a regular basis, we have created an environment that is friendly and accepting of evaluation. As new students and new graduate teaching assistants enter the program, they are introduced to the culture of evaluation and curriculum development. Each semester we review survey results in order to make changes to the syllabi and to update classroom activities. When graduate teaching assistants complete their training, they take with them a positive attitude about evaluation and examples of the tools to perform it. The instruments used for beginning-of-semester, mid-semester, and end-of-semester data collection are now firmly established in the basic language program. Each time these tools are used we consider if and how they should be altered to reflect any changes in the courses or the students. The next step will be to expand our focus beyond the beginning language classes and apply the tools and techniques we have learned in order to develop new graduate level courses. From the standpoint of the evaluation team, this endeavor has been successful in moving the program into a more visible and active role within the area of Latin American Studies. For the first time in some years, Portuguese has been able to generate greater interest in its courses, higher enrollments, and a sense of accomplishment with regard to the quality of the instruction and learning in the classroom.

*Acknowledgements*
The authors thank John Norris, Yukiko Watanabe, and the National Foreign Language Resource Center at the University of Hawai'i for their expertise and support during the development, execution, and completion of this project.

## References

Brown, J. D. (1995). *The elements of language curriculum: A systematic approach to program development*. Boston, MA: Heinle & Heinle.

Carvalho, A. M. (2002). Português para falantes de espanhol: Perspectivas de um campo de pesquisa. *Hispania, 85*, 597–608.

Carvalho, A. M., & Silva, A. J. B. da. (2006). Cross-linguistic influence in third language acquisition: The case of English-Spanish bilinguals' acquisition of Portuguese. *Foreign Language Annals, 39*, 185–202.

Ellis, N. C. (2002a). Frequency effects in language processing. *Studies in Second Language Acquisition, 24*, 143–188.

Ellis, N. C. (2002b). Reflections on frequency effects in language processing. *Studies in Second Language Acquisition, 24*, 297–339.

Green, J. N. (1988). Spanish. In M. Harris & N. Vincent (Eds.), *The Romance languages* (pp. 58–75). New York: Oxford University Press.

Henriques, E. R. (2000). Incompreensão de texto escrito por falantes nativos de Português e de Espanhol. *D.E.L.T.A., 16*(2), 263–295.

Jensen, J. (1999). *Sociolinguistc variations in Portuguese: Challenge to Spanish speakers*. Paper presented at the American Association of Teachers of Spanish and Portuguese. Denver, CO. August 1999.

Milleret, M. (2008). Portuguese program evaluation and Spanish speaker's needs. In L. Wiedmann & M. V. R. Scaramucci (Eds.), *Portuguese for Spanish speakers: Teaching and acquisition* (pp. 257–268). Campinas, Brazil: Pontes Editores.

Odlin, T. (1989). *Language transfer*. Cambridge: Cambridge University Press.

## Appendix A: First week student survey

### I. Indicate which course you are taking:

☐ Portuguese 101  ☐ Portuguese 102  ☐ Portuguese 275–Spanish speakers  ☐ Portuguese 275

### II. Your background

1. Student status: ☐ Freshman ☐ Sophomore ☐ Junior ☐ Senior ☐ Graduate student
2. How many credit hours are you taking this semester? [___] credit hours
3. Are you working ?

    ☐ Yes ☐ No If "yes," how many hours a week? [___] hours
4. What is your major/minor? _____

### III. Your language learning experience

1. Indicate where/how you studied or learned each language that you speak (including your first/native language(s)), and estimate your proficiency level e.g., French, high school, beginner)

| language(s) | where/how learned (at home, in high school, from my spouse, etc.) | beginning | intermediate | advanced | near-native | native |
|---|---|---|---|---|---|---|
|  |  |  |  |  |  |  |
|  |  |  |  |  |  |  |
|  |  |  |  |  |  |  |
|  |  |  |  |  |  |  |
|  |  |  |  |  |  |  |
|  |  |  |  |  |  |  |

2. Are you studying another language this semester? If so, which language and which course(s)?

    Language: _____ Course(s): _____

    Language: _____ Course(s): _____

### IV. About this course

1. How did you find out about this course? (Mark all that apply)

    ☐ University course catalogue ☐ Website ☐ Poster ☐ My advisor
    ☐ Freshman orientation (flier) ☐ Announcement (and flier) in Spanish course
    ☐ A friend taking Spanish ☐ A friend taking Portuguese ☐ Other (please specify)

2. Was the course time convenient for you? ☐ Yes ☐ No (If *No*, please explain your reasons below.)

    _____
    _____

3. Why did you enroll in this particular course (*101* versus *275 for Spanish speakers* versus *275 regular*)?

   ☐ This course fit into my schedule. ☐ I am a Spanish speaker.
   ☐ I wanted to learn quickly. ☐ This course fulfills the core curriculum.
   ☐ other (please explain)._____

4. Mark all your reasons for study Portuguese.

   ☐ To fulfill a requirement ☐ For pleasure ☐ For current work ☐ For my major
   ☐ To work/live abroad ☐ To relate to my cultural heritage
   ☐ other (please explain)._____

5. What do you expect to get out of this particular course? (Use the back of this page if necessary)

   _____
   _____

## Appendix B: Focus group protocol

### I. Purpose

The purpose of the focus group is to obtain mid-semester diagnostic information for maximizing the immediate effectiveness of the three Portuguese courses: Portuguese 101, Portuguese 275(S) for Spanish speakers, and Portuguese 275 for non-Spanish speakers. A facilitator will ask small groups of learners (N=6–10) to provide their perceptions and opinions on the appropriateness of the class to their expectations and needs, and on the design and implementation of the course curriculum (i.e., course content, activities, workload, textbook, instruction, assessment).

### II. Necessary resources:

1. Two classrooms, each with capacity for up to 12 people; classes should be split in two at the beginning (first alphabetic half and second, to keep the distribution relatively random)
2. Personnel: 2 facilitators, one for each class
3. Equipment: two digital or tape recorders, extension cords, extra tapes, and batteries
4. Consent form

### III. Procedures and guided questions

1. Opening: Briefly introduce yourself.
2. Present the purpose of the FG:

   We are here today to talk about your learning experiences so far in this Portuguese course. As you know, this is one of several new courses that have been designed to better meet the needs and interests of different groups of students here at the University of New Mexico. So, the purpose today is to get your perceptions on several aspects of the class so that your instructor and the department can make improvements where they are necessary. Your perceptions are what we want to hear about. There are no right or wrong answers, of course—you should just say what comes to your mind.

3. Ask students to read and sign the consent form. Explain the discussion procedure:

   I will be taking notes and tape recording the discussion so that we do not miss anything you have to say. As you know everything is confidential. No one, including your teacher, will know who said what. This should be a group discussion, so feel free to respond to me and to other members' opinions in the group. It is also important for everyone to have equal opportunity to express their opinions. You can jump in at any time, but I would appreciate it if only one person spoke at once. During the discussion, you can agree or disagree with each other, and you can change your mind. The discussion will last approximately 45 minutes. There are several questions we need to cover, so I will move the discussion along in order to make sure that happens.

4. Key questions

   *Placement*

   Now let's talk about this particular course (Portuguese 101, 275, 275–S) and your decision to enroll in it.

- How did you learn about this course? Has anyone learned about this course through your advisor? Who is your advisor?
- Do you feel this is the right course for you? Why/why not?
- Did the introduction presented by the instructor of the course at the beginning of the semester help you choose the right course for you?
- Is there any information you wish you might have had when enrolling in the course?
- To what extent does the course meet your expectations?

*Textbook*

Let's talk about the textbook you are using.

- What is good about it?
- Tell me what you don't like about the textbook.

*Class activities and materials*

What do you think about the things you do in class?

- Are there particular activities or materials that really help you learn?
- Are there activities or materials that do not help so much?

*Instructor*

Tell me about your instructor

- What does your teacher do that really helps you learn?
- What suggestions do you have for the instructor in order to improve the class?

*Workload*

- How is the workload for this class?

*Assessments*

- Tell me about the assessments: Do they help you to learn?

*Successful learning*

- Based on your experience so far, if you were to give advice to students who are going to take this course, what would you tell them they need in order to be successful in this course?
- How do feel your knowledge or lack of knowledge of Spanish affects your learning?

*Changes*

- Are there any specific changes that you might recommend for improving this course?

5. Wrap-up and recap

Though there were many different opinions about _____, it appears unanimous that _____. Does anyone see it differently? It seems most of you agree on _____, but some think that _____. Does anyone want to add or clarify an opinion on this?

Is there any other information regarding your learning experiences in this class that would be useful for me to know?

6. Closing remark

    Thank you very much for providing us with your perceptions and opinions about this class. Your comments have been very helpful, and I will summarize the results and report them to the department, so that they can make sure that these courses are the best they can be.

## IV. Notes to the facilitators and note takers

1. Notes to the facilitators

    - Keep the discussion focused on the topics of interest.
    - Balance participation.
    - Avoid judgmental responses, such as "great" or "excellent."
    - Attend to participants' responses (nodding, smiling) to maintain conversation flow.
    - Use facilitation probes to clarify, encourage, extend, and compare opinions.

    > **Example Facilitation Probes**
    >
    > Acquiring more information:
    > - Can you tell me more about that?
    > - What made you think so?
    > - How do you know that?
    > - What would be the best avenue(s) for...?
    >
    > Finding discrepancy:
    > - It's interesting that some of you found ( ) effective, while others found them not so effective. What do you think may account for these differences?

2. Notes to the note takers (if available; otherwise these will have to be sought post-hoc by listening to the tapes)

    - Take notes on key words (Try to capture their key ideas and reflect their wording).
    - Take notes on any vote counting that occurs.
    - When topic changes, switch to another page.
    - Record general information of the FG session (Date, course name, group composition).
    - Immediately after the FG session, go through the notes. Identify the major points stated by the participants. Add your impressions and any meta-reflective comments about the FG session (any notable group dynamics or circumstances that may have influenced the discussion?).

## Appendix C: End-of-semester survey

### I. Your background

1. Student status:

    ☐ freshman ☐ sophomore ☐ junior ☐ senior ☐ graduate student

2. If you found out about this course from an advisor, please mark which one.

    ☐ advisor in University College ☐ advisor in Spanish & Portuguese Dept.
    ☐ advisor in Arts & Sciences office ☐ other_____

3. Estimate your Spanish proficiency level.

    ☐ beginner ☐ intermediate ☐ advanced ☐ near-native ☐ native

4. To what extent did your knowledge of Spanish play a role in your ability to learn Portuguese?

    ☐ a lot ☐ somewhat ☐ a little ☐ not at all

    Please comment:_____

### II. Your experience in the course

|  | strongly agree | agree | disagree | strongly disagree |
|---|---|---|---|---|
| I was motivated to study Portuguese in this course. | | | | |
| The course was the right level for me. | | | | |
| The textbook was helpful to my learning. | | | | |
| The CDs were helpful to my learning. | | | | |
| The DVDs were helpful to my learning.. | | | | |
| The course met my expectations. | | | | |

1. List the activities that helped you learn.
2. List the features of the textbook that helped you learn.
3. List the assessments that helped you learn.
4. Do you plan to take another Portuguese course next semester?
    ☐ Yes. ☐ No. Why or why not?
5. If you answered "Yes" to #4, do you feel prepared to continue to the next class?
    ☐ Yes. ☐ No. Why or why not?
6. Would you recommend this course to a friend?
    ☐ Yes. ☐ No. Why or why not?

## III. Your Portuguese language abilities

| To what extent can you… | not at all 1 | 2 | 3 | very well 4 |
|---|---|---|---|---|
| …understand your classmates when they talk about topics beyond their own personal lives? | | | | |
| …contrast cultural themes and behaviors between the Portuguese-speaking world and Spanish-speaking countries? | | | | |
| ..speak with native-like fluency and intonation without relying on Spanish? | | | | |
| …express yourself clearly in writing without the influence of Spanish? | | | | |
| …use your grammatical knowledge to communicate in Portuguese in the present, past, and future? | | | | |
| …feel that you are able to separate Portuguese from Spanish? | | | | |

Please clarify any of your self-ratings above as necessary:
_____
_____

## IV. Your suggestions for course improvements

1. Would you prefer a textbook designed to teach Portuguese to Spanish speakers?
   ☐ Yes. ☐ No. Why or why not?

2. Would you enroll in a 200-level class for conversation and pronunciation?
   ☐ Yes. ☐ No. Why or why not?

3. What topics would you like to study in the future?

4. Please provide any additional comments about the course that you think will be helpful to the Portuguese program.

# Coming to Our Senses:
# The Realities of Program Evaluation

Frauke Loewensen
Rafael Gómez
*California State University, Monterey Bay*

*This chapter explores the use of evaluation as a basis for justifying the creation of a new degree program and as a means for generating awareness about the program at multiple levels. Through surveys of diverse stakeholders and interactions with decision makers, the possibilities and limitations for program change were clarified, and a viable path was charted for the future. The impetus for the project was the need to increase and retain a higher number of students at a time when California State University, Monterey Bay was going through an enrollment and retention crisis. The project provided evidence to help the college dean and university committees make informed decisions about the program change requested by the department. Furthermore, it served to show how evaluation can be a constructive learning experience that lays the groundwork for new program goals and achievements.*

## Program and evaluation context

This project was motivated and conceived within the context of increased accountability pressures in higher education. To a growing extent, there is a recognized need on the part of many in the foreign language profession to approach programmatic changes in a systematic and rational manner, and with an eye towards stating and demonstrating the valued outcomes of our educational efforts (Norris, 2006). This need coincides with advances in the field of language program evaluation over the last two decades (Kiely & Rea-Dickins, 2005), which has begun to provide the profession with the necessary tools to conduct effective and reliable evaluations. Nevertheless, published examples of evaluation at work within college foreign language education are scant to date, and the current work is intended to provide one iteration in that regard.

This foreign language program evaluation project was carried out at the School of World Languages and Cultures (SWLC) at California State University, Monterey Bay (CSUMB).

From the inception of the university in 1994, the SWLC has made a commitment to teach the cultures and languages of the Pacific Rim. As part of this effort, SWLC offers a BA in World Languages and Cultures with emphasis in Japanese or in Spanish. A stand-alone BA degree in Spanish or in Japanese has not been possible due to the small size of the overall student body and the limited number of students interested in majoring in Japanese. Offering only one common degree has given the program the flexibility to support both languages despite differing enrollments in each.

However, although there is a shared degree name, the BA in World Languages and Cultures with emphasis in Spanish is a unique program in terms of its student body and its curriculum. The majority of majors are first generation Spanish heritage speakers with a high degree of language proficiency and cultural knowledge. Due in part to the advanced starting points of these students, the program has a truly interdisciplinary curriculum. Its courses are drawn from culture, literature, art, history, and social sciences, and they cover Peninsular, Latin American, Chicano, and Latino cultures.

The drive for undertaking this program evaluation project was an event external to the department, namely, a campus-wide enrollment and retention crisis that peaked in the academic year 2005–06. The academic and financial health of the university depends on the institution's ability to grow, and CSUMB was not growing as expected. In order to identify the causes and possible solutions to this crisis, the university administration commissioned *Stamats*, a company specializing in market research for higher education institutions, to draw up a strategic enrollment management plan. The results from their research revealed that appropriate and widely recognized degree names affect recruitment and retention of students. Their report pointed out that the distinctive character of the university was not communicated to students: "Students do not understand CSUMB's unique approach to developing degree programs or the degree programs themselves, given their unique names" (*Strategic Enrollment Management Plan 2006–2011*, CSUMB, 2007, p. 3). Therefore, a recommendation was made to develop degree names that could be easily recognized by stakeholders. It became clear that if students, parents, or high school counselors cannot easily find degrees by recognizable names and understand the meaning, goals, and objectives of a degree program, they are not going to choose or recommend it; nor are employers going to hire graduates with such a degree. The findings and recommendations of this study motivated a small group of faculty members in the SWLC Spanish program to evaluate the merits of the recommendations presented in the Strategic Enrollment Management Plan and chart a course for the future.

## First steps in the program evaluation process

At the outset of this evaluation project, the original aim of the faculty was to change the title of *BA in World Languages and Cultures with emphasis in Spanish* to *BA in Spanish*. The main purpose was to make the existing Spanish studies degree more visible. In discussions between the department chair and the dean, it was suggested that a degree name change could only be accomplished through the creation of a new degree, following university procedural regulations. The primary goal of the evaluation project was thus to gain approval for the *Permission to Plan* document for a new *BA in Spanish* degree program. As the name indicates, this document is intended to provide reviewers with an outline of the proposed changes and, once accepted by the reviewers and the administration, gives the requester permission to start planning—in this case to plan for the creation of a new degree called *BA in Spanish*. Such a request would have to pass through several bureaucratic phases and would be initiated with the filing of the *Permission to Plan* document. The team's aim was to create a new *BA in Spanish* that would give stakeholders—students, alumni, parents, administrators, faculty, and employers—a clearer understanding of the degree program as well as its goals and objectives. As a consequence, it would ideally attract and retain more students.

The first step in the project was to identify the key players in the department and the necessary resources. Thus, the department chair set out to persuade a few colleagues to actively participate in the evaluation process. The Spanish program consisted of three tenured professors including the chair, two full-time lecturers, and about ten part-time lecturers. For the evaluation team, the chair was able to recruit his two tenured colleagues and a full-time Spanish lecturer who was the elected representative of the department's lecturers. The composition of this team guaranteed first-hand knowledge of and experience with all aspects of the Spanish program, with the lecturer teaching lower-division Spanish courses and the professors conducting language assessments for incoming students as well as teaching upper-division courses. With respect to resources, the chair was able to secure funding to provide the team training in program evaluation. Three of the four members of the team participated in a summer institute on foreign language program evaluation[1] where much of the groundwork for this evaluation project was laid.

The second step was to use the requirements of the *Permission to Plan* document as a guide to orient the team's efforts in designing and developing the evaluation project. This work was done within the context of the summer institute in Hawai'i. Upon the team's return and after consultation with the college dean, the project changed in an important way. It was suggested that the team file a different document: the *Degree Name Change Request*. The team was told that the new document would better accomplish the desired outcomes (changing the degree name and increasing visibility) because it would speed up the process, skip over the permission phase, and reflect the true purpose of the Spanish program's request. The new goal for the team then became to gain approval of the *Degree Name Change Request* document. Findings from the evaluation project would thus be used to provide evidence/data to meet the evidentiary requirements of this request. The team's main intent was to give university decision makers the necessary information to evaluate the merits of the request. These decision makers included the department (chair and faculty), the dean, upper-administration committees who would have to review and accept or reject the document, and ultimately the CSU Chancellor.

## Evaluation questions

During the spring and summer of 2007, a team of three faculty members (the chair, a tenured Spanish faculty, and a Spanish lecturer) worked together to more precisely identify the purpose of the evaluation. Four key points were distilled from these discussions. The evaluation would gather evidence to examine: (a) whether there was support from a variety of stakeholders for a degree name change, (b) whether a degree name change could add visibility to the existing Spanish program, and (c) whether a degree name change could increase the number of Spanish majors. The fourth aim was to (d) start developing a culture of evaluation. This last aim is particularly important for a relatively new department concerned about documenting student learning. Thus, the exercise was intended not only to train a cadre of faculty members in a systematic approach to program evaluation but also provide a model of how to approach such a task.

---

1 Developing useful evaluation practices in college foreign language programs, National Foreign Language Resource Center (NFLRC), University of Hawai'i at Mānoa, May 28–June 6, 2007

In summary, the main evaluation question addressed in this project was: What evidence exists to support the need for a stand-alone *BA in Spanish* instead of a *BA in World Languages and Cultures with emphasis in Spanish*?

## Methods

In this evaluation, two methods were used to gather evidence for the above mentioned research questions: document analysis and surveys. The team chose document analysis to determine the visibility of the current BA outside the confines of their campus (i.e., in a variety of publicly available documents), and surveys as a means of revealing the views and opinions of various stakeholders.

The evaluation project included several phases. After the initial decision to undertake this project and the recruitment of a team, three of the four team members received training in program evaluation at the National Foreign Language Resource Center summer institute at the University of Hawai'i. There, the project was outlined, with the help of an evaluation consultant,[2] and the first drafts for the surveys were developed. Back at the home campus, the team then conducted the document analyses, and they finalized and administered the surveys. The majority of surveys were completed online using the web-based survey tool SurveyMonkey (www.surveymonkey.com). Some were paper-based as well, in order to access certain respondents, with one of the team members later entering the data into the online survey tool. Once the first survey results were collected and summarized, the entire team gathered to discuss the results. Together with the evaluation consultant, the team engaged in a feedback session, reviewed its survey design, and refocused its evaluation questions. Throughout the Fall semester of 2007, additional surveys were administered and results collected. Much of the information gathered and insights gleaned from the surveys were included in the *Degree Name Change Request* document that was submitted to the college dean for approval, who then sent it forward to the Academic Affairs Council Subgroup (the body charged with adjudicating such requests).

### Document analysis

The aim of this procedure was to gauge the current visibility of the major and by extension the degree program. The team hoped that the results of the analysis might suggest ways to increase program visibility as well as program enrollment. The team focused on the search engine ASSIST.org,[3] a tool for prospective university students, their parents, and counselors to gather information on the degrees granted within the CSU system. ASSIST stands for Articulation System Stimulating Inter-institutional Student Transfer, and it is a free online tool that shows prospective (transfer) students "how course credits earned at one public California college or university can be applied when transferred to another" (ASSIST, n.d.). ASSIST is potentially used by hundreds of thousands of students; the CSU system alone provides an education to over 400,000 students annually. It was therefore of particular interest to the team to determine whether and how SWLC's (and by extension CSUMB's) Spanish major appeared in this "official repository of articulation for California's public colleges and universities" which claims to provide "the most accurate and up-to-date information about student transfer in California" (ASSIST, n.d.). The team searched the database using four relevant key terms: "majors," "Spanish," "languages and literatures," and "Spanish and Portuguese." The site offered a number of primary search terms that could be combined with certain secondary search terms. For this project, the following combinations

---

2  Dr. John Norris and his team (Yukiko Watanabe and Dennis Koyama)
3  http://www.assist.org/web-assist/welcome.html accessed 10–06–08

were used: "majors" with "Spanish," and "language and literatures" with "Spanish and Portuguese."

## Surveys

The evaluation team used surveys as a means to gather information about stakeholder opinions on the proposed degree name change and its related benefits: an increase in program visibility and in program enrollment. The design of questionnaires began at the summer institute, as mentioned above. With the help of an evaluation advisor,[4] the team developed the first drafts that would elicit views from a variety of stakeholders on changing the name of the BA. Back at the home campus, the team finalized the surveys, aiming to distill a format that would be as long as necessary, as short as possible, precise, and to the point. Figure 1 shows and example screen shot from the survey for CSU foreign language department chairs.

---

**2. Survey**

**1. If you had the choice between recommending to your students a "Bachelor's degree in Spanish" versus a "Bachelor's degree in World Languages and Cultures with emphasis in Spanish", which degree would you rather recommend?**

    a. I would recommend a "BA in Spanish".

    b. I would recommend a "BA in World Languages and Cultures with emphasis in Spanish".

    c. I do not perceive a difference and would recommend either one.

    d. Not applicable.

**2. If you answered "a" in question 1, please let us know what factor(s) influenced your decision to prefer the degree name "BA in Spanish".**

**3. If you answered "b" in question 1, please let us know what factor(s) influenced your decision to prefer the degree name "BA in World Languages and Cultures with emphasis in Spanish".**

**4.** If you answered "c" in question 1, we thank you for your input and your time.

**5.** If you answered "d" in question 1, we thank you for your input and your time.

---

Figure 1: Example screen shot from online survey of department chairs

---

[4] Dr. John Norris and his team (Yukiko Watanabe and Dennis Koyama)

The wording of the surveys was slightly adjusted in distinct versions so that it would reflect the situation and interest of the different stakeholders. To exemplify this adjustment, Figure 2 shows part of the survey for upper division Spanish students.

---

**2. If you had the choice for your degree to be called a "Bachelor's degree in Spanish" instead of the current "Bachelor's degree in World Languages and Cultures with emphasis in Spanish", which degree name would you prefer?**

  a. "BA in Spanish".

  b. "BA in World Languages and Cultures with emphasis in Spanish".

  c. I have no preference. Either degree name is fine.

  d. I would like to suggest a different degree name.

**3. If you answered "a" in question 2, please let us know what factor(s) influenced your decision to prefer the degree name "BA in Spanish".**

[                                                                 ]

**4. If you answered "b" in question 2, please let us know whether you have experienced any need to explain the name of the degree ("BA in World Languages and Cultures with emphasis in Spanish") that you are pursuing. Please give specific examples.**

[                                                                 ]

**5. If you answered "c" in question 2,....**

  ...we thank you for your participation.

**6. If you answered "d" in question 2, please tell us what degree name you would suggest.**

[                                                                 ]

---

Figure 2: Example screen shot from online survey of upper division students

The team decided to administer the surveys online since this would greatly facilitate collecting, summarizing, and extracting the data. Once the first survey results were received and a team member had summarized them, the entire team gathered to discuss the results. Later, together with the evaluation consultant, the team engaged in a feedback session, reviewed its survey design and refocused its evaluation questions. Throughout the Fall semester of 2007, additional surveys were administered and results collected.

In the end, seven groups of respondents were surveyed: (a) current upper-division Spanish students (majors and minors), (b) former Spanish majors (i.e., alumni), (c) current lower-division Spanish students (prospective majors), (d) department faculty, (e) tri-county[5] foreign

---

5  CSUMB specifically serves the student population of the tri-county area: Monterey, San Benito, and Santa Cruz.

language educators from K–16, (f) tri-county employers of alumni, and (g) foreign language department chairs on other CSU campuses. A possible degree name change would impact all of these groups, although not in the same way. Current lower-division students might be interested in considering a *BA in Spanish* if such a degree were offered; current upper-division students might not like a change in the degree name, or they might like an option to have their degree carry the new name if the change became effective before their graduation. Alumni holding the current degree might disagree with the name change since it would seem to invalidate their degree, or they might welcome the change because of difficulties they experienced having to explain their degree to employers and graduate schools. The faculty teaching in the program might express well-argued preferences that should be taken into account. The foreign language educators in feeder schools might favor this change to help them recruit more students to their own Spanish classes if they were able to refer them on to the local university. Employers who had previously hired SWLC alumni could provide insights into their interpretation of the current degree, and the skills and knowledge they want in a Spanish BA graduate. Lastly, foreign language department chairs at other CSU campuses could give advice on the transferability of the current degree for graduate studies in Spanish.

Although most of the respondents entered their responses directly into the web-based survey tool, not all of them were contacted in the same way. Lower-division students completed the survey during class time, with one student at a time coming up to the class computer. Upper-division students were contacted via email by their instructor, and alumni were contacted via email by their former capstone course instructor. Similarly, the department's Spanish faculty were sent the web link in an email, after having been informed about the reason for and purpose of the survey in a departmental meeting. Employers were first sent a letter on department stationary explaining the request and asking for their input. Although the letter contained the survey's URL, it was followed by an email that contained the link to the online survey. Input from the foreign language department heads of the 23 CSU campuses was sought in person. Three evaluation team members attended the CSU Foreign Language Council (CSU-FLC) meeting in northern California, briefly presented the survey, distributed a paper version, encouraged their colleagues to respond, and then collected the completed forms. Results were then entered into the survey tool by one of the team members. Foreign language educators were contacted via the Foreign Language Association of Monterey County (FLAMCO). Two different methods were used. First, two team members attended a local meeting, briefly presented the survey, distributed a paper version, encouraged their colleagues to respond, then collected the completed forms and transferred the results into SurveyMonkey. Those FLAMCO members who had not been able to attend the meeting were contacted via email by one of the evaluation team members and asked to access the survey site online and enter their responses electronically.

In all, 141 respondents completed the survey: 24 colleagues from the California State University system, 14 SWLC faculty members, 45 Spanish lower-division students, 23 tri-county Foreign Language school teachers, 8 upper-division Spanish students, 14 alumni holding a BA in World Languages and Cultures with emphasis in Spanish, and 13 local employers.

Throughout the project, communication flowed back and forth between the college dean, the department chair, and the evaluation team. The participation of the department chair in the evaluation team facilitated both decision-making and exchanges with the dean.

## Findings, uses, and recommendations

### Document analysis

As Figure 3 shows, in the ASSIST.org database under the site-provided search terms "majors" and "Spanish," neither the BA offered by the School of World Languages and Cultures nor the department itself are listed, this despite the fact that ASSIST.org claims to provide "the most accurate and up-to-date information available about student transfer in California."

---

**Search Results**

You searched this site for: **Spanish**

**Results**

The following majors are available at university campuses. The campuses that offer the major are identified next to each major name. Click a campus abbreviation next to a major to see more information about that major.

Language B.A. Spanish Option (UCR)
Language Studies - Spanish B.A. (UCSC)
Liberal Studies - Spanish Studies Track B.A. (CSUSB)
Liberal Studies B.A. Concentration in Bilingual/Cross-Cultural-Spanish (CSUSTAN)
Liberal Studies B.A. Concentration in Spanish (CSUSTAN)
Linguistics - Spanish Emphasis B.A. (UCSB)
Linguistics and Spanish B.A. (UCLA)
Literature B.A. (Spanish/Latin American/Latino Literatures Concentration) (UCSC)
Literature, Spanish B.A. (UCSD)
Literatures & Cultures, B.A.-Concentration in Lit. of the Spanish Speaking World (UCM)
Spanish A.B. (UCD)
Spanish and Community and Culture/B.A. (UCLA)
Spanish and Linguistics B.A. (UCLA)
Spanish and Portuguese - Hispanic Languages and Bilingual Issues B.A. (UCB)
Spanish and Portuguese - Iberian or Latin American B.A. (UCB)
Spanish and Portuguese - Luso-Brazilian B.A. (UCB)
Spanish and Portuguese B.A. (UCB, UCLA)
Spanish B.A. (CPP, CSUB, CSUC, CSUCI, CSUDH, CSUEB, CSUFRES, CSUFULL, CSULA, CSULB, CSUN, CSUS, CSUSB, CSUSM, CSUSTAN, HSU, SDSU, SFSU, SJSU, SSU, UCI, UCLA, UCSB)
Spanish B.A. Concentration in Language and Culture (CSUSM)
Spanish B.A. Concentration in Literature (CSUSM)
Spanish B.A. Concentration in Spanish for the Professions (CSUSM)
Spanish B.A. Linguistics Option (UCR)
Spanish B.A. Literature Option (UCR)
Spanish B.A. with Language Option (CSUDH)
Spanish B.A. with Linguistics Option (CSUDH)
Spanish B.A. with Translation Option (CSULB)
Spanish B.A., Preparation for Teaching (SJSU)
Spanish Education B.A. (HSU)

---

Figure 3: Information returned during a search of the Assist.org database for "Spanish"

Another search in this database under the site-provided search terms "languages & literatures" and "Spanish and Portuguese" showed that the degree *World Languages and Cultures B.A* is listed at the very bottom of the page (see Figure 4).

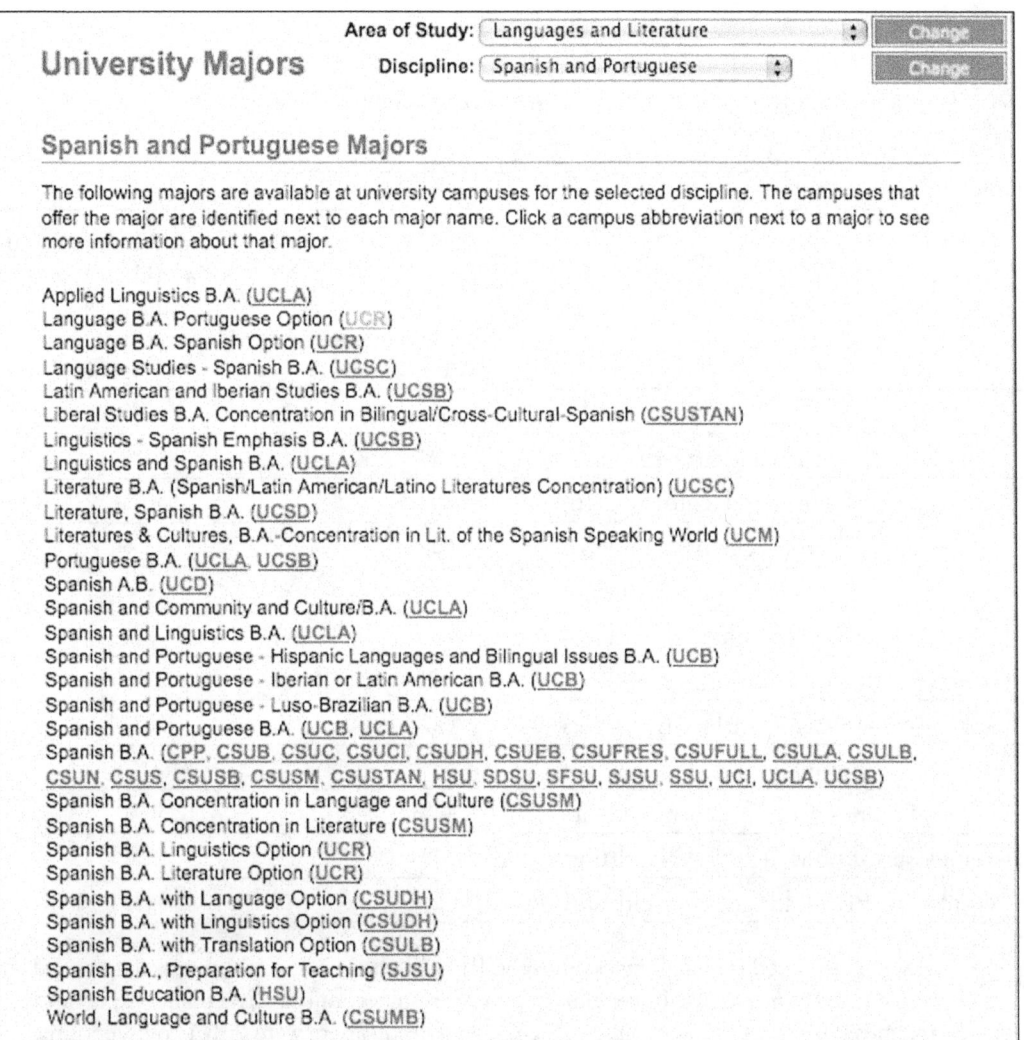

Figure 4: Information returned during a search of the Assist.org database for "Spanish and Portuguese Majors"

It is surprising that the degree *World Language and Culture B.A.* is listed here since it is not overtly connected to either one of the search terms. Further, although the degree name is followed by a link to the CSUMB campus webpage, it does not link to the corresponding department. Only an inquisitive or persistent searcher might follow the link and then try to find the major. The document analysis of this site showed very clearly the nature of the problem: the Spanish major offered by CSUMB is not visible. While the document analysis demonstrated convincingly the problem of lacking visibility, it did not provide the team with sufficient information to propose a possible solution. For that purpose the team turned to the surveys administered to the previously mentioned respondents.

## Surveys

The survey results shown in Table 1 indicate respondents who favored the name *BA in Spanish* versus those preferring the current degree name *BA in World Languages and Cultures with emphasis in Spanish*.

Table 1: Survey results

| | I would recommend a "BA in Spanish" | I would recommend a "BA in World Languages and Cultures with emphasis in Spanish" |
|---|---|---|
| SWLC faculty | 86% | 7% |
| CSU FL department chairs | 79% | 21% |
| tri-county educators (K–16) | 65% | 30% |
| upper-division Spanish students | 63% | 13% |
| alumni | 57% | 29% |
| employers–SPAN language abilities | 62% | 8% |
| employers–oral translation abilities | 62% | 23% |
| employers–written translation abilities | 62% | 15% |
| employers–teach Spanish | 58% | 0% |
| lower-division Spanish students | 44% | 38% |
| employers–knowledge SPAN cultures | 31% | 39% |
| employers–SPAN language & cultures | 31% | 54% |

Groups are ranked by percentages of respondents (highest to lowest) who recommended the degree title *BA in Spanish*. In general, the survey results confirmed the team's expectations. In almost all cases the new degree name was preferred. There were only two exceptions, both of which came from employers. If the desired job qualifications included knowledge of Spanish cultures or knowledge of the Spanish language and cultures, the employers preferred the current degree name by a slight margin.

The strongest supporters in favor of a degree name change appeared to be the department's own Spanish faculty. This was an encouraging result that could strengthen the department's position vis-à-vis the administration. A united department can make a stronger case for requesting a new degree program, and, if approved by the administration, the change can be implemented more easily and effectively. As expected the broad group of the CSU foreign language department chairs heavily favored the new name since it corresponds to the title of the undergraduate degrees offered by their institutions and carries clear expectations with respect to the alumni's preparedness for future graduate study.

While the tri-county educators were a little weaker in their overall preference for the new degree name relative to the current degree name, some of their support for the status quo was tinted by the wide range of reasons provided for their choices. Many of their interpretations of or associations with the current degree title did not align well with the actual academic program. Some respondents thought that the degree required or encouraged the learning of more than one foreign language and culture, which is not the case in reality. "I don't know what the current requirements are," wrote a colleague, "but this name implies to me that more than just Spanish culture has been studied (and possibly more than just the Spanish language). If this is indeed a significant part of the major than this title would be justified, otherwise not." Another foreign language educator wrote: "BA in World Languages and Cultures with emphasis in Spanish implies the student must have to have knowledge in the World Languages and Cultures, therefore, it sounds more well-rounded." The lack of understanding of the meaning of the degree supports (to a certain extent) the findings of the *Stamats* market research that many of the non-traditional degree names at CSUMB caused confusion beyond the institution.

One of the surprising findings of the surveys was the fact that a majority of alumni, whose BA has the current degree name, favored the change (57% vs. 29%). The reasons for this response seem to correlate very well with the employers' answers. Two representative alumni comments in favor of the name change were:

"When I tell to people I have a Bachelor in WLC they don't know what it is exactly. But if the name is changed to BA in Spanish, the name is self-explanatory. And it makes more sense, because the emphasis is Spanish anyways."

"The main factor here is that "WLC" is a very broad and general term. We need specific terms, specially [sic] when it refers to a BA. I studied (mostly) Spanish during my staying in CSUMB. My current job would have preferred to see a BA in Spanish and not the general term called "WCL" [sic]. California needs Spanish professors due to the growth of [sic] Spanish speaking population. So, I think it would make a greater impact—not only to the school, but for the future students—to see a degree in Spanish and not WLC."

The employer survey was longer and more detailed, reflecting the complexity of the job market and variety of possible jobs. The survey highlighted certain skills and areas of knowledge that the employer might seek in an applicant. When in search of employees with "Spanish language abilities" (62% vs. 8%), "oral translation abilities" (62% vs. 23%), or "written translation abilities" (62% vs. 15%), employers clearly expected to find those among graduates with a *BA in Spanish* but less so from graduates with the current degree name. Employers who recruit graduates to teach Spanish would not even consider graduates holding the current degree (58% vs. 0%). This is the most surprising—and shocking—result of the surveys, since many of the Spanish majors at CSUMB expressly intend to become educators, and that finding potentially explains alumni responses in favor of a degree name change as well.

The only substantial support for the current degree name came from employers with specific needs. If they were searching for employees with knowledge of "Spanish cultures" (39% vs. 31%) or "Spanish language and cultures," they preferred the current degree name (54% vs. 31%). However, when asked to describe the Spanish-related abilities they look for in an employee, only one of them mentioned the word culture: "Spanish speaking and writing skills along with being bi-cultural and having sensitivity to the impoverished populations we serve.[6]" It appears, then, that the current degree title does not carry a clear meaning for some employers either.

The lower-division Spanish students were the most evenly divided on the two degree names (44% vs. 39% in favor of change). This result may be because the professional ramifications of a degree name change are the least immediate for this group. They are also most

---

[6] This statement comes from a non-profit employer who provides "social and employment services to individuals on public assistance."

immediately engaged in the current educational system and, by virtue of having chosen this campus, may be most tolerant or supportive of CSUMB's interdisciplinary approach. As CSUMB's website explains, "[e]ach major incorporates several traditional fields of study as well as opportunities for in-depth focus on areas that interest you most" (CSUMB, Broad Majors, n.d.). The reasoning behind this approach is that "[t]oday's interconnected society needs professionals who can examine problems from multiple perspectives and generate creative solutions. A broader knowledge base allows you to think on your feet and apply relevant information, no matter what discipline it comes from" (Ibid). As mentioned in the section above on program context, for SWLC this approach translates into courses that seek to explore the connections between the humanities and the social sciences with faculty who are experts not only in literature and linguistics but also in history and social sciences.

In contrast to the lower-division Spanish students, the upper-division Spanish students were quite clear in their preference for the degree name change (62.5% vs. 12.5%). In fact, the actual preference is even stronger if one assigns one of the comments from the no-preference question to the right category: "I can [sic] think of specific examples but I find that unles [sic] I am talking to someone familiar with CSUMB, I find myself having to explain the name of the degree."

In sum, the project findings responded to the faculty's queries in the following ways. The survey data seemed to indicate that there is strong support from nearly all stakeholders for a degree name change. Conclusions gathered from the document analysis also show that a degree name change would add visibility to the existing Spanish program since it would appear on the ASSIST.org website, could be searched using common key words (such as "major" and "Spanish"), and would bring up CSUMB as one of the degree sites available in California. Taking together the results from both of these sources, it can be expected that over time the degree name change could increase the number of Spanish majors.

## Actions taken

Armed with the evidence assembled through document analysis and surveys, the evaluation team drew up the *Degree Name Change Request* document and submitted it to the college dean, who accepted it without modifications and sent it forward to the Academic Vice President (AVP) of Planning and Educational Effectiveness, who heads the Academic Affairs Subgroup. The AVP rejected the document for the following reason: all degree-related courses must have the same prefix, in this case SPAN for Spanish. Since the current degree is not a stand-alone but a two-pronged degree (SPAN & JAPN), accepting the request would imply that all Japanese courses would have to adopt the prefix SPAN as well. Of course such a change was unacceptable.

Although disappointed by this outcome, the evaluation team sought a new route, as they were unwavering in their intent to change the degree name in response to clear stakeholder preferences and to help the university alleviate its student recruitment and retention problem by making its high-demand degree more visible. After consultation with the college dean, it was decided to prepare yet another request, this time for *a new five-year pilot degree program for a BA in Spanish*. While this request sounds somewhat similar to the team's original plan, namely to propose *a new degree program for a BA in Spanish*, there is one important difference. The approval of a pilot degree program is a campus-internal process. Once approved by the Campus Senate, the pilot program runs for five years, then seeks permanent status, at which time the CSU Chancellor's Office will decide whether or not to accept it as an approved CSU degree program. Relying on the promise of a faster (because campus-internal) approval process and near-term implementation, the team completed and submitted the request for *a new five-year pilot degree program for a BA in Spanish*, using evidence gathered in the previously conducted evaluation. At the time of this writing, the team is awaiting adjudication of this proposal.

**Reflection on evaluation process and its impact on people and programs**

Although the evaluation project did not progress in a straight line to the desired goals, it did complete all of the major phases and culminated in the production and submission of proposals that went beyond the department level to the college dean, university-wide committees, and even the CSU Chancellor's Office. In this sense, it demonstrates that faculty can take concrete action that is well-planned, effectively and efficiently designed, and carried out thoroughly to address campus-wide as well as internal issues. It also shows how evaluation can enable faculty to support and interact with the administration proactively in pursuing their goals for the university and in their efforts to find solutions to problems. Whether or not the upper administration has perceived this evaluation project as helpful is not clear at this time since no direct feedback, other than encouragement from the college dean, has come back to the team. The more immediate impact, however, was felt at the department level in terms of faculty development. All team members, including the tenured Spanish professors, became aware of the entire range of stakeholders of the Spanish program—from the enrolled student to the counselors at high schools and junior colleges, prospective students, parents, employers, and administrators beyond the campus. The department chair, Spanish professors, and the lecturer representative had the opportunity to work together much more closely. Additionally, three Spanish faculty members received thorough training in program evaluation.

It goes almost without saying that this project has set the tone for any future program evaluation endeavors in the department. Instead of relying on personal anecdotes, assumptions, politics, or individual preferences, future evaluation questions will be addressed using appropriate instruments to collect as much empirical information as possible. This fundamental shift is especially important and useful with regard to controversial issues where it is advisable to circumvent or neutralize departmental politics. This project has also helped to foster a culture of evaluation in the department. This is a desirable and achievable goal, as it is in line with the values and vision of the university (and no doubt most other U.S. universities). CSUMB is characterized by a culture of scholarship that is supposed to have reflection at its core. Each of the four areas of a professor's job responsibilities is defined in terms of scholarship, and every academic review includes a self-reflection on the scholarly approach to those four areas. Program evaluation shares that central concept of reflection.

This project has also demonstrated how securing pertinent data can help decision makers make informed decisions, and it shows that data can be used repeatedly as long as they are relevant to the issue at hand. Each of the submitted proposals was able to clear the college dean's level of review due to the strength of the evidence presented. As mentioned, the evaluation team most recently has submitted to the college dean the proposal for *a new five-year pilot degree program for a BA in Spanish*. If the proposal is accepted and implemented, a new phase of the evaluation project will need to be designed in order to examine the effectiveness of the pilot in attracting students to the program, and to make a case for permanency of the new degree program. Further, the entire department will engage in an accreditation-mandated departmental program review in the next two academic years, and the evaluation team will offer its recently gained expertise to help make this as meaningful and useful a process as possible. Lastly, the Japanese program has been inspired by the Spanish program evaluation project described here to propose an independent degree in

Japanese. They argue that their current enrollment issues also can be overcome with a stand-alone *BA in Japanese* since it will be more visible and more attractive to more students than the current joint degree.

**References**

ASSIST. (n.d.). *Welcome to ASSIST*. Retrieved October 6, 2008 from http://www.assist.org/web-assist/welcome.html

California State University, Monterey Bay (2007). *Strategic Enrollment Management Plan 2006–2011*. California State University, Monterey Bay. CA.

California State University, Monterey Bay (n.d.) *Broad majors*. Retrieved February 9, 2009, from http://csumb.edu/site/x18417.xml

Kiely, R., & Rea-Dickins, P. (2005). *Program evaluation in language education*. New York: Palgrave Macmillan.

Norris, J. M. (2006). The why (and how) of student learning outcomes assessment in college FL education. *Modern Language Journal, 90*(4), 576–583.

# 4

# Using Evaluation to Design Foreign Language Teacher Training in a Literature Program

Alessandro Zannirato
Loreto Sánchez-Serrano
*Johns Hopkins University, Baltimore, Maryland*

*The intent of this evaluation was to gather useful information that would facilitate the creation of a formal foreign language teacher training pilot program for graduate teaching assistants (GTAs) working towards a PhD in literature. The evaluation addressed the different stakeholders' perceptions of their professional roles within the department and their ideas on desirable teacher training practices of the GTAs. This information enabled the evaluators to design a pilot course with fitting content and format that could meet the needs and expectations of the different stakeholders. This study also documents how unforeseen external factors may require a modification of the initial evaluation plan.*

## Introduction: Program context and impetus for evaluation

Foreign language (FL) departments in the United States are undergoing an important period of transformation, as documented in a recent Modern Language Association report on the state of language teaching (MLA, 2007). The report highlights the challenging fact that cooperation between language faculty members and their humanities colleagues is minimal, and that the role of applied linguists and second language acquisition (SLA) experts within a department of foreign languages and literatures is often unclear, as are the qualifications deemed necessary to teach a foreign language. This issue is, of course, not new. The ambiguity of the role of SLA, applied linguistics, and foreign language teaching within university foreign language departments has been at the center of numerous reflections in recent years (e.g., Katz, 2005).

In a related vein, the issue of foreign language graduate teaching assistant (GTA) training and mentoring has been debated at length. A collection edited by Rifkin (2001) discusses some of the tensions and challenges that language program directors face when dealing with GTA teacher training. For instance, what are the purposes and effective approaches

---

Zannirato, A., & Sánchez-Serrano, L. (2009). Using evaluation to design foreign language teacher training in a literature program. In J. M. Norris, J. McE. Davis, C. Sinicrope, & Y. Watanabe, (Eds.), *Toward useful program evaluation in college foreign language education* (pp. 97–116). Honolulu: University of Hawai'i, National Foreign Language Resource Center.

to mentoring in the foreign languages (Siskin, 2001)? How do departments reconcile tensions that arise when graduate students concentrating on *content* training (such as literature or linguistics) are asked to dedicate time and energy to teaching language skills (Guthrie, 2001)? How do departments deal with the fear some GTAs have that foreign language teacher training may diminish individual creativity and result in 'robotic' teaching (Leaver and Oxford, 2001)? As this evaluation will reveal, many of these challenges remain unresolved and their resolution will require a thorough cultural change at all academic levels.

The specific scenario presented here will document how an evaluation effort provided useful and meaningful information to address the development of GTA training in the department of German and Romance Languages and Literatures at Johns Hopkins University. The department of German and Romance Languages and Literatures offers both majors and minors in language and literature, as well as a PhD degree in French, German, Italian, and Spanish literature. Although minors in language studies are offered for some languages at the undergraduate level, the department defines itself as a strongly literature-oriented entity. As in many other institutions, graduate teaching assistants in the literature program begin teaching language courses immediately after being admitted to the PhD program in literature. Most of them have no training in SLA or language pedagogy. The only foreign language pedagogical training GTAs receive is through a weekly meeting with language program directors (LPD) or coordinators. This status quo has resulted in some tensions: students specializing in literature are required to teach foreign language courses for which they have no formal training, while the department requires that their performance be evaluated. Furthermore, given that several LPDs and coordinators hold degrees in SLA and/or foreign language pedagogy, their expectations are quite high in this respect.

In the context of these challenges during the last few years, several coordinators and LPDs specializing in SLA and/or language pedagogy have targeted the objective of fashioning a more research-based and less traditional foreign language program. While some literature faculty welcomed this change as an opportunity to increase teaching quality and academic standards of the department, others saw this change as either irrelevant or plainly undesirable. Notably, this kind of tension has also been observed *within* and *across* language programs, between long-term lecturers and coordinators with a non-linguistic background and the newer faculty with formal training in language teaching, who may be better equipped to articulate the need for specific changes in programs. The perceived threat from such changes resulted in several tumultuous events that led to the abrupt closure of an existing FL teaching methods course in Spring 2007.

More recently, the lack of a training program has been perceived by many LPDs and coordinators, in particular by those specializing in SLA/foreign language teaching, as extremely detrimental. Given that the department does not consult LPDs when new graduate students are selected, LPDs sometimes find themselves working with GTAs they judge as lacking in foreign language proficiency and/or pedagogical training. To address this issue, LPDs suggested that an evaluation of the feasibility of a new methods course be carried out, and the Italian and Spanish LPDs (the evaluation team for the project and authors of this report) made themselves available to lead this process, which was approved by both the department's head and the university's internal review board. The initial objective of this evaluation was to gauge the feasibility and utility of a future training program so that a decision could be reached about whether such a program should be pursued. Given the tensions mentioned above, the evaluation aimed to study in a structured way the different stakeholders' perceptions of their professional roles within the department and their ideas on desirable professional development practices for GTAs in terms of foreign language teaching. The evaluation team thought it unproductive to push for the creation of a new foreign language training course if the evaluation were to show a lack of interest and support from decision-makers. At the same time, the initiators of this evaluation wanted to gather information on possible formats and content for a training program *if* the evaluation showed sufficient support for such a process.

Coincidentally, while this evaluation effort was still in process, the department underwent a review by the academic council of the university in Spring 2008, which had an unexpected effect on the evaluation process. The review committee shared some of the concerns mentioned above and recommended that "the language program directors need the authority to decide who is and who isn't prepared to teach language to undergraduates, and develop appropriate training courses to prepare graduate students to teach language courses." (JHU Academic Council, 2008). As a result, the Spanish language program director, the most senior member of the department holding a terminal degree in SLA/foreign language teaching, was asked to design a methods of foreign language teaching course, on an experimental basis, during the 2008–09 academic year, with the approval and insight of the department's head, and with the help of the Italian LPD. While this was a much welcomed outcome, the evaluators realized that the original evaluation would need to be adjusted to reflect this new situation. Collecting information on stakeholders' perceptions of the usefulness of GTA training was still relevant for the purposes of the new evaluation project, though the focus could no longer be the *feasibility* of a training program—at this point a de facto occurrence—but rather its usefulness and its curricular implications. Therefore, the evaluators discussed the recommendations of the Academic Council with the department chair and proposed to use existing and as yet to be collected evaluative information to facilitate the design of a training program that would reflect as much as possible the perceptions, values, and beliefs of the different stakeholders. The chair approved their recommendations.

## Stakeholders, intended uses, and intended users

The stakeholders for this evaluation project were the language program directors and coordinators, the section heads, the directors of graduate studies (DGS), the department chair, and the GTAs. Originally, the primary users of this evaluation—those who would have needed to make decisions about the possible creation of a training program—were the language program directors, the section heads, the DGSs, and the department chair. The GTAs were defined as secondary users of this evaluation because, while part of the decision-making process, they were not the primary decision makers.

However, the change in the evaluation project described above required something of a redefinition and further specification of intended users and uses, that is, what the evaluation was intended to accomplish. The evaluation team thus identified language program directors and coordinators as the new primary intended users for the redirected evaluation project. Graduate student teaching assistants remained as secondary users. LPDs and coordinators would use project findings for three main purposes: (a) identify content and format for a FLT training course that different stakeholders would find appropriate; (b) provide an empirical basis for the integration into coordinator/GTA weekly meetings of meaningful foreign language teacher training content addressing the real needs of the GTAs; and (c) judge the quality of undergraduate foreign language teaching.

## Evaluation questions

Based on the identification of the evaluation's users and uses, two general evaluation questions were formulated and broken down into sub-questions, which are summarized along with the corresponding indicators (i.e., observable phenomena that would shed light on the issues raised in the evaluation questions) in Table 1.

Table 1: Evaluation questions and indicators

| evaluation questions | indicators |
| --- | --- |
| Could we improve the quality of our undergraduate courses through structured GTA training in foreign language teaching? | Review of classroom observations carried out by program directors or coordinators |
| | Classification of negative comments in classroom observations reports in order to verify whether methodological considerations are predominant |
| What kind of training course could best respond to the department's needs?<br>• What are the training needs of the GTAs in terms of foreign language teaching?<br>• What are the needs of the coordinators in terms of their interaction with the GTAs?<br>• What training program format and content could better accommodate the needs of the stakeholders? | GTA reflections on satisfaction with teaching responsibilities |
| | GTAs' training in foreign language teaching before admission to the program |
| | GTAs' perceptions or misconceptions about the usefulness of FLT training |
| | language coordinators' reflections on their interactions with the GTAs and on their own experience in the department. |
| | language coordinators perceptions of foreign language teacher training |
| | language coordinators reflections on teaching performance of GTAs |
| | DGSs and section heads' reflections on the training needs of the GTAs |
| | DGSs and section heads' perceptions of the importance of FLT training |

## Methods

This evaluation project involved analysis of data from three questionnaires, one prepared for each of the following groups: (a) directors of graduate studies and sections heads; (a) language program coordinators; and (c) graduate teaching assistants. Additional sources of data included recent GTA classroom observation feedback and classroom recordings.

### Identifying indicators/sources of information

The first step in implementing the evaluation consisted of identifying relevant sources of information: four DGSs, four section heads, seven language coordinators, and 57 potential GTA respondents were identified. The identified individuals were approached, via email, to establish their interest in participating in the research project.

### Questionnaires and classroom observation reports

Evaluation questions were answered through the implementation of three questionnaires, which attempted to gather information about the respondents' background with regard to foreign language teacher training, perceptions of their roles as foreign language teachers, as well as experiences and expectations as a GTA or supervisor. Additional information came from recent GTA classroom observations feedback as well as classroom recordings.

An important consideration was to use a methodology that would guarantee respondent anonymity as well as the confidentiality of classroom observation data. Given the evolution of the project, as recounted above, some questionnaire items relevant for the original evaluation plan became less pertinent after the departmental academic review. Such information has not been reported in the findings section of this chapter.

*Questionnaires*

The questionnaire prepared for the section heads and DGSs attempted to gather information about their perceptions on the importance of FL teacher training and the relationship between graduate studies in literature and formal training in foreign language teaching. The questionnaire prepared for the coordinators intended to collect information on their views of graduate students' preparation for and attitudes towards teaching foreign languages, as well the ideal training the department should provide GTAs. The questionnaire prepared for the graduate teaching assistants attempted to collect data about their preparation in foreign language teaching, their experiences teaching in the program, their responses to the possibility of creating a methods course, and their opinions on how it should be shaped. The questionnaries included both open-ended and closed-ended questions and were disseminated using the online survey tool SurveyMonkey (www.surveymonkey.com). A link to each questionnaire was sent by email to all respondents. As the team had no institutional financial support for the project, web-based questionnaires were a cost effective means to gather data and provide both the autonomy and the anonymity needed to ensure pressure-free and trusworthy answers. The respondents were given two weeks to respond. After two weeks, the evaluators retreived the data from the server. The three questionnaires are available in Appendix 1.

*Classroom observation reports*

Coordinators in the department are required to routinely visit and observe graduate teaching assistants' classes. Alternatively, GTAs' classes may be video recorded and reviewed. Following an observation, most coordinators write a report, which is later discussed with GTAs. Twenty recent classroom observation reports were analyzed to reveal common issues that coordinators or LPDs encountered in the GTAs' teaching. Classroom observations were hoped to reveal whether weaknesses in GTA performance could be attributed to lack of training in foreign language teaching. In selecting the sampling of reports, it was decided to use those that had been compiled during the past 12 months by coordinators with a specialization in applied linguistics or SLA. For this reason and due to logistical implications, only reports available to the Italian and Spanish LPDs were reviewed. These two programs host the majority of the graduate teaching assistants within the department and, therefore, represent a significant portion of the graduate student population. Issues that were encountered at least twice in different reports were selected and categorized. Analysis concentrated on areas of GTAs' performance that coordinators judged unsatisfactory, and did not take positive comments into consideration.

## Data analysis

Information from questionnaires and classroom observation reports were reviewed to identify emergent categories and units of analysis. Questionnaire data were subject to a 3-step analysis: open, axial, and selective coding (Dey, 1999). Open coding is a first pass through the collected data, and is "the process of breaking down, examining, comparing, conceptualizing and categorizing data" (Strauss & Corbin, 1990, p. 61). Axial coding is a second pass through the data, and is "a set of procedures whereby data are put back together in new ways after open coding, by making connections between categories" (Ibid., p. 96).

Selective coding is the final pass through the data, and is "the process of selecting the core category, systematically relating it to other categories, validating those relationships, and filling in categories that need further refinement and development" (Strauss and Corbin, 1990, p. 116). Any possible personal identifiers were altered to protect the privacy of the respondents. After questionnaire coding was completed, the 20 classroom recordings and their corresponding observation reports were coded using the same system. All questionnaires and primary documents were then coded using word abbreviations, with appended numbers, to organize the information and to easily identify each category along with its properties.

## Findings

The following narrative summarizes the outcomes of our analyses of the classroom observation reports and three questionnaires.

### Classroom observation reports

The analysis of classroom observation reports was intended to identify useful information about the teaching performance of GTAs, with the purpose of judging the quality of undergraduate foreign language teaching offered by the language programs. This information would help users know whether the quality of undergraduate courses could be improved through structured GTA training in foreign language teaching. The areas of concern highlighted by coordinators were classified into two broad categories: (a) issues related to general teacher training; and (b) issues specific to foreign language teaching.

*General teacher training issues*

The recurring issues in this category were further divided into three sub-categories: (a) lesson planning issues; (b) pedagogical issues; and (c) classroom management issues. Coordinators frequently lamented a deficiency in the application of lesson planning principles; areas that required attention included "class objectives not presented," "transition between one activity and the other not coherent," and no "recall," "correct closure," or "summary" provided. Coordinators also advised GTAs to avoid following the book too closely and to concentrate more on logical and coherent development of class activities, rather than the order provided by the textbook. Another area of concern had to do with the timing of the various activities, which was sometimes described as "not balanced" (e.g., 20 minutes of warm-up activities in a 50-minute class).

Additional pedagogical issues identified by coordinators included the following:

- The instructor asks students to perform a task or an activity without providing clear instructions or a model.
- The instructor's talking time is excessive. The instructor dedicates most of the class time to explicit grammatical explanations and/or providing input, but does not encourage group work, independent reflection, and student output.
- The instructor introduces new information in a decontextualized fashion. No communicative framework is introduced and no clear objectives and desired outcomes are presented to the class.
- The instructor does not use the environment and technologies available to facilitate learning. For example, in most cases technology is used as a back-up reminding the GTA of the grammar content he/she needs to present instead of fostering activities that facilitate students' learning.

- The instructor displays a lack of presence or authority in the class. For example, in response to a student's out-of-context question, the instructor provides an extremely long answer, making it difficult to bring the original discussion back on track.

*Issues specific to foreign language teaching*

A second category of comments related to linguistic and information-processing issues. Instructors who were second language speakers were often advised to strengthen their L2 knowledge and to monitor their L2 production in class, which according to coordinators often contained an excessive amount of non-standard forms. Moreover, the instructors sometimes provided incorrect explicit grammar information, which created confusion and caused students to question the qualifications of the instructor.

Comments regarding methodological issues were generally related to the strategies used by the GTAs to present the input, or to the output elicited in relation to the input provided. Examples of coordinators' comments included:

- The instructor proposes activities focusing simultaneously on forms and meaning.
- Students are asked to produce output without having received a sufficient amount of input, and, therefore, are not able to perform the task well.
- The instructor does not provide comprehensible input and speaks in the L2 all the time without checking for student comprehension.
- The instructor seems interested only in eliciting students' language samples, and often shifts to a focus on form. There seems to be insufficient focus on an actual exchange of information, and little is done to reflect the purpose of the task.
- The instructors' error correction strategies disrupt communication. Students become discouraged by continuous corrections by the instructor.
- The instructor provides explicit grammar information during the input phase, and, contrary to what was announced at the beginning of the year, students are not encouraged to formulate their own hypotheses and, therefore, revert to a passive note-taking mode.
- Issues with listening comprehension activities: No information-processing directions are given before the listening phase (i.e., what are students supposed to do with the information they are going to listen to?).

## DGSs and section heads questionnaires

Two important indicators for answering the evaluation questions were DGS and section head perceptions of the importance of foreign language teacher training, and their ideas on training program format and content. Information from these sources was used to answer the following question: What format and content could better accommodate the needs of the stakeholders? However, the questionnaires for graduate studies directors and section heads were answered by only three out of eight members. Why the response rate was so low for these important informants is unknown as of the writing of this report. Further research may be necessary to identify the reasons. Nevertheless, issues raised by those who did respond are summarized here.

When asked if they saw any relationship between graduate studies in literature and formal training in foreign language teaching, all of the respondents addressed the benefits that language training would provide students in the job market. One of the respondents pointed out that "it enhances the student's entry-level job qualifications." In terms of competitiveness in the job market, one of the respondents explained that the benefits of this training could provide "an edge in competition for some jobs, particularly those at smaller, although still elite schools, where faculty also teach language. Many such jobs are attractive to our graduates."

All of the respondents generally agreed that the integration of foreign language teacher training into the graduate curriculum would produce benefits. However, the challenges of such training were unanimously recognized to include the potential "course overload" that this training could generate and the effect on the graduate students' ability to focus on their literary studies. One participant asserted, however, that this training would pose such a risk "only if it is overly stacked with non-essential tasks. [The course] should emphasize practicality, even in theoretical work." The respondents also agreed that the integration of foreign language teacher training into the graduate curriculum could have positive effects on the competitiveness of their PhD program, with one participant promoting it as an "an attractive selling point." Nevertheless, it was clear from respondent comments that the more important issue was the appropriate balance between training and graduate students' literary work.

## Language coordinators questionnaires

The language coordinators questionnaires targeted two project indicators: (a) coordinators' perceptions of foreign language teacher training; and (b) levels of satisfaction with GTA performance. This information helped answer the following evaluation questions: "What are the needs of the coordinators in terms of their interaction with the GTAs? What training program format and content could better accommodate the needs of the stakeholders?" The language coordinators questionnaires were answered by nine out of eleven possible respondents.

### *Graduate students' profile*
Most language coordinators offered a positive general description of graduate students. Most graduate students start the PhD program with a Master's degree already in hand, and a considerable number of them are multilingual with a clear focus on literary, theoretical, and philosophical studies.

### *Strengths and weaknesses*
Based on their coordination work, the coordinators ranked the main strengths of current GTAs in the following descending order: cooperative, motivated, flexible, and creative. The most descriptive comments about the strengths of the GTAs included:

> "Some demonstrate natural talent and excellent sense of pedagogy."

> "Most of them are quite hard working."

> "For most, the willingness to cooperate is commendable."

With regard to weaknesses in GTA teaching, seven respondents mentioned their insufficient level of language proficiency, followed by a lack of commitment to learning about foreign language teaching (4 respondents), a lack of teaching experience (3 respondents), a lack of teaching methodology training (3 respondents), and poor time management (2 respondents).

When language coordinators were asked to describe the level of preparation demonstrated by the GTAs who were just beginning to teach for their programs, seven out of nine respondents acknowledged an obvious lack of preparedness, and three out of nine respondents indicated the need for mentorship. One of the coordinators observed that the GTAs "are basically learning as they go." Another described the situation as follows:

> "They are absolutely NOT prepared to teach a foreign language. How could they be? They are asked to do something for which they have received no formal training and that, in many cases, they find themselves doing for the first time. I guess this happens in foreign language teaching only. Would a vet be allowed to teach a university-level cardiology course?"

While most acknowledged that the GTAs are expected to teach literature upon graduation, language coordinators did not agree on GTAs' preparedness to enter the job market as foreign language teaching professionals. Four out of nine respondents expressed their satisfaction with GTAs' language teaching preparedness at the end of their graduate studies, while three out of nine expressed dissatisfaction. However, language coordinators that did not see GTAs as foreign language professionals did express a positive view of the process of professionalization some graduate students undergo, for example, describing their potential in the following terms:

> "A few of them could, with adequate training, function capably as foreign language instructors."

> "Through the interactions with the coordinators, about half of them will have acquired a level of theoretical knowledge and experience allowing them to do a decent job as foreign language instructors."

### Coordinators' job responsibilities and time usage

In order to ascertain the overall level of satisfaction of language coordinators' with their interaction with GTAs, and to identify issues and possible training needs, the questionnaire contained questions about the coordinators' daily responsibilities and duties within the language program. Table 2 includes the main job responsibilities of the nine language coordinators who responded to the survey. Findings indicated that language coordinators spend most of their time dealing with GTA supervision and curriculum development, followed closely by GTA pedagogical training.

**Table 2: Most time-consuming coordination activities**

| duties | # of respondents |
|---|---|
| GTAs supervision, help in management of GTA teaching duties, ensuring task completion. | 7 |
| Participating in curriculum development. | 7 |
| GTA training and pedagogical feedback. | 6 |
| Complying with administrative duties and problem solving. | 4 |
| Creating a collaborative and motivated team. | 2 |

### Institutional support

Language coordinators were asked to describe the teacher training support provided by the institution to GTAs. Coordinators acknowledged that GTAs rely primarily on their assistance in addition to that of the program directors. They generally described the assistance that the university provides to GTAs as insufficient and recommended a first year fellowship without teaching duties, as explained by one of the respondents: "Ideally, they should not have to teach their first year. It would make much more sense to have them free the first and last years and have them teach the three years in between." Three language coordinators assessed the department's current GTA training practices as "fairly good" while another three described it as "functional" and "survival." Yet another two coordinators indicated that the department was going through a period of transition in relation to GTA language training.

### *Views on foreign language teacher training*

Language coordinators unanimously agreed that the integration of foreign language teacher training into the graduate curriculum would have a positive effect on graduate students' competitiveness in the job market. Their supporting statements can be represented by the following quote from one respondent:

> Absolutely, even though many of them do not believe it. Few of our students will be going to their first job at a research university and will be teaching at liberal arts colleges where they will have to teach 2/3 language and 1/3 literature. For those types of institutions, they will often have to teach a language class as part of their interview. It could be a make or break situation.

Seven out of nine language coordinators believed that the integration of foreign language teacher training into the graduate curriculum would also have positive effects on the quality of the undergraduate courses they coordinate. One of the coordinators who did "not anticipate great effects" conceded that it could "hopefully improve consistency in teaching." Another coordinator acknowledged that it could "enable me to focus on other aspects of coordination and on teacher training that is more targeted to my curriculum."

When language coordinators were asked to describe the format for the most appropriate type of training, five out of nine recommended hands-on workshops. Three out of nine wanted to see case studies implemented into workshops as well as a review of the most important SLA theories. The most important topics that the language coordinators wanted covered in a training program were ranked as follows:

1. Lesson planning (8 out of 9 respondents)
2. In-classroom and out-of-classroom time management (8 out of 9 respondents)
3. Second Language Acquisition (SLA) theory and practice (5 out of 9 respondents)
4. In class grammar/content implementation (5 out of 9 respondents)
5. Assessment design and implementation (5 out of 9 respondents)
6. Other relevant topics (2 out of 9 respondents):
    a. Recognizing different learning styles
    b. Discovering a personal teaching style
    c. Using real-world material in the classroom
    d. Creating student-centered activities
    e. Using new technologies in and out of the classroom appropriately
    f. Creating activities that motivate students.

## Graduate student questionnaire

The aim of this questionnaire was to gather information about GTA training in foreign language teaching from the perspective of GTAs before they were admitted to the program, their satisfaction with their teaching responsibilities, and their perceptions or misconceptions about the usefulness of foreign language teacher training. This information was used to identify the content and format for the FLT training course that different stakeholders would find appropriate, and to partly answer the following evaluation question:

"What are the needs of the GTAs in terms of foreign language teaching?" On average, each questionnaire item prepared for GTAs was answered by 25 of the 57 graduate students in the department (maximum response rate: 28; minimum: 9). Table 3 summarizes responses to closed-ended questions.

Table 3: Summary of responses to close-ended questions

| question | strongly disagree | disagree | neither/nor | agree | strongly agree | N |
|---|---|---|---|---|---|---|
| During the first year of my teaching assistantship, I felt/feel ready to teach a foreign language. | 7.1% | 17.9% | 25.0% | 35.7% | 14.3% | 28 |
| By the end of my PhD program, my teaching assistantship experience will allow me consider myself a professional foreign language instructor. | 3.7% | 11.1% | 33.3% | 25.9% | 25.9% | 27 |
| The weekly interactions with my coordinator have helped me improve my teaching skills. | 3.7% | 7.4% | 25.9% | 40.7% | 22.2% | 27 |
| I feel the department should do more to train me in foreign language teaching | 7.7% | 30.8% | 38.5% | 23.1% | 0.0% | 26 |

The data summarized in Table 3 show that about half of the respondents felt ready to teach a foreign language during the first year of teaching assistantship, and that by the end of the PhD program they would consider themselves professional foreign language instructors. More than half of the respondents agreed that the interactions with the coordinators helped them improve their teaching skills. However, only 23% of them thought the department should offer more teacher training opportunities. Note also that only approximately one third of the respondents claimed to have received previous formal training in foreign language teaching, which varied in quality and length (e.g., training as high school teachers in their native countries, short training courses to become volunteer teachers or to work in private language academies). Two thirds of the respondents had received no training whatsoever prior to teaching in the department.

*Graduate teaching assistants' self-perception as foreign language instructors*
Almost half of the respondents felt that they were ready to teach a foreign language without having received any sort of previous formal training. Only a fourth clearly categorized themselves as unprepared. This expression of self-confidence was further echoed when the respondents were asked what teaching obligations had been the most difficult to fulfill. The largest group of respondents (28%) answered that they had not perceived any obligations as difficult. A positive working environment and a passion for teaching were cited as elements that made teaching for the department an easy task. While this was the most recurrent response, others disagreed and expressed some concerns. Five respondents mentioned that finding a balance between teaching and research obligations was challenging. One respondent expressed frustration over the teaching workload, mentioning that preparing lesson plans and designing exams take a very long time to do well and that "unfortunately, either the lesson plans or my work as a literature student suffered." Time constraints and

grading were also mentioned as other areas of difficulty. Respondents (16%) expressed concerns about their ability to grade objectively and systematically, and the excessive amount of time that it takes to do so. Other respondents (12%) stated that the most difficult aspect of their teaching was providing corrective feedback to students, particularly on an individual basis. They found it challenging to correct students without obstructing their language production, and also to find the time to do so while following the lesson plan.

Respondents were able to further elaborate on the less positive aspects of their teaching by responding to the following item: *What teaching obligations have you found the most difficult to fulfill?* Responses to this item reinforced previously collected information. Nearly one third of the respondents (31%) suggested that there is no aspect of their teaching practice with which they struggle. The second largest portion of respondents (20%) mentioned "explaining the grammar." Another area of concern had to do with student motivation (12%). Some respondents reported struggling to motivate students to speak in the target language, especially while learning difficult grammar.

The evaluators were also interested in eliciting information on the teaching obligations graduate students found to be the least difficult to fulfill. The most recurrent idea (31%) had to do with engaging the students in class discussion and facilitating group work. Many respondents felt that this was not only the least difficult but also the most fulfilling aspect of their teaching.

### Class preparation time

When asked how graduate students spend most of their class preparation time, most answers (50%) focused on the preparation of lesson plans. Preparation activities that were mentioned included:

- Deciding on the best activities that would cover the content of each session.
- Establishing an adequate sequence of activities in order to both make the best of each class hour and maximize the level of motivation in students.
- Selecting and including activities that review previous content as much as they provide practice time for new information.

Some respondents also mentioned that among the most time-consuming activities in lesson planning was reflection on how the grammar should be taught and "come[ing] up with more dynamic exercises than what the textbook asks." The teaching of grammar was the second most frequently mentioned aspect (20%) for this item.

### Language versus literature

When asked whether they saw any relationship between graduate studies in literature and formal training in foreign language teaching, the majority of respondents (68%) claimed that such a relationship did exist, though with varying degrees of assertiveness. The main idea (40%) was that teaching a foreign language provides the kind of pedagogic and didactic framework that can be applicable to the teaching of any subject. This could prove to be an advantage in their careers as literature professors given that "even in literature courses, an instructor must be well-versed in foreign language pedagogy so as to be able to stimulate conversation and create relevant and interesting activities for the students." Another respondent agreed that "the skills which we practice (such as lesson planning, being organized, learning to work with our peers/coordinators) are all skills which will be crucial to our teaching literature and/or language in the future."

Those who did not see any relationship between the two disciplines (32%) supported their responses with less detailed explanations than did those who saw a link between the two. One respondent claimed that the "two subjects require very different teaching methods."

Another expressed the opinion that "most professors are hired based on their writing abilities, dissertation and publications" and that teaching "relates only minimally to graduate studies in literature."

### *Integration of a foreign language teaching course into the graduate curriculum*

The respondents were asked to express their opinions on the possible benefits of integrating formal foreign language teacher training into the graduate curriculum. The majority of respondents (72%) said that it would indeed be beneficial for new and experienced students alike, in several respects. Foreign language teacher training was seen as an advantage, given that most graduate students will teach language when they graduate. One respondent reported on the difficulty of starting to teach a foreign language without having received any sort of formal training, adding:

> When I first came to the university with no experience, I was merely handed the course materials a couple of days before the semester started, we conducted an hour long meeting and then I was off and teaching. The main problem for me at that point was a lack of confidence due to a lack of instruction and direction from the department.

However, several respondents expressed their concerns about the feasibility of a training program in terms of time commitment. Some suggested that it be offered during the first year of training, or at least during the summer, and, in any case, before graduate students start to teach. Several others stated that it would be interesting only if structured "in an effective way" and concentrating on "concrete examples and not [on] a bunch of silly theories." Preferences were expressed for a training course in which "PRACTICAL advice is given and TA's have the opportunity to discuss REAL LIFE problems and challenges they face in the classroom." Eight respondents, on the other hand, claimed that the integration of formal foreign language teacher training in the graduate curriculum would produce few, if any, benefits.

Conversely, a majority of respondents (68%) claimed that such integration would also pose risks. Two main concerns were expressed; the first had to do with time constraints (56%). Respondents suggested that in order for the course to be feasible, it should count toward the graduate seminar degree requirement. The second recurring idea was the fear that training in foreign language teaching would result in "robotic teaching." One respondent claimed that "if the formal training imposes too many rules, guidelines and restrictions, TAs will be overwhelmed and discouraged." Another saw a possible training course as something far removed from the real world in which they would find themselves working:

> The risk is that make-up lesson plans and tests might become more important for the instructor of the course than the real thing that TAs have to do for their own students. There is also a risk of instructor-required repetition: training should help TAs come up with effective and various ways to make foreign language accessible to undergraduate students, not simply clone the method of the instructor of the course.

Putting it more bluntly, another respondent said that such a course would overload "our curriculum with useless things." Even those (30%) who did not see any risks said that a training course should be conceived in a way that does not overwhelm students.

While a majority of respondents acknowledged the usefulness of a possible training course in FL teaching, only 23% of the respondents felt that the department should offer anything beyond the training already offered through weekly meetings with coordinators. When asked if the integration of foreign language teacher training in the graduate curriculum would have any effect on the quality of current undergraduate courses, 64% of the respondents answered affirmatively. One respondent claimed that the benefits on the quality of courses could be tangible only if the training course really addressed the needs and questions of the GTAs. However, "if the TA were not willing, from day one, to dedicate themselves to the teaching requirements, then no amount of training will have an effect." Those who believed it would involve no benefits for the undergraduate curriculum highlighted the view that the burden of a training course for graduate teaching assistants would make it impossible to transfer its benefits to undergraduate courses. Four respondents said that it would actually worsen the quality of the undergraduate courses: "While it may have improved my teaching, I am sure it would have hurt my studies, and so in the end, I would probably have been a worse teacher due to feeling overwhelmed or like a failure in my literature studies."

Finally, respondents were asked for suggestions on the design of a possible training course in foreign language teaching. The majority of respondents expressed a preference for a *how-to* style:

- interactions with senior teaching assistants on "what students have responded well to in the past" or on "good or bad experiences of activities that work or don't work"
- analyzing concrete cases and ways of dealing with teaching difficulties
- demonstrating real life situations
- classroom visits (by all new teachers to other new and experienced teachers)
- how to make efficient lesson plans and prepare their own lesson plans
- how to prepare exams
- how to motivate students
- discussing how grading would be completed, what would constitute a mistake
- presenting different teaching methods
- how to teach grammar

### Data triangulation and interpretation

The information from the three questionnaires showed that most of the respondents in this evaluation agreed with the potential benefits of a formal teacher training program for GTAs. However, a primary point of concern was the importance of achieving an ideal balance between time invested in training and the GTAs' graduate studies. Indeed, time constraints were a major issue mentioned by all groups. This perception will be important to address when implementing foreign language teacher training, as echoed by Siskin and Davis (2001), who expressed their concern that even in institutions that have foreign language GTA training programs in place, students may resent having to dedicate extra time to teaching-related matters, given that "the general impression [might be] that time spent on improving teaching is time taken away from writing books and articles" (p. 10).

Coordinators and GTAs agreed on the lack of experience and formal training that prevails among the GTAs' ranks when entering the program. However, the two groups disagreed on their level of preparation. More than half of the GTAs felt ready during their first year of teaching, while more than half of the coordinators held a contrary perception. GTAs may still hold the view that many in universities have about foreign language teaching: while teaching expectations may be high when it comes to literature or even linguistics, language teaching by contrast is "so simple that virtually anyone can do it" (Chaput, 2001, p. 193).

A quarter of the graduate students did not find any of their teaching obligations difficult. However, when asked to expound on the areas in which they struggled, the GTAs enumerated some of the most basic tasks related to foreign language teaching:

- objective grading
- lesson planning elaboration and execution
- providing clear grammar information
- providing appropriate feedback
- motivating students

These tasks were also listed by coordinators, and included in the information from classroom observation reports, as major areas of needed improvement. Many of these points were also cited by GTAs themselves as tasks that took the most time during class preparation or post-class obligations. All respondents also agreed the training program should focus on practical matters that can be immediately applied. The responses from both the DGSs and the GTAs, however, highlighted some resistance to the teaching of SLA and foreign language teaching theory, which was described by several respondents as "non-essential," involving risks of "robotic teaching," and a "bunch of silly theories." This resistance to a more academic facet of foreign language teaching was also highlighted by a contradiction which emerged in the GTAs questionnaire analysis: While most of the GTAs agreed on the usefulness of some sort of formal training in foreign language teaching, only 23% of them agreed or strongly agreed that the department should do more than just continuing to offer weekly meetings with coordinators. Understanding the reasons behind this contradiction would probably require more evaluation work. However, it may be hypothesized that GTAs consider what "goes on between a TA and his/her students [as] more private and 'inviolable' than what is, for instance, written on literary theory by the same person" (Siskin & Davis, 2001, p. 11). More training would probably reveal the basic needs that GTAs have in terms of teaching preparation, and reduce inflated levels of self-confidence as well as thinking that little training is necessary to teach a foreign language.

## Recommendations, evaluation uses, and conclusions

From the outset, one of the main uses of information from this evaluation was to identify a teacher training program format and content that would reflect the values and needs of all stakeholders. To this end, the following recommendations were made.

1. The very basic teaching skills of in-coming and practicing GTAs revealed that much is still needed in terms of GTA foreign language teacher training. The evaluation team recommends that these concerns be taken into consideration, and also suggests that the training program contribute to a change in perception of the importance of formal academic training in SLA and foreign language teaching. Further evaluation may be necessary to identify the best ways in which this could be accomplished.

2. Given the perspectives of stakeholders, the team recommends that a flexible program, including short bi-weekly workshops and a mentoring component, be offered in the following year. While the program should highlight how SLA and foreign language teaching theory can help shed light on the decisions that every foreign language teacher needs to make on a daily basis, efforts should be geared towards more general educational principles that can find immediate application in the language classroom. The main topics that language coordinators and GTAs agreed should be included in such a teacher training program are:

    - teaching methodology in practice
    - assessment design and implementation

- grammar content implementation
- elements of applied SLA theory

The information obtained in this evaluation will help guide the design of a new teacher training program entitled *Methodology and instructional practices in foreign language teaching*. This course was approved by the executive committee that governs the department and will be mandatory for both incoming graduate students and current graduate students. Further, the information will also be used for a future evaluation project having two main objectives: (a) evaluating the effectiveness of the training program; and (b) motivating other decision makers to support future training efforts in ways that will be effective and work toward consensus among all stakeholders involved. The low response rate from the faculty suggests that more should be done to draw their attention to aspects of foreign language teaching assistant training. To reach this aim, the evaluation findings will be further disseminated to the different stakeholders as follows: (a) through presentations offered during future department-wide faculty meetings; (b) through meetings between LPDs and language coordinators in order to harmonize the content of the weekly training the coordinators hold with their GTAs and the Methods course; and (c) through the training program itself. While much will be done at the local level, this evaluation has also highlighted that the issue taken into consideration is much broader than the specific case under consideration. The uncertain status of SLA, applied linguistics, and language teacher training within Languages and Literatures departments poses a challenge to the evolution (and effectiveness) of the teaching of foreign languages and deserves continued attention from the academic community at large.

## References

Dey, I. (1999). *Grounding grounded theory: Guidelines for qualitative inquiry*. San Diego: Academic Press.

Guthrie, E. (2001). New paradigms, old practices: Disciplinary tensions in TA training. In B. Rifkin (Ed.), *Mentoring foreign language teaching assistants, lecturers, and adjunct faculty* (pp. 19–40). Boston: Heinle

JHU Academic Council (2008). *2008 Academic review of the Department of German and Romance Languages*. Baltimore: unpublished document.

Katz, S. (2005). Toward an understanding of the role of applied linguistics in foreign language departments. *Modern Language Journal, 89*, 490–502.

Leaver, L., & Oxford, R. (2001). Mentoring in style: Using style information to enhance mentoring of foreign language teachers. In B. Rifkin (Ed.), *Mentoring foreign language teaching assistants, lecturers, and adjunct faculty* (pp. 55–88). Boston: Heinle.

Modern Language Association of America (2007). *Foreign Languages and Higher Education: New Structures for a Changed World*. Retrieved July 2008, from http://www.mla.org/mlaissuesmajor

Rifkin, B. (2001). *Mentoring foreign language teaching assistants, lecturers, and adjunct faculty*. Boston: Heinle.

Siskin, H. J., & Davis, J. (2001). Historical, theoretical and programmatic perspectives on mentoring. In B. Rifkin (Ed.), *Mentoring foreign language teaching assistants, lecturers, and adjunct faculty* (pp. 1–17). Boston: Heinle.

Strauss, A., & Corbin, J. (1990). *Basics of qualitative research: Grounded theory procedures and techniques*. London: Sage.

## Appendix: Questionnaires

### Literature faculty questionnaire

(to be distributed to the directors of graduate studies and the section heads through www.surveymonkey.com)

*Thank you for your participation in the study. Your collaboration is highly appreciated. Filling this questionnaire will only take you about 10 minutes. All the information provided will be used exclusively for statistical purposes. Confidentiality is guaranteed.*

1. Do you see any relationship between graduate studies in literature and formal training in foreign language teaching?
2. Would the integration of foreign language teacher training into the graduate curriculum produce any benefits?
3. Would the integration of foreign language teacher training into the graduate curriculum pose any risks?
4. How would you assess your graduate students' preparedness to enter the job market as foreign language teaching professionals?
5. Would the integration of foreign language teacher training into the graduate curriculum have any effect on the graduate students' competitiveness in the job market?
6. Would the integration of foreign language teacher training into the graduate curriculum have any effect on the competitiveness of your PhD program?

### Foreign language coordinator questionnaire

(to be distributed to language coordinators via www.surveymonkey.com)

*Thank you for your participation in the study. Your collaboration is highly appreciated. Filling this questionnaire will only take you about 20 minutes. All the information provided will be used exclusively for statistical purposes. Confidentiality is guaranteed.*

1. How would you describe the general profile of your graduate students?
2. Judging from your coordination work, what are the main strengths of your graduate teaching assistants?
3. Judging from your coordination work, what are the main weaknesses of your graduate teaching assistants?
4. How prepared do you think your graduate teaching assistants are when they start teaching for your program?
5. How do you assess your graduate teaching assistants' preparedness to enter the job market as foreign language teaching professionals when they graduate?
6. What do you think the institution requires of the language teaching coordinator?
7. How do you spend most of your coordination time?
8. Can you describe the support that that the institution gives the graduate teaching assistants to help overcome possible obstacles encountered, both immediately preceding and during their years of training?

9. Can you describe the support that that the institution gives you as coordinator to help overcome possible obstacles encountered, both immediately preceding and during your graduate teaching assistants years of training?
10. How do you assess the Department's current training practices of your graduate teaching assistants?
11. Have there been any issues with the evaluation of graduate students teaching that you have encountered repeatedly?
12. Do you believe graduate students make good use of your coordination time, feedback and evaluation?
13. Would the integration of foreign language teacher training in the graduate curriculum have any effects on the graduate student's competitiveness in the job market?
14. Would the integration of foreign language teacher training in the graduate curriculum have any effects on the quality of the undergraduate courses you coordinate?
15. If you think that formal foreign language teacher training of your teaching assistants is beneficial, what are the five most important topics you would like to see covered in a training program?
16. If you think that formal foreign language teacher training of your teaching assistants is beneficial, what do you think the most appropriate training format would be?

## Graduate teaching assistant questionnaire

(to be distributed to graduate teaching assistants via www.surveymonkey.com)

*Thank you for your participation in the study. Your collaboration is highly appreciated. Filling this questionnaire will only take you about 20 minutes.*

1. At what stage of your doctoral program are you?

    ☐ 1st year  ☐ 2nd year  ☐ 3rd year  ☐ 4th year  ☐ 5th year  ☐ 6th year

2. Before starting your PhD program, did you receive any formal training in foreign language teaching? Please explain.
3. How do you spend most of your class preparation time?
4. What teaching obligations have been the most difficult for you to fulfill?
5. What teaching obligations have been the least difficult for you to fulfill?
6. During the first year of my teaching assistantship, I felt/feel ready to teach a foreign language

    ☐ strongly disagree  ☐ disagree  ☐ neither agree nor disagree
    ☐ agree  ☐ strongly agree

7. If you are past your ABD, how do you assess your preparedness to enter the job market as a foreign language teaching professional? (Please skip if not applicable..
8. Are there any aspects of your foreign language teaching that you still struggle with?

9. The weekly interactions with my coordinator have helped me improve my teaching skills.

   ☐ strongly disagree  ☐ disagree  ☐ neither agree nor disagree
   ☐ agree  ☐ strongly agree

10. By the end of my PhD program, my teaching assistantship experience will allow me consider myself a professional foreign language instructor.

    ☐ strongly disagree  ☐ disagree  ☐ neither agree nor disagree
    ☐ agree  ☐ strongly agree

11. Do you see any relationship between graduate studies in literature and formal training in foreign language teaching?

12. I feel the Department should do more to train me in foreign language teaching.

    ☐ strongly disagree  ☐ disagree  ☐ neither agree nor disagree
    ☐ agree  ☐ strongly agree

13. Would the integration of formal foreign language teacher training in the graduate curriculum produce any benefits?

14. Would the integration of formal foreign language teacher training in the graduate curriculum pose any risks?

15. Would the integration of foreign language teacher training in the graduate curriculum have any effects on the quality of the undergraduate courses you teach?

16. Receiving formal foreign language teacher training as part of my graduate education would give me a competitive edge in the job market

    ☐ strongly disagree  ☐ disagree  ☐ neither agree nor disagree
    ☐ agree  ☐ strongly agree

17. If you think that formal foreign language teacher training would be beneficial, how would you envision it? Feel free to share any ideas you may have about your ideal foreign language teacher training experience.

# 5
# Developing and Implementing an Evaluation of the Foreign Language Requirement at Duke University

Ingeborg C. Walther
*Duke University, Durham, North Carolina*

*This chapter describes the first stages of a multi-year project to evaluate the impact on student learning of the foreign language requirement at Duke University. The project was designed to investigate and assess student performance in the areas of language proficiency and cultural knowledge and understanding, and to use the information gathered for purposes of validating and improving our foreign language requirement curriculum. Following an account of the objectives of the requirement, and the intended uses and users of the evaluation, the chapter provides an overview of our project design and reports on our experiences during the beginning stages of implementation. It concludes with a reflection on the process of evaluation and its impact thus far on our people and programs.*

In the year 2000, Duke University instituted a new general education curriculum in Trinity College of Arts and Sciences.[1] Within this curriculum, a foreign language requirement was instituted as one method of developing cross-cultural understanding and competencies needed for successful interaction in a pluralistic, globally interconnected world. More specifically, the ability to learn a foreign language was viewed as an important way to acquire a deeper understanding of another culture. The ultimate goal of the foreign language requirement was articulated as developing in students a level of competency in a second language sufficient to enable them to engage meaningfully with another culture in its own language. Once the curriculum was implemented, the Dean of Trinity College and Vice Provost for Undergraduate Education initiated a systematic evaluation of the various components of the required curriculum. The major goal of the evaluation has been to document and understand what students have learned upon completion of the

---

1  Trinity College is the name of the undergraduate college of the School of Arts and Sciences. Duke undergraduates are enrolled either in Trinity College of Arts and Sciences or in the Pratt School of Engineering. The curriculum described here applies only to undergraduates in Trinity College and does not affect engineering students.

Walther, I. C. (2009). Developing and implementing an evaluation of the foreign language requirement at Duke University. In J. M. Norris, J. McE. Davis, C. Sinicrope, & Y. Watanabe (Eds.), *Toward useful program evaluation in college foreign language education* (pp. 117–138). Honolulu: University of Hawai'i, National Foreign Language Resource Center.

general education requirements for the ultimate purpose of engendering programmatic and curricular improvements.

In evaluating the foreign language requirement, the dean worked closely with Duke's Office of Assessment and with several language program directors to develop an evaluation plan that would document student learning objectives and chart student progress at various stages of their foreign language learning. Because the new curriculum provided specific outcomes for the foreign language requirement, it was important to gather information on the extent to which these were being met, and to use the evaluation process to determine the kinds of information that would be useful to language program faculty in the ongoing process of curricular and course development.

What follows is an account of the work that has been accomplished thus far, in developing a project design and evaluation questions that would be most useful to the primary users of the information obtained: administrators and faculty who share the responsibility of ensuring that students are meeting the objectives of their programs and curricula, and who are in a position to effect change. The underlying philosophy of the project from the outset has been that evaluation and assessment are part and parcel of the intellectual agenda to enhance undergraduate education. Thus, it was important that the evaluation plan not be imposed "top down" by administrators, but rather that it be the result of a collaborative process involving those who are most directly involved with designing and developing educational programs, curricula, and courses. After presenting a more detailed description of our program context and intended uses of the evaluation, this chapter will describe the evaluation questions and the various methods selected to gather the desired information. It will conclude with an account of our experience thus far with several of these methods, and some reflections on the evaluation process itself.

## Program context and impetus for evaluation

The curriculum that was instituted in 2000 was framed as a response to extraordinary and extraordinarily rapid changes caused by technological advances, the globalization of nations and markets, advances in science and genetics, and the emergence of entirely new fields of scholarly investigation (Curriculum 2000 Report, 1998a).[2] The previous curriculum, implemented in 1988, had required students to fulfill requirements in five of six areas of knowledge (arts and literature, civilizations, social sciences, natural sciences, quantitative reasoning, and foreign languages), and a review conducted in 1997, in connection with our reaccreditation through the Southern Association of Colleges and Schools, found that some 20% of students opted out of foreign language study.[3] The committee charged with the development of a new curriculum was thus asked to consider, among other things, "whether, in a world of increasing complexity and cultural interchange, to require students to be exposed to a diversity of world cultures" and "whether, in a world that depends on international communication, to re-institute a foreign language requirement" (Ibid). Having concluded that foreign language study indeed has a crucial role to play in preparing students to face the multiple and

---

2 The Curriculum 2000 Report gives a full account of the context, rationale, and design of this curriculum.
3 A study prepared by Duke's Office of Institutional Research revealed that at least 47% of 1996–97 graduating seniors had omitted completing at least one course in one of the six areas of knowledge during their entire undergraduate career (19% omitted foreign language, 10% omitted quantitative reasoning, 13% omitted natural sciences, 3% omitted civilizations, 2% omitted social sciences, and 0% arts and literature, see report.)

complex challenges of the 21st century, the new curriculum included a foreign language requirement as one of its components.[4]

The rationale and objectives of the foreign language requirement, as articulated in the Curriculum 2000 Report, are as follows:

### Rationale

Duke has set internationalization as an institutional priority in order to prepare students to live in an increasingly diverse and interdependent world. Internationalizing the institution means that students must be given opportunities to engage with other cultures and to be exposed to ways of thinking other than their own. These perspectives come not only from around the globe but also from multicultural communities within the United States. By developing proficiency in a foreign language, students can develop cross-cultural competency and become more successful members of their increasingly complex local, national, and international communities. Through foreign language study, students have access to materials and cultures not otherwise available and which inform and enrich both the undergraduate experience and post-graduate life.

Beyond providing an additional language resource for communication, foreign language study substantially broadens students' own experiences. As students engage another language, thought, and culture, they can develop their own intellect, gain respect for other peoples, and learn new ways of thinking. Students need an awareness of how language frames and structures understanding and effective communication, and a study of foreign language improves students' native language skills.

### Objectives

We seek for students to:

- Develop sufficient proficiency in a second language to engage foreign cultures, histories and literatures.

- Gain an understanding of the nature of culture in as far as it is embodied in language.

- Bring a cultural perspective to bear to enhance understanding of issues of similarity and difference (Curriculum 2000 Report, 1998a).

As part of the process in creating this new curriculum, a Language Task Force consisting of faculty from within the language departments in Arts and Sciences was charged with determining the specific criteria for fulfilling the foreign language requirement. The members of the Language Task Force advocated for a proficiency-based requirement, which would require "all Duke students to have a level of competency in a second language sufficient to enable them to engage meaningfully with another culture in its own language" and determined that such engagement normally requires the advanced level of proficiency typically needed in our 100–level (5th semester and beyond) courses (Curriculum 2000 Language Task Force Report, 1998b).[5] Thus, the criterion for fulfilling the foreign language requirement became the successful completion of one 100–level

---

[4] In this curriculum, slightly revised in 2004, students are required to take two courses in each of five areas of knowledge (arts, literature and performance; civilizations; social sciences; natural sciences; quantitative studies) and two to three courses in each of six modes of inquiry (cross-cultural inquiry; ethical inquiry; science, technology and society; foreign languages, writing, and research).

[5] At Duke, introductory language courses are typically numbered 1 and 2, intermediate level courses in the 60's and/or 70's, and advanced level courses in the 100's.

(advanced level) course. It was also recognized that some students would want to begin the study of a new language but might be deterred from doing so if this required a five course commitment. Thus, the requirement was set at completing one 100–level course for students who enter their language study at Duke at the intermediate level or above, and the completion of three courses for students who begin their study of a foreign language at Duke in an elementary language (first or second semester) course.

The criteria for fulfilling the foreign language requirement are described in the *2008–2009 Bulletin of Undergraduate Instruction* as follows:

> To satisfy the foreign language competency requirement students must complete one of the following:
>
> 1. For students who enter their language study at Duke at the intermediate level or above, and intend to complete their requirement in that language:
>
>    Completion of a 100–level course that carries the FL designation. Therefore, students who place into the first semester of the intermediate level will take three full courses, students who place into the second semester of the intermediate level will take two full courses, and students who place into the 100 level will take one course. […]
>
> 2. For students who begin their study of a foreign language at Duke in an elementary language (first or second semester) course, and intend to complete their requirement in that language:
>
>    The successful completion of three full courses in the same language that carry the FL designation. […] (Bulletin of Undergraduate Instruction, 2008, p. 26)

A central principle of our curriculum is that each requirement reflects an intellectual engagement that is expected of all graduates of Trinity College. Thus, no student is exempted or allowed to test out of any requirement. In the case of the foreign language requirement, it was argued that since our advanced level classes aim to teach not just literacy (which not all native speakers necessarily possess) but also cross- or trans-cultural literacy (which even literate native speakers may not necessarily possess), no student should be exempted from taking at least one course at the advanced level. Thus, students place into, rather than out of, foreign language classes. Students who already possess some proficiency in a foreign language are not motivated to place artificially low, since it would require more courses to get to the advanced level.

Following the graduation of the first classes subject to the new curriculum, Robert Thompson, the Dean of Trinity College and Vice Provost for Undergraduate Education at the time, undertook an initial study to determine the impact of the foreign language requirement. Using data gathered for the graduating class of 2002–03, the last class under the old curriculum, and the four classes of 2003–04 through 2006–07 who graduated under the new curriculum, comparisons were made for the highest level of language course completed by students in each graduating class, the percentages of students completing a first or second major or minor in a foreign language, and students' self-assessments of their language skills (Thompson and Schlosberg, 2007, p. 2). The findings indicated that, in addition to having all students engage in the study of a foreign language, the percentage of the graduating class completing an advanced level course increased from 34% for the class of 2004 to an average of 55% for the class of 2007, and that an additional 8% to 12% of students now persisted in the study of language beyond the level required. Responding to a question on the annual survey for graduating seniors, the percentage of students indicating that their language skills were stronger increased from 29% to 39%, while the students reporting that their skills were much stronger remained relatively constant at around 14% (Ibid, p. 3).

Included in the plan to evaluate the impact of the foreign language requirement at Duke was to find ways of documenting and assessing actual student learning outcomes in terms of language proficiency, and cultural knowledge and understanding, as articulated in the objectives stated above. To this end, in the summer of 2007 Dean Thompson gathered a study group comprised of himself, the director of the Office of Assessment (Matt Serra), and the directors of the four language programs he selected for the initial evaluation: Chinese (Carolyn Lee), French (Clare Tufts), German (Ingeborg Walther), and Spanish (Liliana Paredes).[6] It was particularly fortuitous that Carolyn Lee and Ingeborg Walther had been accepted to participate in the National Foreign Language Resource Center 2007 summer institute at the University of Hawai'i, *Designing useful evaluation practices in college foreign language programs*. They were thus able to use their time at the institute towards learning more about evaluation practices and developing an initial planning document for the study. Particularly helpful was the emphasis placed in the workshop on the uses and usefulness of an evaluation, and on the development of multiple methods that are closely linked to intended users and uses. What follows here describes the collaborative work that has taken place thus far on this evaluation project. A more complete report that includes specific information with regard to study design and results will be published at a later date.

## Evaluation goals, intended uses, and users

As indicated above, the major goal of the evaluation project is to document and understand what students have learned upon completion of the foreign language requirement. The findings will be used as part of the formal evidence regarding general education learning outcomes that the university is submitting as part of the reaccreditation process through the Southern Association of Colleges and Schools. Important here is the fact that these accreditors in December of 2007 significantly revised their comprehensive standards to require that institutions identify expected student learning outcomes, assess the extent to which they achieve these outcomes, and provide evidence of improvement based on analysis of the results (Southern Association of Colleges and Schools Commission on Colleges, 2008). For the dean of the college, however, it was important that evaluation and assessment be motivated not merely by accreditation but rather by the intellectual agenda of establishing a culture of experimentation and evidence, which fosters continuous improvement in undergraduate education. From the very beginning, therefore, he involved those who would be in the best position to establish this culture and to effect curricular improvements in language teaching at Duke: language program directors. The directors of the four languages selected for the initial evaluation were thus invited to work with the dean and the Office of Assessment in designing an evaluation plan that would be useful and mutually beneficial. In principle, then, there has been a general commitment to the idea of utilization-focused evaluation as developed by Michael Quinn Patton (1997), elaborated here by Weiwei Yang (2009):

---

6 Duke offers some 20 languages in five departments: Asian and Middle Eastern Studies (offering Arabic, Chinese, Hebrew, Hindi, Japanese, Korean), Classical Studies (offering Greek and Latin), Germanic Languages and Literature (offering primarily German), Romance Studies (offering French, Italian, Portuguese, and Spanish), and Slavic and Eurasian Studies (offering primarily Russian, but also Hungarian, Persian, Polish, Romanian, Turkish, Pashto, and Ukrainian). The Dean's selection of Chinese, French, German, and Spanish for the initial study was based largely on enrollments.

> Utilization-focused evaluation starts with identifying primary intended users (PIU) of an evaluation, negotiating with them the purposes and intended uses of the evaluation, and generating among the PIUs a commitment to these uses. In this manner, uses of the evaluation are clarified and built in from the very beginning, with evaluation users committed to participation throughout the process. Subsequent evaluation activities, including the design, data collection, analysis, and presentation of evaluation findings, all find their guidance from and strong association with the pre-specified intended uses. (p. 540)

Working together and using the insights gained from the NFLRC summer institute, we (members of the study group) identified some key primary uses of our project. First, we intend to use the information we obtain to better understand the extent to which our foreign language programs prepare students to meet the objectives and learning outcomes articulated by the curriculum, for the purposes of engendering programmatic and curricular improvement. Second, by documenting student learning outcomes and charting student progress at various stages of their foreign language learning we hope to be able to demonstrate the merit and value of the foreign language requirement in meeting its stated objectives. Ultimately, we intend to use the results of our evaluation to enhance the profile of foreign language programs within the university at large, as integral to the humanities and to a liberal arts education. Furthermore, developing a methodology for assessing language proficiency and cultural understanding will enable subsequent evaluation projects to effectively gauge the impact of curricular and pedagogical innovations on these important outcomes.

In formulating our evaluation questions, we felt it important to be mindful of the multiple stakeholders and their uses of evaluation findings, as well other potential audiences. Thus, university administrators will use the information gathered not only to provide evidence of program effectiveness and of the value of our curriculum, but also to demonstrate the ways in which the university is maintaining standards of accountability in its educational practices, and using evaluation to engender programmatic improvements. Intended audiences are not only our accrediting body, the aforementioned Southern Association of Colleges and Schools, but also the general public both within and outside the university, including students, alumni, faculty in other departments, parents, schools, and communities. Within foreign language departments, chairs, directors of undergraduate studies, and other faculty will benefit from evaluation practices that require a perhaps deeper reflection not only of the foreign language curriculum, but of their own individual course content and pedagogical practices.[7] Duke's Office of Study Abroad, which works closely not only with foreign language programs but with all departments and programs across the university towards better integration of study abroad into their curricula, will have a vested interest in gaining knowledge and understanding of the role of study abroad in students' linguistic and intercultural development.[8] Keeping all of these uses in mind, then, our study group

---

7 Because many of our language programs at Duke are directed and coordinated by non-tenure track regular rank faculty, with beginning and intermediate level courses taught by graduate students, lecturers, and adjunct instructors, the direct involvement of tenured faculty in language programs tends to be rather minimal. However, with increased pressure on departments to develop and implement assessment plans for the major (at Duke this has been for the most part a direct result of our reaccreditation process), along with national organizations such as the Modern Languages Association calling for new departmental structures and greater curricular cohesion between lower and upper division courses, there is much at stake and much to be learned from gathering information on student learning at the end of the required sequences, as well as from the evaluation process itself.

8 A high percentage of Duke students participate in study abroad at some point during their undergraduate career. 47% of the class of 2008 had studied abroad. Because of the different endpoints

developed the evaluation questions, methods, and assessments discussed in detail in the sections that follow.

## Evaluation foci, instrumentation, and timeline

Reflecting the intended uses outlined above, the working group decided to focus in the first iteration on four areas for the evaluation project. First, it was obviously important to know what levels of language proficiency students are achieving in oral and written communication by the end of the required sequences and to determine the gradient of gains across the various exit points (intermediate and advanced levels) within each language. Second, because cultural and intercultural understanding play such a central role in the articulation of our foreign language requirement, we needed to know just what cultural knowledge, understandings, and perspectives students are gaining at each level of the curriculum. Third, because we know that very diverse experiences and encounters with foreign languages will factor into student learning outcomes (in other words, we cannot be sure that students' language proficiency and [inter]cultural understanding are necessarily the direct result of their having taken our courses), we wanted to know to what extent factors such as study abroad, heritage, and previous language learning experiences play a role in students' learning outcomes performance. And fourth, we wanted to know how students themselves perceived the impact of the foreign language requirement, in terms of their gains in language proficiency, and cultural knowledge and understanding, and the various dispositions their foreign language study has engendered. A guiding principle in our evaluation project is the use of multiple sources of empirical information to address each question. In particular, we felt it important to use a combination of direct and indirect, external and internal assessment methods and tools. While realizing the limitations of such external direct assessments as the Simulated Oral Proficiency Interview, or SOPI (Center for Applied Linguistics, 2007), the Intercultural Development Inventory, or IDI (Intercultural Communication Institute, 2008), and the Global Perspectives Inventory, or GPI (Global Perspective Institute, 2008) in capturing the full measure of student learning, we also acknowledged the importance of being able to gauge our students in relation to external norms. At the same time, we felt it necessary to obtain a more complete picture by using our own, internal direct assessments obtained from course-embedded materials, as well as indirect methods in the form of student self-assessments and perceptions. (These instruments will be discussed in detail in the following section.)

Another guiding principle has been to resist the temptation to do everything at once. It is important to emphasize that effective evaluation is a cyclical process that involves continual phases of prioritization, data collection, and use, which in turn engender new prioritization with new foci (Norris, 2006). We conceived the project from the outset as a multi-year, ongoing process to be accomplished in stages. Thus, for example, we decided to focus in the initial stage of our evaluation on oral communication for directly assessing language proficiency, and to limit our engagement in the first two years primarily to the piloting and implementation of three external direct assessments (the SOPI, IDI, and the GPI), and one indirect assessment (a self-designed student questionnaire). The fall semester of 2007 was used for initial planning, determining appropriate cohorts of students, and developing and piloting our student questionnaire. In the spring semester of 2008 we analyzed the results of the questionnaire and made

---

possible under the foreign language requirement, it is likely that some students will have studied abroad before completing the requirement, while others may study abroad after completing it.

revisions and adjustments accordingly.[9] At the end of the semester, we piloted the SOPI and administered the revised questionnaire. At the beginning of the fall semester of 2008 we held training sessions for instructors and graduate students on rating the SOPI, and administered both a pre-course and post-course version of the student questionnaire. In addition, we are piloting the IDI and the GPI with different cohorts of students. Over the course of next spring and summer our group will discuss internal, direct assessments which will be piloted and implemented over the course of the following year.

## Evaluation questions, methods, and actions

This section provides an overview of the methods planned for gathering data in response to each of the evaluation questions as well as the actions that will ensue. In the section that follows we describe in greater detail our experience thus far with utilizing some of these methods.

### Evaluation question #1: Language proficiency outcomes

What levels of language proficiency are students achieving in oral and written communication by the end of the required sequences? In order to address this question, we discussed the merits of various external direct assessments, and concluded that the Simulated Oral Proficiency Interview (SOPI) would best serve our immediate purposes due to relative ease of administration, availability across the languages in focus at Duke, and its widespread use in institutions of higher education in the United States. The SOPI is a performance-based, tape-mediated speaking test that follows the general structure of the oral proficiency interview (OPI) used by government agencies and the American Council on the Teaching of Foreign Languages to measure speaking proficiency.[10] Its use has required and will require ongoing training of instructors and graduate students who will be rating the samples. For the reasons mentioned above we will also be using various course-embedded assessments for oral and written communication, and determining sets of comparable tasks and rubrics. The idea ultimately is to collect student work in speaking, reading, and writing in electronic portfolios in accordance with a common protocol across languages. As an indirect measure, we have included in the student questionnaire sets of statements that require self-assessments of language abilities in speaking, reading, and writing (see Appendix). We thought it important to measure direct outcomes against student self-perceptions, and student questionnaires were selected due to relative ease of administration in class, thus yielding a high response rate and facilitating subsequent analyses.

With the data obtained from the SOPI, we will be able to analyze proficiency ratings by course and in terms of multi-course development over required sequences, and to compare the performance of Duke students with available data on students at other institutions. As with the information we gather from the course-embedded assessments, we will compare performance with course and program outcomes. The data from the student questionnaire will allow us to map student perceptions against curricular outcomes and actual performance. All of this will provide meaningful information

---

9  This involved mostly shortening the questionnaire by deleting items that asked for information that could be obtained elsewhere (e.g., registrar), and items we found to be redundant.

10  More information can be found through the Center for Applied Linguistics website. See also Elizabeth Bernhardt's article on student learning outcomes as professional development and public relations (Bernhardt, 2006).

upon which to make course and curricular adjustments and improvements. Table 1 provides a summary of methods, procedures, and projected actions to be taken with the collected data.

Table 1: Evaluating spoken and written language proficiency outcomes

| methods | procedures | actions (tied to uses) |
|---|---|---|
| **external, direct assessment:** SOPI for oral proficiency | • research and discuss advantages/disadvantages of SOPI; <br> • determine cohorts and procedures for administering; organize workshop(s) for instructors on ACTFL proficiency guidelines and rating SOPI; <br> • set up timeline and procedures for rating | • analyze proficiency ratings by course and development over required sequences; <br> • compare performance of Duke students with available data on students at other institutions; <br> • compare performance with course/program outcomes; <br> • clarify/adjust course outcomes and make improvements as needed |
| **internal, direct assessments:** student portfolios (course-embedded materials for speaking, reading, writing) | • determine content of student portfolios, and process for collecting and evaluating them; <br> • create rubrics that are comparable across languages | • compare performance with course/curricular outcomes; <br> • make course/curricular improvements as needed |
| **indirect assessment:** student questionnaire | • develop questions regarding student perceptions of their proficiency in speaking, reading, writing <br> • pilot questionnaire and revise as needed | • map student perceptions against curricular outcomes and actual performance; <br> • make course/curricular improvements as needed |

## Evaluation question #2: Cultural learning outcomes

What cultural knowledge, understandings, and perspectives are students gaining? Our Office of Assessment has identified two external instruments to address this question, the Intercultural Development Inventory (IDI) and the Global Perspectives Inventory (GPI), which were piloted at the end of the fall 2008 semester. Because of the limitations of such generic external instruments in assessing the extent to which students are meeting our course- and program-specific outcomes with regard to (inter)cultural understanding, we will also be investigating ways to use course-embedded materials (see above) collected in student portfolios for this purpose. This step will allow for triangulation of the data gathered from the standardized instruments and the data gathered from the assessment of the course-embedded materials. To aid us in this endeavor, we invited a language program evaluation and assessment expert to give a workshop on assessing (inter)cultural learning in the spring of 2008. As an indirect method, we have also included a set of statements on the student questionnaire for student self-assessment of their cultural and intercultural learning (see Appendix).

As with the first evaluation question, the data gathered here will allow us to compare the performance of Duke students with available data on students at other institutions, with our own course and curricular outcomes, and to make course and curricular improvements as needed. Table 2 presents a summary of methods, procedures, and projected actions.

Table 2: Evaluating cultural knowledge, understandings, and perspectives

| methods | procedures | actions (tied to uses) |
|---|---|---|
| **external, direct assessment:**<br>Intercultural Development Inventory (IDI)<br>Global Perspectives Inventory (GPI) | • research and discuss advantages and disadvantages;<br>• determine cohort groups and processes for administration;<br>• pilot and make adjustments as needed | • analyze data by course level and development over required sequence;<br>• compare performance of Duke students with available data on students at other institutions;<br>• compare performance with course/curricular outcomes;<br>• make course/curricular improvements as needed |
| **internal, direct assessments:**<br>course-embedded materials (student portfolios) | • determine content of student portfolios, and process for collecting and evaluating;<br>• create rubrics that are comparable across languages | • compare performance with course/curricular outcomes;<br>• make course/curricular improvements as needed |
| **indirect assessment:**<br>student questionnaire | • design questions regarding student perceptions of cultural knowledge and understanding gained as result of FL study;<br>• pilot questionnaire and revise as needed | • map student perceptions against curricular outcomes and actual performance;<br>• make course/curricular improvements as needed |

## Evaluation question #3: Effects of learner and learning factors

To what extent do outside factors such as study abroad, heritage status, and previous language learning experiences play a role in students' learning outcomes? In order to gain a fuller picture of the various factors that play a role in student learning, both with regard to language proficiency and (inter)cultural learning, we intend to use information obtained from the student questionnaire, as well as data collected by our Office of Assessment from various other offices (admissions, study abroad, registrar) on student background, study abroad, or other experiences that may factor into student learning. While it is perhaps never completely possible to determine the extent to which our programs are solely responsible for the skills, knowledge, and dispositions our students demonstrate, we can attempt to control for other factors that might play a role and evaluate the contribution of different experiences.

We also hope to be able to map such information to data gathered on learning outcomes (questions #1 and #2). By comparing the results of students with and without prior or outside experience in FL learning, we can determine to some extent the impact of study abroad and other experiences in achieving FL requirement outcomes. Table 3 summarizes the methods, procedures, and projected actions for using the information gathered.

Table 3: Evaluating the relationship between outside factors and learning outcomes

| methods | procedures | actions (tied to uses) |
|---|---|---|
| student questionnaire | • design questions re. study abroad and language background outside of Duke;<br>• determine cohort; pilot questionnaire and revise as needed | • map information to data gathered in questions #1 and #2;<br>• compare results of students with and without prior or outside experience in FL; analyze to determine impact of study abroad and other experiences in achieving FL requirement outcomes |
| data from the office of the registrar and the office of study abroad | • collect and analyze data from the registrar's office and the office of study abroad on students' prior language background and/or study abroad experience | • (see above) |

### Evaluation question #4: Student perceptions, behaviors, and dispositions

What are student perceptions of the value of their foreign language learning, and what behaviors and dispositions has it engendered? To demonstrate the value of the foreign language requirement, the study group felt it was important to gather information not only on student learning outcomes, but also on student perceptions of the value of their foreign language study and its impact on their lives. One obvious way of gathering such information is from student surveys, and we have included in our student questionnaires a section that addresses their perceptions and dispositions with regard to their foreign language study. We will also be collecting information and data from the registrar, study abroad, and alumni offices to determine what students do with their foreign language post-requirement. As a further measure we intend to conduct interviews with focus groups of current students and alumni.

Because our foreign language programs aim to have a positive impact on students attitudes, behaviors, and dispositions with regard to the value and use of foreign languages beyond the classroom, the information obtained here will help us evaluate the extent to which our courses are meeting these goals, and to make improvements accordingly. Tracking the extent to which foreign language study at Duke correlates with students' future study or work abroad, or their use of foreign language in their future careers will also be helpful in demonstrating the value of the requirement to all stakeholders. Table 4 summarizes the methods, procedures, and projected actions for using the information gathered.

Table 4: Evaluating students' perceptions, behaviors, and dispositions

| methods | procedures | actions (tied to uses) |
| --- | --- | --- |
| **student questionnaire** | • design questions re. value of foreign language study and impact on present and projected future lives;<br>• pilot and revise as needed | • analyze data by course level and development over required sequence;<br>• make course/curricular improvements as needed |
| **interviews with focus groups of current students and alumni** | • design, pilot, revise questions for focus groups<br>• identify and solicit volunteer focus group participants; set up process for interviews | • analyze extent to which FL study at Duke correlates with experience abroad or use of FL in career |
| **data from the registrar, study abroad, and alumni offices** | • collect data on numbers of students studying or participating in career or other experiences abroad, by language, country, and cohort group | • (see above) |

## Our experience thus far

### Student questionnaire

The post-course student questionnaire was developed in the fall semester of 2007 by the four language program directors, with the assistance of the director of the Office of Assessment. It was designed primarily as an indirect measure that would ask students to self-assess their learning in the areas of language proficiency and cultural knowledge, and to agree or disagree with statements concerning the value of foreign language study and their future engagement with the language. It is a paper-based questionnaire, administered in class, and takes approximately ten to fifteen minutes to complete. The most recent version of the questionnaire is provided in the Appendix.

Following a series of items requesting students' background information such as their current stage in fulfilling the requirement, previous experience with the language and experience outside of Duke foreign language courses, time spent living, studying, working in a country where the language is spoken, and identity as a heritage or native speaker of the language, the questionnaire asks students to indicate their competency with respect to cultural knowledge and understanding on a 5-point Likert-type scale ranging from *not competent* to *competent*. Sample items are:

> "understanding the culture(s) in which the language is spoken (e.g., routines of everyday life, traditions, values, attitudes, beliefs, etc.),"

> "knowing some of the major social and political issues of the countries or communities where the language is spoken,"

> "knowing how global events are viewed or understood in the target language countries or communities," and

> "understanding the relationship between language and culture (i.e., the extent to which language and culture are interrelated)."

The next section asks students to rate their competency with respect to speaking and writing skills, and comprehending written and spoken communication. Items are based on ACTFL proficiency guidelines and include such descriptors as:

> "engaging in simple, casual conversations in the target language on topics of everyday life (family, hobbies, daily routines and activities, etc.),"

> "reading and understanding the main ideas of most written texts encountered in everyday life (newspapers, magazines, internet, short novels or plays) with minimal help of glossaries or dictionaries,"

> "writing short, simple communications, compositions, descriptions, and requests for information in loosely connected sentences on topics related to everyday life and personal experiences," and so on.

The final section targets students' perceptions, dispositions, and future plans with regard to foreign language learning. It asks them the extent to which their foreign language study at Duke (including in Duke study abroad programs) has increased their interest in such activities as:

> "engaging with the target language and culture,"

> "using foreign language texts to access knowledge in other areas of interest," or

> "seeking out interaction with people of another culture,"

and to agree or disagree with statements such as:

> "it is important to be able to communicate in languages other than English" or

> "I would like to live, study, or work in a foreign country at some point in the future."

The post-course survey was piloted at the end of the fall 2007 semester with students in the three courses in each of our four languages in which students were potentially completing their requirement: intermediate I and II, and one advanced level course. In revised versions it has been administered in the spring and fall 2008 semesters as pre-course surveys to all students in elementary, intermediate, and one advanced level course, and as post-course surveys for students completing the requirement. While we cannot publish results at this time, we can say that student responses have already had a positive impact on some of our programs. For example, whereas most students generally felt competent or somewhat competent in knowledge of the culture and society of the language in question, they felt less competent in knowing how global events are viewed or understood in the target language countries or communities. Thus, some of us will no doubt be adjusting our courses and syllabi to better address this area.

## Simulated Oral Proficiency Interview (SOPI)

During the 2007–08 academic year we explored various possibilities for administering the SOPI. Given the limitations of our budget,[11] which precluded hiring professional testers/raters, we purchased the disclosed tests and test booklets for our four languages from the Center for Applied Linguistics (CAL), and scheduled through CAL rater training workshops for our instructors and graduate students to obtain certification. These workshops were held in the summer and fall of 2008, and all participants in Spanish, French, and German received certification. Because a trainer could not be located for Chinese, the Chinese faculty participated in an OPI workshop that was being given for the Chinese program at

---

11 For the entire project we have a working budget of approximately $30,000 obtained through Trinity College curriculum development/assessment grants.

nearby University of North Carolina at Chapel Hill. Having piloted the SOPI at the end of the spring 2008 semester to several sections in each language of intermediate I, intermediate II, and an advanced level class, we administered it again at the end of the fall 2008 semester and will be rating students over the course of next semester.[12]

We plan to administer the SOPI again at the end of the spring 2009 semester. Given the cost in time and money, and the challenge of maintaining a cadre of certified or trained raters, we do not plan to make administration of the SOPI a regular component of our language programs. Rather, guided by the findings of this evaluation, the SOPI will be selectively employed in smaller scale evaluations to address questions about the impact of specific pedagogical innovations and curricular or program components in one or more language programs. It will be important to compare and calibrate the SOPI results with our own course-embedded assessments to determine whether these will yield useful information and be cost-effective for long-term use.

## Cultural inventories

As noted above, the Intercultural Development Inventory (IDI) had been identified as the best external instrument for our purposes that is available at this time, and because of its standing in the field for high reliability. As Sinicrope, Norris, and Watanabe (2007) report: "in-depth evaluations of the Intercultural Development Inventory (IDI) and studies using the instrument have lent support to the validity and usefulness of the IDI for estimating changes in intercultural competence" (p. 18), though they also warned about its indiscriminate use without articulation to specific program learning outcomes. Developed by Mitchell Hammer in cooperation with Milton Bennett, it is a 50–item, theory-based paper and pencil instrument which assesses five of the six major stages of Bennett's Developmental Model of Intercultural Sensitivity (DMIS): denial, defense, minimization, acceptance, and adaptation. Students are asked to respond, using a 5-point Likert-type scale ranging from disagree to agree, to statements such as:

> "cultural differences are less important than the fact that people have the same needs, interests, and goals in life,"

> "it is appropriate that people from other cultures do not necessarily have the same values and goals as people from my culture," or

> "family values are stronger in our culture than in other cultures," which correspond to the various developmental stages.[13]

As a result of further research on cultural competency inventories, an additional assessment was identified during the fall semester of 2008 that appeared to be a viable, cost-effective alternative to the IDI. The Global Perspectives Inventory (GPI) is a 46 item survey designed to provide self-reports of students' perspectives in three dimensions of global learning and development: cognitive, intrapersonal, and interpersonal.[14] Here, too, students are asked to respond to statements on a 5-point Likert-type scale ranging from strongly agree to strongly disagree. The cognitive domain consists of two scales, knowing and knowledge, and is measured by items such as "when I notice cultural differences, my culture tends to have the better approach," or "I understand the reasons and causes of conflict among nations of different cultures." Likewise, the intrapersonal domain addresses identity and affect

---

12 Raters will be paid per student rated.
13 For more information, including a full description of the IDI, see the Intercultural Communication Institute website.
14 More information can be found on the Global Perspective Institute website. For a descriptive guide and sample inventory, see https://gpi.central.edu/supportDocs/Interpretative_guide.pdf.

with such statements as "I see myself as a global citizen," and "I avoid disagreements with people from backgrounds different from my own." The interpersonal domain assesses social interaction and responsibility with items such as "I intentionally involve people from many cultural backgrounds in my life," and "I work for the rights of others."

We piloted both inventories at the end of the fall semester 2008. To obtain a basis of comparison for the project cohort of students, a control group of volunteer students who have not completed the foreign language requirement were invited to participate. Half of our study cohort and control groups were administered the IDI, and the other half the GPI. Piloting two assessments provides an opportunity to compare the findings and determine whether there are differences in sensitivity to the background, curricular, and other educational experiences of Duke students, which will inform decisions about which instrument would be the more useful for future evaluations.

## Course-embedded assessments

While there is some degree of skepticism among members of our group with regard to the ability of such external instruments as the IDI and GPI to assess student learning that is a direct result of taking our foreign language courses,[15] the findings we gain—positive or negative—will nevertheless be of interest to us and the larger foreign language teaching community. But precisely because we would like to more closely align our assessments with our program learning outcomes and with what is actually happening or intended to happen in our courses, we feel it is especially important to include course-embedded assessments of both performance and cultural understanding in our evaluation study. To this end, we have begun the arduous but satisfying and rewarding process of comparing syllabi, student assignments, and rubrics for evaluating spoken and written performance, to our mutual benefit. While it is not our purpose, given the differences in languages and programs, to create or impose a set of uniform tasks and grading rubrics across languages and courses, it will be necessary to reach agreement on the types of student performances that will be used to assess the kinds of knowledge, skills, and dispositions we hope to foster in our students, as well as on common components for rating. Our Office of Assessment has been helping us identify some of these components and developing assessments that can be compared across languages. We have also begun discussions about electronic portfolio collection and use.

## Reflections on the evaluation process and its impact on people and programs

Perhaps the most immediate and welcome impact of the evaluation project is the close collaboration it has engendered among the four language program directors involved. Since the forming of the Language Task Force in the context of the creation of the new curriculum, our dean has continued and supported its existence—now as the Trinity Language Committee—ever since. As an ad hoc standing committee charged with addressing matters related to the study of foreign languages at Duke, its members, comprising representatives from all language departments, have been meeting regularly for the past ten years and have enjoyed the opportunity to address common issues and share ideas and concerns. The dean has also given the committee a small annual budget to invite guest

---

15 One concern is that the kinds of attitudes, behaviors, and dispositions these instruments attempt to grasp are typically acquired over a much longer period of time than a few semesters of college study. The development of intercultural competence is a long term prospect, and usually attained only by living and interacting for an extended time within a foreign culture or even within a relatively intercultural domestic one. We worry that growth over the developmental stages will not be evident in our students over the course of only a few semesters of foreign language study. However, we may find that curricular experiences heighten awareness and sensitivity or stimulate changes or transformations in attitudes or dispositions.

speakers for continued ongoing professional development. Further, whereas we have always mutually benefited from our regular contact, the project has required us to move from more global and general concerns to delve more deeply into discussions at the curricular and course level. It has been wonderful to compare our various rubrics, for example, for evaluating different kinds of writing and speaking assignments, to learn more about the kinds of tasks each of our programs has students perform at each level of instruction, and to use this information to enhance our own pedagogical practices.

The evaluation project has also required us to take a closer look at our language programs in the context of the rationale and objectives for the foreign language requirement described in the Curriculum 2000 Report, particularly with regard to the development of cultural knowledge and understanding. While we are all aware of the sometimes unrealistic expectations placed on our beginning and intermediate level courses for fostering both language proficiency and (inter)cultural knowledge, we strive to do both throughout our curricula. The results of our survey thus far have indicated, however, that we might do a better job of communicating to students that we are teaching them much more than language skills in our beginning and intermediate courses. Some of us are thus considering ways to include more cultural content, or to more explicitly engage students on the nature of the relationship between language and culture.

As rewarding as the process has been on many levels, it has not been without its challenges. Aside from the considerable resources required in terms of time and money, it has been challenging to schedule class time each semester for the completion of various instruments: instructors complain that this is taking away valuable instructional time, and we worry about students becoming weary of the questionnaire after repeated encounters. As noted above, it will be difficult and expensive, in the long term, to maintain a cadre of trained raters for the SOPI, although it contributes to the professional development of our instructors and graduate student teaching assistants. If, however, we are able to map the results of our external assessments onto our internal ones in a meaningful and transparent way, we would likely limit their use to periodic intervals (every five years, for example), whereas course-embedded assessments would become a regular part of the curriculum.

It is also becoming increasingly clear that the timeline we have set may be overly ambitious. We are fortunate to have an Office of Assessment to help collect and analyze data, but administering the various instruments and putting the information gathered to meaningful use in our programs and curricula is an enormous challenge that requires sustained commitment of time and energy on the part of the primary users. If evaluation and assessment are to be part of an ongoing culture of experimentation and evidence, the goals and expectations must be carefully and realistically measured against available financial, institutional, and above all human resources.

As we hope to have shown, however, even in its initial planning stages, the evaluation project has already been useful in helping individual language programs address issues of curricular outcomes, content, and coherence, faculty development, and articulation with other programs and departments across the university. We hope it will also have the added value of communicating more precisely to the outside world (administrators, faculty, students, parents, communities) just what it is our foreign language programs do and what students learn, enhancing the profile of foreign language programs within the university and beyond as an integral part of the humanities in a liberal arts education, and contributing to the growing research in the field of foreign language education and program evaluation.

*Acknowledgements*

This is a collaborative project initiated in 2007 by my colleague Robert J. Thompson, Jr., then Dean of Trinity College of Arts and Sciences and Vice Provost for Undergraduate Education. I gratefully acknowledge him and my fellow collaborators, Carolyn Lee, Liliana Paredes, Matt Serra, and Clare Tufts, for their valuable support and editorial suggestions in writing this account of our work. In particular, I would like to acknowledge my colleague Carolyn Lee, who participated with me in the 2007 NFLRC workshop on *Designing useful evaluation practices in college foreign language programs*. This account follows closely on the work we accomplished together at the workshop. I would also like to thank John Norris of the University of Hawai'i for his invaluable guidance, encouragement, and support.

# References

Bernhardt, E. B. (2006). Student learning outcomes as professional development and public relations. *Modern Language Journal, 90*, 588–590.

Center for Applied Linguistics (2007). *Simulated oral proficiency interviews.* Retrieved September 2, 2008, from http://www.cal.org/topics/ta/sopi.html

Duke University (2008). *2008–2009 Bulletin of undergraduate instruction.* Retrieved September 2, 2008, from http://registrar.duke.edu/bulletins/undergraduate/

Duke University (1998a). *Curriculum 2000 report.* Retrieved September 1, 2008, from http://www.aas.duke.edu/admin/curriculum2000/report.html

Duke University (1998b). *Curriculum 2000 language task force report.* Retrieved September. 1, 2008, from http://www.aas.duke.edu/admin/curriculum2000/ltf/requirement.html

Global Perspective Institute (2008). *Global perspective inventory.* Retrieved November 1, 2008, from https://gpi.central.edu/index.cfm

Intercultural Communication Institute (2008). *Intercultural Development Inventory.* Retrieved August 13, 2009, from http://www.idiinventory.com/

Norris, J. M. (2006). The why (and how) of student learning outcomes assessment in college FL education. *Modern Language Journal, 90*(4), 576–583.

Sinicrope, C., Norris, J., & Watanabe, Y. (2007). *Understanding and assessing intercultural competence: A summary of theory, research, and practice.* Technical Report for the Foreign Language Program Evaluation Project. University of Hawai'i at Mānoa. Retrieved September 10, 2008, from http://nflrc.hawaii.edu/evaluation/

Southern Association of Colleges and Schools Commission on Colleges. (2008). *The principles of accreditation: Foundations for quality enhancement.* Retrieved September 1, 2008, from http://sacscoc.org/pdf/2008PrinciplesofAccreditation.pdf

Thompson, R. J. & Schlosberg, L. (2007). *Impact of instituting a foreign language requirement.* Duke University: unpublished Report.

Yang, W. (2009). Evaluation of teacher induction practices in a US university English language program: Towards useful evaluation. *Language Teaching Research, 13*(1), 77–98.

## Appendix: Student questionnaire

Please indicate your responses on the answer sheet provided. Responses submitted on the survey will not be accepted.

1. Please indicate which of the following best describes you:
   (a) With this course included, I have not yet fulfilled the FL requirement.
   (b) After completing this course, I will be finished with the FL requirement.
   (c) The FL requirement is not applicable (e.g., I am a graduate student)

2. Of the courses you have taken to fulfill your FL requirement, how many were taken at Duke (including this course and Duke-in study abroad programs)? *Please count only those courses that fulfill the FL requirement, not requirements of a major.*
   (a) 0 courses
   (b) 1 course
   (c) 2 courses
   (d) 3 courses

Items 3–7 refer to your plans to major in a foreign language. Please respond to each of the questions. If you do not intend to major in the language, select "I do not plan to major."

3. Do you plan to major or minor in Chinese?
   (a) I plan to *major* in Chinese.
   (b) I plan to *minor* in Chinese.
   (c) I do not plan to major or minor in Chinese.
   (d) I am undecided.

4. Do you plan to major or minor in French?
   (a) I plan to *major* in French.
   (b) I plan to *minor* in French.
   (c) I do not plan to major or minor in French.
   (d) I am undecided.

5. Do you plan to major or minor in German?
   (a) I plan to *major* in German.
   (b) I plan to *minor* in German.
   (c) I do not plan to major or minor in German.
   (d) I am undecided.

6. Do you plan to major or minor in Spanish?
   (a) I plan to *major* in Spanish.
   (b) I plan to *minor* in Spanish.
   (c) I do not plan to major or minor in Spanish.
   (d) I am undecided.

7. Do you plan to major or minor in another language?
   (a) I plan to *major* in another language.
   (b) I plan to *minor* in another language.
   (c) I do not plan to major or minor in another language.
   (d) I am undecided.

Please indicate your competency with respect to each of the following skills.

|     |                                                                                                                                                                            | not competent | | somewhat competent | | competent |
|-----|----------------------------------------------------------------------------------------------------------------------------------------------------------------------------|---|---|---|---|---|
|     |                                                                                                                                                                            | a | b | c | d | e |
| 8.  | Understanding the culture(s) in which the language is spoken (e.g., routines of everyday life, traditions, values, attitudes, beliefs, etc.).                              | ☐ | ☐ | ☐ | ☐ | ☐ |
| 9.  | Knowing some of the major cultural products of the country or countries where the language is spoken (e.g., music, art, literature, theater, pop songs, films, TV shows, etc.). | ☐ | ☐ | ☐ | ☐ | ☐ |
| 10. | Knowing some of the major social and political issues of the countries or communities where the language is spoken.                                                        | ☐ | ☐ | ☐ | ☐ | ☐ |
| 11. | Knowing how global events are viewed or understood in the target language countries or communities.                                                                        | ☐ | ☐ | ☐ | ☐ | ☐ |
| 12. | Knowing the history of the countries or regions where the language is spoken.                                                                                              | ☐ | ☐ | ☐ | ☐ | ☐ |
| 13. | Understanding cross-cultural similarities and differences.                                                                                                                 | ☐ | ☐ | ☐ | ☐ | ☐ |
| 14. | Understanding the relationship between language and culture (i.e., the extent to which language and culture are interrelated).                                             | ☐ | ☐ | ☐ | ☐ | ☐ |
| 15. | Empathizing with individuals possessing different beliefs, behaviors, and social norms.                                                                                    | ☐ | ☐ | ☐ | ☐ | ☐ |

Please indicate your competency with respect to each of the following skills.

|     |                                                                                                                                             | not competent | | somewhat competent | | competent |
|-----|---------------------------------------------------------------------------------------------------------------------------------------------|---|---|---|---|---|
|     |                                                                                                                                             | a | b | c | d | e |
| 16. | Engaging in simple, casual conversations in the target language on topics of everyday life (family, hobbies, daily routines and activities, etc.). | ☐ | ☐ | ☐ | ☐ | ☐ |

| | | | | | | |
|---|---|---|---|---|---|---|
| 17. | Engaging in more complex conversations and discussions on a variety of topics, including family, interests, work, travel, current events and social issues. | ☐ | ☐ | ☐ | ☐ | ☐ |
| 18. | Reading and understanding the main ideas of simple written texts encountered in everyday life from a variety of media (e.g., newspaper ads, signs, internet media, simple stories, song texts, or poems) with the help of glossaries and/or dictionaries. | ☐ | ☐ | ☐ | ☐ | ☐ |
| 19. | Reading and understanding the main ideas of most written texts encountered in everyday life (newspapers, magazines, internet, children's books, short novels or plays) with minimal help of glossaries and/or dictionaries. | ☐ | ☐ | ☐ | ☐ | ☐ |
| 20. | Understanding the main ideas of simple conversations encountered in everyday life (face-to-face conversations; short radio, film and video clips, internet). | ☐ | ☐ | ☐ | ☐ | ☐ |
| 21. | Understanding the main ideas of most speech encountered in everyday life (face-to-face interactions, short speeches or presentations, radio, film and video, internet). | ☐ | ☐ | ☐ | ☐ | ☐ |
| 22. | Writing short, simple communications, compositions, descriptions, and requests for information in loosely connected sentences on topics related to everyday life and personal experiences. | ☐ | ☐ | ☐ | ☐ | ☐ |
| 23. | Writing longer texts consisting of connected paragraphs about familiar topics related to interests and events of current, public, and personal relevance with fair to good control of major time frames and basic grammatical structures. | ☐ | ☐ | ☐ | ☐ | ☐ |

Please indicate your current interest level in the topics listed below.

| | | not interested | | somewhat interested | | interested |
|---|---|---|---|---|---|---|
| | | a | b | c | d | e |
| 24. | Engaging with the target language and culture. | ☐ | ☐ | ☐ | ☐ | ☐ |
| 25. | Using foreign language texts to access knowledge in other areas of interest. | ☐ | ☐ | ☐ | ☐ | ☐ |
| 26. | Seeking out interaction with people of another culture. | ☐ | ☐ | ☐ | ☐ | ☐ |
| 27. | Developing a better understanding of cultural stereotypes. | ☐ | ☐ | ☐ | ☐ | ☐ |

| | | | | | | |
|---|---|---|---|---|---|---|
| 28. | Developing a better understanding of my own language and culture. | ☐ | ☐ | ☐ | ☐ | ☐ |
| 29. | Pursuing additional courses or research related to the countries or cultures of the target language after completing this course. | ☐ | ☐ | ☐ | ☐ | ☐ |

Please rate the extent to which you agree with the following statements:

| | | strongly agree | | neutral | | strongly disagree |
|---|---|---|---|---|---|---|
| | | a | b | c | d | e |
| 30. | As the world becomes more culturally and linguistically diverse, it is important to be able to communicate in languages other than English. | | | | | |
| 31. | Studying a foreign language has enhanced my education. | | | | | |
| 32. | I plan to continue studying this language beyond the foreign language requirement, either at Duke or elsewhere. | | | | | |
| 33. | My foreign language skills have enhanced my career opportunities. | | | | | |
| 34. | My foreign language skills have enhanced my potential for personal growth. | | | | | |
| 35. | I would like to live, study, or work in a foreign country at some point in the future. | | | | | |

On the back of the answer sheet, please provide any additional comments regarding the topics covered in the above sections. Please do not write your comments here.

# 6

## Improving Educational Effectiveness and Promoting Internal and External Information-Sharing Through Student Learning Outcomes Assessment

Antonio Grau Sempere
M. Chris Mohn
Roger Pieroni
*University of Evansville, Indiana*

*In the fall of 2005, the University of Evansville Department of Foreign Languages appointed a three-member committee to oversee the development of an assessment strategy to measure the educational effectiveness of the department in terms of student learning outcomes. This effort responded both to an internally identified need for reflecting and improving upon the program, as well as an external need to ensure and disseminate information about the program's educational quality and value. Over the course of the following two years, the committee—in consultation with the rest of the department—established student learning outcomes statements, created tools designed to measure those outcomes, and pilot-tested a portfolio assessment process. As a result of this undertaking, the foreign language department now has in place a set of instruments and procedures for assessing the effectiveness of the program and enhancing its overall quality, and it is in a much better position to engage in related evaluation activities for the benefit of students and staff.*

During the fall of 2005, a new chair in the Department of Foreign Languages at the University of Evansville (UEDFL) encouraged faculty members to reflect on the status of the foreign language program and to target needed changes for the future. In the internal evaluation that followed, over the course of the ensuing semester, faculty identified academic excellence as a goal that was clearly supported by all. Identifying academic excellence as an overall goal, however, was only the first stage in charting a course for the future of the department. The next step involved clarifying and articulating the path to achieve that excellence. Clarification began with the framing of a vision and mission statement that targeted eventual public and institutional recognition of the UEDFL as one of the top language programs among universities in its category (see Appendix A). The department

---

Grau Sempere, A., Mohn, M. C., & Pieroni, R. (2009). Improving educational effectiveness and promoting internal and external information-sharing through student learning outcomes assessment. In J. M. Norris, J. McE. Davis, C. Sinicrope, & Y. Watanabe (Eds.), *Toward useful program evaluation in college foreign language education* (pp. 139–162). Honolulu: University of Hawai'i, National Foreign Language Resource Center.

then sought and received an internal grant from the university to initiate a project to improve academic excellence in pursuit of that vision. At the urging of the chair, the project was pursued by following an explicitly evaluative approach, based on the gathering of empirical evidence that could be utilized for shedding light on aspects of the program that were functioning well and others in need of attention. Stages of the project included stating specific program goals, determining project components in consultation with an external evaluator, and exploring ways to evaluate the department's effectiveness in meeting high-priority goals, primarily through the process of student learning outcomes assessment. The UEDFL is currently engaged in the cyclical process of conceiving, developing, and implementing various forms of student learning outcomes assessment, so that multiple stakeholders are provided with empirical assessment-based information to illuminate and improve upon the effectiveness of UEDFL degree programs and courses. The details of this project, from inception to current implementation, form the content of this chapter.

## Background, context, and impetus for evaluation

### About the university

With a population of approximately 2400 undergraduates, the University of Evansville is composed of a College of Education and Health Sciences; a School of Business Administration; a College of Engineering and Computer Science; and a College of Arts and Science, the largest of the four schools, which houses the Department of Foreign Languages. The department offers majors and minors in French, German, and Spanish, as well as minors in Japanese Studies, Russian Studies, and Latin American Studies. Faculty from the departments of Archaeology and Philosophy and Religion offer course work in Latin, Greek, and Hebrew in conjunction with the department's programs as well (including a classical studies major or minor, or a classical languages minor). The UEDFL faculty consists of five full-time equivalencies (FTEs) and one adjunct in Spanish, two and a quarter FTEs in French, and one FTE respectively in Japanese, Russian, and German. It also hosts four Fulbright language teaching assistants (FLTAs) on a rotating annual basis, one each for Russian, Spanish, French, and German. Students preparing a Bachelor of Science or a Bachelor of Fine Arts degree at the university are required to take one year of a foreign language, while students enrolled in a Bachelor of Arts program have a two-year requirement. As of the writing of this report, the department had a total of 48 majors: three in German, 14 in French, and 31 in Spanish.

### The impetus for a fresh start

The development of the evaluation project was directly linked to the objective of improving academic excellence, as set for the department during its 2005 internal evaluation. On the one hand, there was a clear internal need to forge agreements about what excellence might mean for the department's various language programs, and to begin collecting evidence to understand the extent to which excellence so defined was being achieved. At the same time, beyond the department, there were also institutional and larger concerns with perceptions of the value contributed by the foreign language programs to undergraduate studies at the university, and these needed to be addressed on the basis of something other than intuitions, traditional arguments about the value of language study, and so forth. The project therefore focused on creating an assessment approach that would objectively demonstrate to students, instructors, administrators, and others the progress, success, and value of the UEDFL program. A committee of three tenured and tenure-track faculty members was created for the purpose of keeping the project moving, though the entire department was regularly consulted for feedback and kept abreast of progress.

## Setting the stage for useful evaluation: Focus, uses, users

Because of their commitment to the vision and mission statements developed in the fall of 2005, the UEDFL faculty members were eager to work together to identify and articulate the evaluation needs of the department in order to pursue the challenging agenda implied. After several department meetings, brainstorming sessions, and discussion of the issues, faculty identified the following high-priority needs that were potentially related to evaluation:

- A means for the improvement of teaching methods, class content, and course offerings;
- An evidentiary basis for making requests to the administration; if we cannot show data that we are doing a good job, then we cannot justify resources, positions, and the like;
- An evidentiary emphasis on *student learning* in the validation of all our programs and efforts in the UEDFL;
- A process for helping faculty to understand what the department currently does (or does not do) well in order to improve curriculum and instruction; and
- A way for students to understand what a UEDFL degree means to them and to others, how it is or should be useful to them, and what they will be able to do with it after graduation.

Faculty members also raised questions related to study abroad, student recruitment, and validation of the intensive and specialized efforts of the language majors. After further discussions, the full department reached consensus on the program evaluation issue with the highest priority, namely putting into place a student learning outcomes assessment framework that would meet the immediate needs of the department and others as listed above. The department decided to focus in the first iteration of this project on the core of its program, the undergraduate majors, and to title the project *Understanding the educational effectiveness of the UEDFL in terms of student learning outcomes*. The primary intended evaluation use was to illuminate the educational effectiveness of the UEDFL degree program in the most meaningful terms possible. Educational effectiveness was to be measured according to what students know and are able to do, as well as their disposition to act in certain ways, upon completion of the degree in foreign languages.

The first item of business for the committee was to gather preliminary information in preparation for a summer institute on program evaluation in foreign language education, hosted at the University of Hawai'i National Foreign Language Resource Center in 2007. In anticipation of this event, the UEDFL committee worked with an evaluation consultant (John Norris) to define the primary and secondary users of evaluation findings. The committee and the external consultant identified the primary users as the UEDFL faculty, who would act on information to make needed improvements in curriculum and instruction, while the dean, students (current and prospective), other departments, the administration, and the community constituted secondary but nevertheless quite important users, as they would use information to make judgments about the value of the foreign language programs.

Throughout the evaluation process, the information needs of these distinct user groups were kept in mind. Specifically, UEDFL faculty members would use student learning outcomes assessments to: (a) come to consensus regarding the basic learning expectations for the degree program; (b) validate the good work that was going on within the program; (c) improve the institutional and public image of the department; (d) justify funding and additional resource requests to the administration; (e) identify strengths and weaknesses in program outcomes for the purpose of improving program delivery; and (f) ensure the quality of student learning that takes place within the program, both by motivating students toward high expectations, and by better designing curriculum and instruction to match the intended outcomes of the degree program.

The dean would use the resulting data to meet basic quality assurance demands, including institutional accreditation, and to understand more comprehensively the role of the UEDFL vis-à-vis the institution and its mission. The administration would also project a public image in part on the basis of the students' outcomes and use this particular assessment plan as a means for educating other departments within the college on the ways in which such assessments may be done effectively. Current UEDFL students would use student learning outcomes assessments to understand what they had achieved through the degree program and to project what they would be able to do with their degree. In addition, students would use assessments to further their post-graduation plans (e.g., professional portfolios that include a variety of indicators of students' knowledge and abilities may be used for job or graduate school applications). Prospective UEDFL students would use basic information about student learning outcomes to understand the value of foreign language study at UE and to make decisions about pursuing classes or degrees therein based on indicators that are easy to interpret (such as proficiency levels achieved by graduates; professional/academic success of graduates; alumni testimonials; and evidence that quality assurance is taking place through assessment).

Following the identification of intended users and uses, the next stage was to have the UEDFL committee take concrete steps towards developing and implementing a sound methodological approach to meeting these demands. From the outset, of course, setting the outcomes assessment project as one of our main goals already initiated something of an evolution in departmental practices, in the sense that it established a heretofore absent or unfocused sense of collective program ownership. All members of the department, tenured, tenure track, contract, and adjunct instructors were given the chance to offer input and feedback in weekly department meetings, and they became highly invested stakeholders throughout the project. However, beyond this developing sense of shared commitment, the next phases in the project included: (a) developing common student learning outcomes; (b) mapping learning outcomes to the curriculum; (c) developing learning outcomes assessments; (d) pilot-testing assessments; and (e) acting upon initial findings.

### Developing student learning outcomes statements

The committee's next charge was to produce student learning outcomes (SLOs) statements for students completing a major in a foreign language. Given the size and broad scope of the department, simplicity, manageability, and clarity in the outcomes assessment process were essential; thus, while the UEDFL houses distinct language programs, they all adhere to the same core pedagogic principles and expectations for undergraduate majors. Therefore, these outcomes needed to be common to all individuals completing a major, regardless of language, area of specialization, or courses taken. Committee members devoted several department meetings to brainstorming sessions and discussions that produced three successive and more refined versions of SLOs that would in fact be amenable to all languages being taught. During these meetings, individual faculty were first encouraged to review and offer feedback on outcomes statements, prior to full group discussion and decision-making. Subsequently, the final draft of the SLOs was sent to seven foreign language majors with a request for suggestions and reactions. The response rate was 100% from the students, and the overall tone of the feedback can be summarized by this statement from one major:

"I'm excited that the department is eager to improve its services to students." Another department meeting saw the final vetting of the document, taking into account all the feedback that had been received from different stakeholders: students, colleagues, and the external consultant who had made campus visits and provided constant feedback. In early May 2007 the committee produced the following list of common SLOs for undergraduate majors in the UEDFL:

1. Students express themselves confidently in a variety of oral and written registers, keeping in mind the communicative context and conventions of the particular cultures.
2. Students read and comprehend texts in the target languages tailored to a variety of communicative needs.
3. Students write documents in the target languages tailored to a variety of communicative needs, keeping in mind the conventions of the particular cultures.
4. Students understand native speech.
5. Students employ a variety of coping strategies to communicate both verbally and non-verbally in the target languages.
6. Students demonstrate a familiarity with the current events, the pop culture, and the social structures of the countries/cultures in which the target languages are spoken.
7. Students demonstrate understanding of language variation (social, dialectal, and contextual).
8. Students are able to perform a linguistic (synchronic and diachronic) analysis of language.
9. Students read literary texts in the target languages and analyze them critically using a theoretical framework.
10. Students understand literary and artistic movements and the history of ideas.

At that time, the entire department felt that it had developed a solid base upon which to build and a convenient framework with which to examine the curriculum and the targeted 'educational effectiveness' more closely.

## Mapping outcomes to the curriculum

Once the student learning outcomes were established, the next step was to map them first to the French and Spanish curriculum, in order to help the department ascertain to what extent the courses offered at UEDFL adequately addressed and encompassed all of the targeted outcomes (i.e., to what extent did students have the opportunity to achieve these outcomes). We limited this initial mapping to the French and Spanish programs because the German major was in a transitional stage at the time of the project. For curricular mapping, the committee members first reviewed the contents of the current course offerings as stated in the course descriptions and class syllabi, and they identified which of the stated outcomes were met in each of the courses or sequences of courses. This mapping was intended to help delineate clearly the areas where the overlap between course content and learning outcomes was sufficient and the areas where it might be predicted to fall short. In addition, it also enabled the identification of likely areas in need of attention on the basis of future assessment findings (i.e., locating the sources of any identified weaknesses in outcomes would be facilitated through curricular maps). Thus, the critical decision of which new courses might need to be offered, how existing course curricula might need to be revised, and the qualifications listed on the job description for the next vacant teaching position would be based on the necessity to eliminate any identified gaps (a summary of the curricular map for the Spanish curriculum can be found in Appendix B). Mapping the currently-offered courses in the sequence for Spanish and French majors to the stated outcomes resulted in the following immediate findings:

1. All courses included in the upper-level sequence for the Spanish major, including the grammar, composition, and conversation courses, the courses for the professions, the culture and civilization courses, as well as the literature and linguistics offerings (and the study abroad programs), met Outcomes 1 through 5.

2. Only the culture and civilization courses and the literature seminar aligned themselves with Outcome 6, while only the linguistics and senior capstone courses aligned themselves with Outcomes 7 and 8.

3. The introductory literature and culture courses, along with the literature seminar and the study abroad courses, were mapped to Outcomes 9 and 10.

4. This mapping exercise suggested that the Spanish major program addressed all the outcomes in one or more courses. The committee determined that, because no immediately apparent gaps existed, no changes to the Spanish curriculum needed to be made at that time.

5. In a similar mapping of French courses to the outcomes, we discovered that we lacked the linguistics courses necessary for the students to achieve parts of Outcomes 1–7. As a response to the lack of a French linguistics sequence, a phonetics component has been added to the French conversation class, and a translation class has been developed that integrates linguistics into its content. Additionally, faculty members are steering students toward taking linguistics courses in their study abroad sequences. Similarly, the expected results of the next assessment cycles are a curriculum and a sequencing of all courses that will eventually allow our majors in every language to achieve the SLOs established by the UEDFL over the course of their academic career at the University of Evansville.

## Developing outcomes assessment: Planning within an evaluative framework

### Initial design

With the development of SLOs and corresponding curricular maps completed, the committee turned to designing a set of outcomes assessments. Such assessments would allow the UEDFL to discover the degree to which learning outcomes data illuminated the educational effectiveness of the Department of Foreign Languages degree program. However, in addition to providing data, the assessments would inform particular interpretations and actions by particular users, as described above. That is, beyond measurement functions, outcomes assessments had evaluative functions and needed to be designed accordingly (see Norris, 2006). Accordingly, the plan for the UEDFL assessment project was derived from ideas and lessons learned during the National Foreign Language Resource Center Summer Institute in May-June 2007. Guiding our efforts was a definition of program evaluation developed at the summer institute and agreed upon by the committee: evaluation was understood to be the "ongoing process of reflecting upon what faculty members do in the UEDFL, based on systematic and objective evidence; promoting internal (among faculty and students) and external (administrators) communication, information, and education; and judging the effectiveness of the program to evaluate its development and improvement."

Having established a clear definition of program evaluation for ourselves, we began to develop evaluation questions that articulated a specific project focus. Drawing from previous committee discussion and information received at the Summer Institute, three evaluation questions were developed:

- To what extent do UEDFL majors graduate with the basic knowledge and skills that faculty expect?
- To what extent does the program provide the students with the necessary resources to graduate with expected knowledge and skills?
- To what extent are UEDFL majors able to compete with other students graduating from similar programs?

The next step was to prioritize the three questions in relation to urgency, utility of findings, and feasibility (Patton, 1997). The committee decided to answer only the first evaluation question in the initial round of this project. It was determined that we could address the second question adequately only after multiple assessment cycles. Likewise, the third question was better left to a later round; the time and resources necessary to identify and collect data on "students graduating from similar programs" were not readily available.

The committee needed, then, to identify relevant indicators and methods to determine the answer to our first question, that is, to what extent UEDFL majors graduate with the basic knowledge and skills that faculty (and students) expect. Indicators are observable sources of information that provide meaningful evidence related to various components of programs under evaluation.

In our outcomes assessment project, then, indicators needed to provide information about students' achievement of the learning outcomes in ways that would be meaningful to the various intended users. Thus, indicators could include tests and measures, but they also might include a variety of other observable phenomena (e.g., teacher subjective ratings, interviews, student attitudinal questionnaires) and a host of other possible information sources.

The committee decided to focus on two indicators in the first iteration of the outcomes assessment project: (a) students' perspectives on their own accomplishments within the language degree, and (b) actual oral and written student performances in the target language. Both indicators were feasibly observable and provided us not only the desired evidence of student performance, but also the students' own awareness of that performance. Methodologically, then, data would be collected in two ways. First, we would gather feedback from the students reflecting their own observations about the knowledge and skills they had developed. This information would be collected through one-on-one exit interviews, conducted in English (the emphasis being on the students' perceptions of their abilities in the target language rather than the interviewers' evaluation of those abilities). The second method of data collection, focused on the evaluation of students' abilities, would be a performative portfolio. This portfolio would provide enough measurable information for the purpose of assessment. It would also provide the students tangible evidence of their academic accomplishments. The basic approach to assessment was initially designed according to the following guidelines:

1. Students in FL 401 (a senior capstone course) choose a committee of three faculty members of the UEDFL (one member must be the student's adviser, who serves as the committee's director).
2. Students submit to their committee directors at least three relevant examples of their previous work at UEDFL (i.e., papers, tests, publications in the language of their major on current events, civilization, literature, and linguistics) and a five-page original essay in the target language summarizing their student career at UE.
3. Students arrange a date and time with their committee for the portfolio presentation to be conducted in the target language. At the presentation, the students give a five minute oral review of their materials. The presentation is followed by a question and answer session based on the artifacts. Finally, the committee prompts the students to formulate questions on a given topic.
4. Each committee evaluates student performance and the quality of the portfolio materials according to an internally developed rubric (see Appendix C).
5. Each student must also arrange a one-on-one exit interview with his/her committee director. This interview is conducted in English and is used to elicit the student's opinion about his/her learning.

Committee members initially expected that the Q/A session following the portfolio presentation would provide data for learning Outcomes 1, 4, and 5 (oral expression and listening comprehension). Data for Outcomes 3, and 6–10 (written production and knowledge of literature, linguistics, and current events) were to be taken from analysis of the students' written portfolio materials. The exercise in which students generated their own questions would provide data on Outcomes 1 and 4 (oral expression and understanding native speech).

The department completed the assessment plan at the start of the fall semester of 2007. At the first department meeting of the fall semester, committee members presented the results of the summer institute and proposed that the outcomes assessment project be piloted in the fall in the senior capstone course. The committee also prepared for the scheduled September visit by the external assessment consultant. At that site visit the consultant reviewed and discussed the work of the committee, the implementation of the project plan, and the data collection and analysis procedures. A project timeline was also established. The following section summarizes the revisions to the initial assessment framework that were made in response to the analysis and feedback of the consultant.

## Revising assessments

Discussions between the consultant and the committee resulted in a critique of various aspects of the assessment plan, including the portfolio creation process, the portfolio presentation itself, data solicitation, time and logistics, and aspects of the one-on-one exit interview in English. Related issues and subsequent revisions are detailed in this section.

Committee members had envisioned that the one-on-one exit interview conducted in English would take place at the end of the semester as the final step in the assessment process. Its purpose was to allow students to reflect on their own learning in order to determine their status in terms of language development and skills. Faculty members were thus seeking information that would allow for triangulation of the other assessment data, and also wanted to know students' perceptions of their own outcomes. Furthermore, we wanted the students to reflect on the totality of their coursework and whether and how their world-views had changed. However, the committee became aware that the exit interview process was prone to inconsistent elicitation and potentially idiosyncratic interpretation of responses (i.e., varying from one advisor to the next). The solution agreed upon was to create a very structured one-on-one interview protocol, thereby reducing the possibility of inconsistent elicitation and to record the interview to allow for subsequent review and hopefully guarantee accuracy.

Another issue concerning the exit interview was the challenge of eliciting full and honest responses from students who might be more or less comfortable sharing their opinions with a faculty member. A proposed solution was to complement the personal exit interview with an anonymous web-based survey. In this way, we could gather detailed information from students regarding their perceptions of their academic performance and of the department while still providing them the anonymity to express negative observations. We developed a multiple-choice choice survey administered internally by our Department of Institutional Research. Once that tool had been developed, the committee realized the value it could provide in addressing an important lack that had also been identified during the consultant's site visit: our assessment framework did not include an intentional developmental component. There was no targeted measure of students' progress over time. It was decided to administer the survey at both the mid-point and the end of the students' time at UE in order to introduce some degree of progress assessment in terms of students' perspectives on their own learning.

With the portfolio, as well, there was an important aspect of time that we had not considered. Because students were to choose the samples of their work for inclusion in the portfolio, they would need to be so informed upon declaration of the major. This step would ensure the students' early and active involvement in the selection of the artifacts to be included in the portfolio. Another issue regarding the artifacts in the portfolio had to do with task variability. To ensure that there would be enough evidence across the different tasks to warrant interpretations about the target learning outcomes, it was necessary that the portfolio artifacts be somewhat consistent for all students. Therefore, the committee established common guidelines for what to include in the portfolio, created a framework for the writing of exemplar papers, including style and length, and established a standard for paper grading in terms of coherence, cohesion, creativity, grammatical accuracy, and lexical choice.

Regarding the original essay in the target language to be included in the portfolio, the committee agreed that its purpose was not only to allow students to highlight their foreign language writing skills, but also to use the portfolio itself as a tool for reflection on their learning, on the value of their degree, and on the manner in which they had changed over the course of their learning experience at UE. In order to guide the students in that self-reflection, the committee decided to provide a prompt directing students to write a justification for their writing selections and address specific questions (see Appendix C). All students would receive the prompt and write the essay during the senior capstone course. The committee also wrote a prompt for the portfolio presentation and created a general rubric for performance assessment.

Additionally, while the speaking and listening skills demonstrated in the presentation of the portfolio to a faculty committee would provide more data for analysis, we lacked a direct measure of reading comprehension (one of the learning outcomes). Recognizing this lack, the committee considered various options for standardized language proficiency tests, and ultimately, because of convenience, cost effectiveness, and manageability, decided on DIALANG. This web-based battery of proficiency tests in 14 European languages was created by the European Commission and is available online at no charge (http://www.dialang.org). An additional benefit to this online reading test was that it provided an external evaluation tool that added credibility to the assessment findings, since the rest of the tools had been created internally.

Data elicitation created another challenge regarding portfolio assessment. The committee needed to confirm that the data gathered would actually provide an answer to the evaluation question being asked, and would be sufficiently reliable to make claims about results. Other points for consideration included the manner in which elicitation would occur. Since any faculty member could potentially be involved in the portfolio presentation process, it was necessary that none be the source of observed variability during their participation in the Q/A session following the student presentation. The solution here was to create a standardized assessment rubric, print guidelines that clearly described the procedures (see Appendix C), and provide training for the faculty at department meetings.

Because our assessment project could be categorized as institutional research, we also took the step of seeking clearance from our institutional review board and requested guidelines for research on human subjects. We were advised that, because we were assuring anonymity, confidentiality, and no harm to those interviewed, we would not be violating guidelines for ethical human research. If we were to convert the assessment findings themselves for outside presentation, guidelines for research on human subjects would be followed.

The final issue raised during the site visit, and one with which we are still grappling, was an internal one: that of biased reviewing. Because all assessment procedures, with the exception of DIALANG, were internally developed and reviewed by UEDFL faculty, the results could be seen from the outside as (most likely positively) biased. If assessment results were intended for use beyond the university, the reliability and validity of the information might be questioned. We considered that one possible response to this perceived bias would be to include the use of student opinion data from the web-based survey and outside collaboration on the portfolio project (i.e., by faculty from other institutions). For portfolio reviews, the committee is now considering collaborating with colleagues from the University of Southern Indiana (a cross-town state university). The committee realized that, if assessment results are to be used beyond the university, an outside review of some sort must be arranged in order to validate the process.

Following this extensive review and revision to our assessment plan, and with our tasks clearly defined and a timeline established, discussion with the consultant who helped us refine our assessment activities came to a close. The next step was for the committee to create rough drafts of all needed assessment materials, and then, once again, to present these to our colleagues at department meetings. After feedback from faculty and an external reviewer, we completed the design of assessment tools, piloted the project, and analyzed initial results.

## Assessment piloting: Data collection, analysis, and reflection

Once the department agreed on methods proposed by the evaluation committee, it was important to pilot-test the instruments and procedures. The committee decided to engage UEDFL majors enrolled in FL 401, the capstone course offered each fall that all students take in their senior year. Because there were only four foreign language majors in the fall 2007 graduating class, all of them Spanish majors, only Spanish faculty members took an active role in the assessment piloting phase. However, every UEDFL faculty member was encouraged to participate indirectly in the process. All were informed of the developments taking place and asked for their feedback. They were also invited to attend the portfolio presentations.

The department completed the pilot data collection phase of the project with these four students in December of 2007. At this point, it was important to map out the data analysis phase. First, the committee needed to consider the available evidence outcome by outcome, across the four students. Second, we had to consider the data collected (and the different ways it was collected) for each outcome and determine whether each of the four students had met the different outcomes expectations. Third, we wanted to determine whether the data met our needs in terms of quality, quantity, and relevance. In sum, we sought to answer these questions:

- What evidence had we collected for each outcome (across the four students)?
- What did the evidence tell us about the extent to which the outcome was achieved (or not)?
- Were our expectations met for the outcome, or if not, in what ways were they not met?

After answering these questions with the help of a rubric (included in Appendix C), the committee met to analyze results, summarize findings, and present them to the department for feedback. The assessment pilot was deemed generally successful. On reflection, however, the department reached the conclusion that there were still adjustments to be made (a positive outcome of the decision to engage in pilot testing in the first place!). First, to further ensure that all the materials included in portfolios were consistent, we agreed all papers written in advanced level classes would have the same format, that is, a five-page paper written in MLA style. Second, we observed that the one-on-one exit interview in English was problematic logistically and that it provided essentially the same data as the web-based survey, so we decided to eliminate it. Third, because all language majors take the same capstone course, the faculty member teaching that course was responsible for the assignment and development of all the portfolios. It was decided that every adviser would guide his or her own advisees through the assessment processes, and that the assessment would take place in the advisees' final semester at UE. Fourth, we discovered that enough data was generated during the portfolio presentation and the following Q/A session in the target language to make the student question generation exercise at the end of the session redundant. Therefore, we decided to eliminate this element. Finally, we realized that the DIALANG test was problematic because it did not provide data meeting our standards: some of the multiple choice answers are ambiguous. We agreed to continue looking for better tests in line with our needs.

This discussion resulted in changes to our data gathering process, making it more streamlined and providing us with focused, meaningful, and useful information. In addition, after considering the summary of results from the first group of student assessments (Appendix D), we concluded that in general the students we assessed were graduating with almost all of the learning outcomes we had designed for them. However, importantly, we found the following initial patterns that bear further attention:

- Several students were not able to complete their portfolios because they had not had the opportunity to write a paper in all major fields. Advisers need to be aware that all majors must take literature, linguistics, and culture courses, either on campus or during their study abroad.
- We realized we had no accurate method to gather data to assess SLO 5, "Students employ a variety of coping strategies to communicate both verbally and non-

verbally in the target languages." Therefore, until we find an effective way to assess it, we decided to put aside this outcome.

- None of the students applied literary theory in their papers. We decided that we needed standards for literature instructors and that theory must be included in literature classes and in papers so that SLO 10, "Students read literary texts in the target languages and analyze them critically using a theoretical framework" can be met.

**Lessons learned along the way**

At the conclusion of our work on this initial phase of outcomes assessment, we realized that our departmental conversations throughout the project, whose focus was ultimately on students' needs, brought forward some interesting and not completely anticipated results and benefits. The first result was the recognition that the relative importance we currently place on the study of literature in our curriculum does not match its place, 9 and 10, in our ranking of student learning outcomes. Our inherited curriculum, somewhat literature-heavy (especially in French), will therefore be scrutinized closely during future curricular revisions. The creation of job descriptions for future faculty hires will also take this factor and related decisions about outcomes and curricular emphases into account. Additionally, we realized we must focus our attention, as professionals working in a multi-language department, on the need to maintain similar goals, standards, and practices across the different languages so that the claims we make as a cohesive department, regarding our goals and successes, are valid and reliable.

More importantly perhaps, these months of hard work sparked very animated and fruitful conversations among all department members (adjunct, contract, junior tenure track, and tenured faculty). The key to our success was the dynamic that animated a small committee of faculty members, each of whom brought different skills to the team (attention to details, energy to keep work on track, *big picture* outlook, writing and editing skills, etc.). These individuals worked well together and always kept departmental colleagues involved. As a result, the entire group experienced an enhanced *can-do* attitude, a positive feeling of team work, a sense of collective ownership of the project, and a better understanding of our identity and goals as a department. Who could have predicted that an evaluation project would elicit faculty excitement? This work and excitement has also filtered through to colleagues outside the department and the university administration. It has raised the visibility of the department on campus, with one member of the team now serving on the university-wide assessment committee.

Another benefit has been the interest generated among prospective students and their parents when presented with our list of SLOs. "I have never seen anything like this in any of the schools we've been to," is the most frequent comment we hear. This clear articulation of the UEDFL outcomes seems to carry a lot of weight in convincing clients that we have a well-defined product. But most importantly, our belief is that our majors have been particularly pleased to be involved in the design of the SLOs. The set of assessment tools they have been working with seems to give them a sense of accomplishment and a much clearer understanding of what it is they have learned and what we want to do as a department. These outcomes were important goals we set for ourselves when we started this process. And process is the correct word: each year, with each graduating class, our majors will continue to bring us data assessing their work and evaluating our own. The analysis of these data will create a feedback loop that will impact future curriculum development and revision, and the fine-tuning of our assessment tools.

## Conclusion

After piloting the outcomes assessment project for two semesters, both the fall semester of 2007 and the spring semester of 2008, we are generally pleased with the results. Plans now include separating the project from the senior seminar and allowing the students to work on its completion throughout the course of their senior year. We acknowledge that our work has only begun, and we continue to think about ways to improve the process. Our plans include expanding the evaluation project to include our minors as well as our study abroad programs. We feel that now we have an assessment tool and procedure that allows us to measure the success of our programs and to improve the quality of the product that we offer. Our participation in the University of Hawai'i Foreign Language Program Evaluation Project enabled us to take vital steps in pursuing our vision; to be recognized as one of the top language programs among universities of our category in the United States—an attainable goal, indeed.

### *Acknowledgement*

The authors would like to thank John Norris for his help and support throughout this project.

## References

Norris, J. M. (2006). The why (and how) of student learning outcomes assessment in college FL education. *Modern Language Journal, 90*(4), 576–583.

Patton, M. Q. (1997). *Utilization-focused evaluation: The new century text* (3rd ed.). Thousand Oaks, CA: Sage.

## Appendix A: Department vision, mission, and goals

### Vision

The Department of Foreign Languages at the University of Evansville will be recognized as one of the top language programs among universities in its category. The department embraces and enhances the University's global vision by

- emphasis on interdisciplinary programming
- internship/study abroad opportunities
- innovative language instruction
- experiential and service learning projects
- a wide range of language offerings
- outstanding faculty members interacting with a culturally diverse student body.

### Mission

Foreign languages are an essential component of the great tradition of teaching and learning in the liberal arts. By teaching students to communicate in other languages, allowing them to gain knowledge and an understanding of other cultures, helping them to make connections with other disciplines, providing them with insight into the nature of language and culture, and requiring them to participate in multilingual communities both at home and abroad, the programs in the Department of Foreign Languages play a critical role in preparing students for the personal and professional challenges of a multicultural society and a global marketplace.

### Goals

- to prepare majors for successful competition in professional programs, graduate school and the workplace.
- to provide programs of study leading to a Bachelor of Arts in Liberal Arts or a Bachelor of Science in Education in French, German and Spanish, Japanese Studies, Latin American Studies and Russian Studies.
- to foster the development of the four language skills- speaking, writing, reading and comprehending the living languages currently offered on campus; French, German, Japanese, Russian and Spanish.
- to impart a knowledge of the literatures and cultures represented by these languages.
- to continue its excellent record of teaching through a diverse and innovative curriculum that meets the expectations and needs of our students.
- to foster interdisciplinary studies with the other departments, i.e., Business, Communication, Education, International Studies, Political Science, Theatre, and so forth.
- to expose students to an environment that fosters the development of the linguistic, communicative, and semiolinguistic competencies to be applied to conversing, reading, and writing critically about the general object of study.
- to provide academic support for graduation and degree requirements that involve language study through the first, second or third year.
- to support areas of the university curriculum-notably the World Cultures sequence and the major and minor in Classical Studies, and a Liberal Arts minor in Classical Languages: Latin, Greek and Hebrew.

**Appendix B: Mapping of outcomes to the Spanish curriculum**

**SLO 1.** Students express themselves confidently in a variety of oral and written registers, keeping in mind the communicative context and conventions of the particular culture.
SPAN 311 Spanish Grammar and Composition
SPAN 314 Business and Legal Spanish
SPAN 316 Spanish Conversation
SPAN 320 Latin American Social Issues
SPAN 321 Introduction to Hispanic Literature
SPAN 333 Introduction to Hispanic Culture
SPAN 350 Medical Spanish
SPAN 433 Hispanic Civilization
SPAN 438 Spanish Seminar
SPAN 450 Spanish Linguistics
Study Abroad

**SLO 2.** Students read and comprehend texts in the target languages tailored to a variety of communicative needs.
SPAN 311 Spanish Grammar and Composition
SPAN 314 Business and Legal Spanish
SPAN 316 Spanish Conversation
SPAN 320 Latin American Social Issues
SPAN 321 Introduction to Hispanic Literature
SPAN 333 Introduction to Hispanic Culture
SPAN 350 Medical Spanish
SPAN 433 Hispanic Civilization
SPAN 438 Spanish Seminar
SPAN 450 Spanish Linguistics
Study Abroad

**SLO 3.** Students write documents in the target languages tailored to a variety of communicative needs, keeping in mind the conventions of the particular cultures.
SPAN 311 Spanish Grammar and Composition
SPAN 314 Business and Legal Spanish
SPAN 316 Spanish Conversation
SPAN 320 Latin American Social Issues
SPAN 321 Introduction to Hispanic Literature
SPAN 333 Introduction to Hispanic Culture
SPAN 350 Medical Spanish
SPAN 433 Hispanic Civilization
SPAN 438 Spanish Seminar
SPAN 450 Spanish Linguistics
Study Abroad

**SLO 4.** Students understand native speech.
SPAN 311 Spanish Grammar and Composition
SPAN 314 Business and Legal Spanish
SPAN 316 Spanish Conversation
SPAN 320 Latin American Social Issues
SPAN 321 Introduction to Hispanic Literature
SPAN 333 Introduction to Hispanic Culture

SPAN 350 Medical Spanish
SPAN 433 Hispanic Civilization
SPAN 438 Spanish Seminar
SPAN 450 Spanish Linguistics
Study Abroad

**SLO 5.** Students employ a variety of coping strategies to communicate both verbally and non-verbally in the target languages.
SPAN 311 Spanish Grammar and Composition
SPAN 314 Business and Legal Spanish
SPAN 316 Spanish Conversation
SPAN 320 Latin American Social Issues
SPAN 321 Introduction to Hispanic Literature
SPAN 333 Introduction to Hispanic Culture
SPAN 350 Medical Spanish
SPAN 433 Hispanic Civilization
SPAN 438 Spanish Seminar
SPAN 450 Spanish Linguistics
Study Abroad

**SLO 6.** Students demonstrate a familiarity with the current events, the pop culture and the social structures of the countries/cultures in which the target languages are spoken.
SPAN 320 Latin American Social Issues
SPAN 333 Introduction to Hispanic Culture
SPAN 433 Hispanic Civilization
SPAN 438 Spanish Seminar
Study Abroad

**SLO 7.** Students demonstrate understanding of language variation (social, dialectal and contextual.)
SPAN 450 Spanish Linguistics
SPAN 401 Senior Seminar

**SLO 8.** Students are able to perform a linguistic (synchronic and diachronic) analysis of language.
SPAN 450 Spanish Linguistics
SPAN 401 Senior Seminar

**SLO 9.** Students read literary texts in the target languages and analyze them critically using a theoretical framework.
SPAN 321 Introduction to Hispanic Literature
SPAN 333 Introduction to Hispanic Culture
SPAN 438 Spanish Seminar
Study Abroad

**SLO 10.** Students understand literary and artistic movements and the history of ideas.
SPAN 321 Introduction to Hispanic Literature
SPAN 333 Introduction to Hispanic Culture
SPAN 433 Hispanic Civilization
SPAN 438 Spanish Seminar
Study Abroad

## Appendix C: Guidelines for faculty members

### UNIVERSITY OF EVANSVILLE
### Department of Foreign Languages Assessment Project

**Directions for examiners**

Now that students are in their last semester, it is time for them to show how much they have achieved through their degree in Foreign Languages at UE. For this purpose, we invite them to complete the following exercises:

1. Online survey
2. Online reading comprehension test
3. Portfolio
   a. Original essay
   b. Three significant research papers
   c. Presentation
   d. Q+A session

|  | purpose | language | when | where |
|---|---|---|---|---|
| online survey | self evaluation | English | anytime during the semester | home |
| online reading comprehension test | | | | |
| portfolio | test proficiency in Spanish | target language | anytime during the semester. arrange appointment | TBD |

Name: _____

Committee: 1. _____

2. _____

3. _____

**Exercises students complete on their own:**

1. Online survey

    To be completed by the student at any point in the semester. Results will be collected and tallied by AGS.

2. Online reading comprehension test

    To be completed by the student at any point in the semester. Collect result sheets.

**Exercises requiring faculty assistance**

1. Portfolio evaluation
   a. Portfolio essays: An original essay and three research papers

      *Directions for students*
      In a thoughtful, well-organized essay in the target language, analyze the changes you have experienced in the last four to five years. What were your

expectations of yourself and the university community when you entered as a freshman, and how have those expectations changed? How have you changed, both as a person and as student of a second language and culture? What impact has your education at the University of Evansville had on your life to this point, and how will what you have learned here continue to affect you in the future? Please share both positive and negative examples of specific instances from all areas of your campus life (classroom, instructor, student life etc.) and Study Abroad that have helped shape you as a human being.

In the second section of your essay, please comment on the material you have chosen for inclusion in your portfolio. How does the material included in the portfolio represent both you and your learning experience at the University of Evansville?

In your essay conclusion, please share your plans for the future. What do you see yourself doing with the education you have received at the University of Evansville?

The essay must be written in the target language and must adhere to MLA style in terms of presentation and citation. It must be a double-spaced, computer-generated document, five pages in length, written in Times New Roman, 12 pt. font. We are interested in your own experiences. You may get no editorial help.

Three research papers reflecting your best work in and on the target language must be turned in. One paper must deal with literature, one with linguistics and one with cultural issues. You may get no editorial help excluding the corrections the professors may have given you in class.

### Directions for the examiners

The student must contact you to set an appointment. Students must turn in their portfolio materials at least a week before the portfolio presentation.

Generally comment on the students' writing abilities as well as their knowledge of the three topics (linguistics, literature and cultural issues). Compare with the other committee members' comments.

**Comments:** _____
_____
_____

b. Essay presentation

### Directions for students

In a well-designed and efficiently delivered oral presentation in the target language not to exceed 15 minutes in length, please summarize the contents of your written essay for the faculty panel. You may use as much or as little technology as you wish, from a PowerPoint presentation to only 3 x 5 note cards, according to your personal style. Keep in mind, however, that your presentation may not be read. It should be delivered in a comfortable, yet professional manner.

### Directions for the examiners

Comment on the students' oral performance.

After session, examiners compare their comments.

**Comments:** _____
_____
_____

c. Q+A session

   *Directions for the interviewers*
   Ask the questions below in the target language. Generally comment on the students' performance.

   Other questions may be asked (follow up…) but answers to those not included in comments.

   After session, examiners compare their comments.

   **Q+A session prompts**
   *Nine questions on the original essay:*

   1. What made you decide to come to UE?
   2. How much did you know about UE?
   3. How did you feel when you were about to begin your freshman year? Were you excited, nervous…?
   4. Was it hard for you to adjust during your freshman year? Why?
   5. What was the most important challenge for you in adjusting to college life?
   6. What did you think of classes, instructors, classmates… your first semester?
   7. What's the one thing you'll always remember about UE?
   8. What's the one thing you can't wait to forget about UE?
   9. How would you summarize your UE experience to an incoming freshman?

   *Six questions on the three research papers:*

   1. To what extent has the study of linguistics contributed to your understanding of the Spanish language?
   2. Are there any linguistic areas you wish you had studied more in depth? Why?
   3. How do you think your literature classes helped you in understanding more the Spanish language and culture?
   4. What book or author did you enjoy the most? Why?
   5. Do you think learning culture has been an important aspect in your foreign language education? Why?
   6. What aspect of Hispanic culture interested you most? Why?

Comments: _____
_____
_____

2. Rubric for portfolio assessment

   Once all the different activities are completed, the advisor completes the following evaluation:

   Circle the most appropriate choice. Explain if necessary.

   1. Students express themselves confidently in a variety of oral registers, keeping in mind the communicative context and conventions of the particular culture.
      Was this outcome met?

      0     1     2     3     4     5
            no                      yes
      0=not enough evidence found

   2. Students read and comprehend texts in the target languages tailored to a variety of communicative needs.
      Was this outcome met?

      0     1     2     3     4     5
            no                      yes
      0=not enough evidence found

   3. Students write documents in the target languages tailored to a variety of communicative needs, keeping in mind the conventions of the particular cultures.
      Was this outcome met?

      0     1     2     3     4     5
            no                      yes
      0=not enough evidence found

   4. Students understand native speech.
      Was this outcome met?

      0     1     2     3     4     5
            no                      yes
      0=not enough evidence found

   5. Students demonstrate a familiarity with the current events, the pop culture and the social structures of the countries/cultures in which the target languages are spoken.
      Was this outcome met?

      0     1     2     3     4     5
            no                      yes

   6. Students demonstrate understanding of language variation (social, dialectal and contextual.)
      Was this outcome met?

      0     1     2     3     4     5
            no                      yes
      0=not enough evidence found

7. Students are able to perform a linguistic (synchronic and diachronic) analysis of language.
   Was this outcome met?

   | 0 | 1 | 2 | 3 | 4 | 5 |
   |---|---|---|---|---|---|
   |   | no |  |  |  | yes |

   0=not enough evidence found

8. Students read literary texts in the target languages and analyze them critically using a theoretical framework.
   Was this outcome met?

   | 0 | 1 | 2 | 3 | 4 | 5 |
   |---|---|---|---|---|---|
   |   | no |  |  |  | yes |

   0=not enough evidence found

9. Students understand literary and artistic movements and the history of ideas.
   Was this outcome met?

   | 0 | 1 | 2 | 3 | 4 | 5 |
   |---|---|---|---|---|---|
   |   | no |  |  |  | yes |

   0=not enough evidence found

## Appendix D: Results of the pilot program
### 1. Fall 2007 portfolio evaluation: Individual student results

Four students participated in this original assessment cycle.

0–5 in the vertical axis refer to the following scale:

0   1   2   3   4   5
    no                                yes

0=not enough evidence found

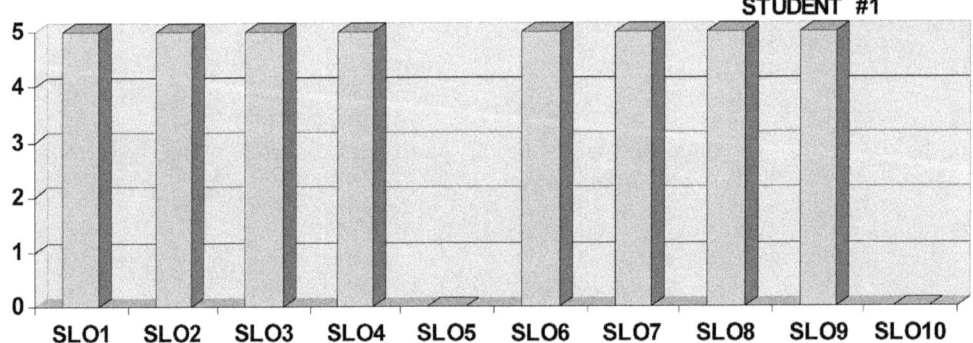

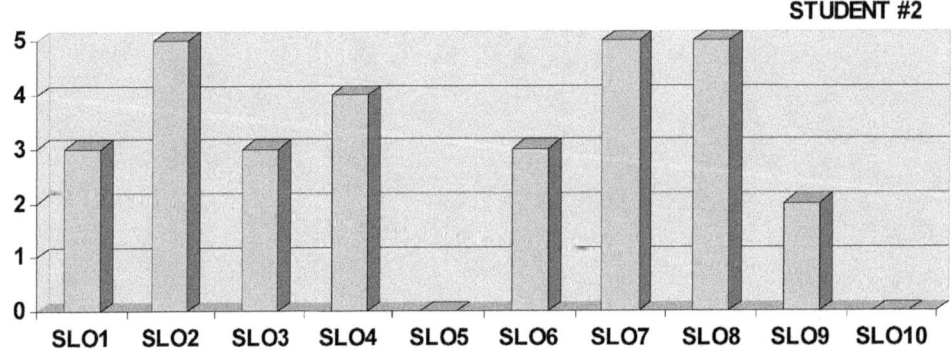

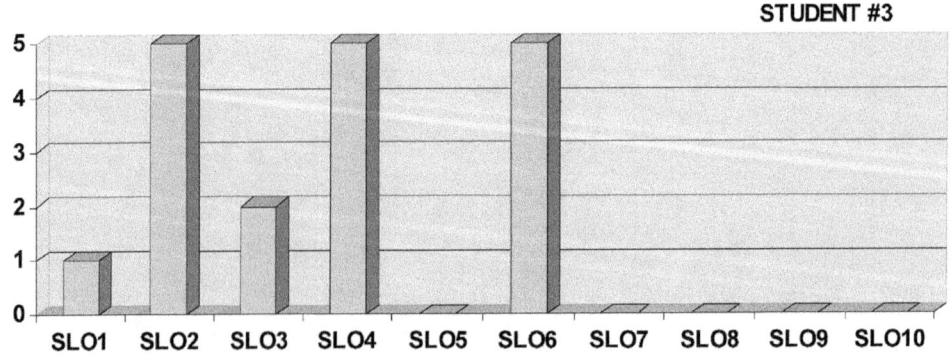

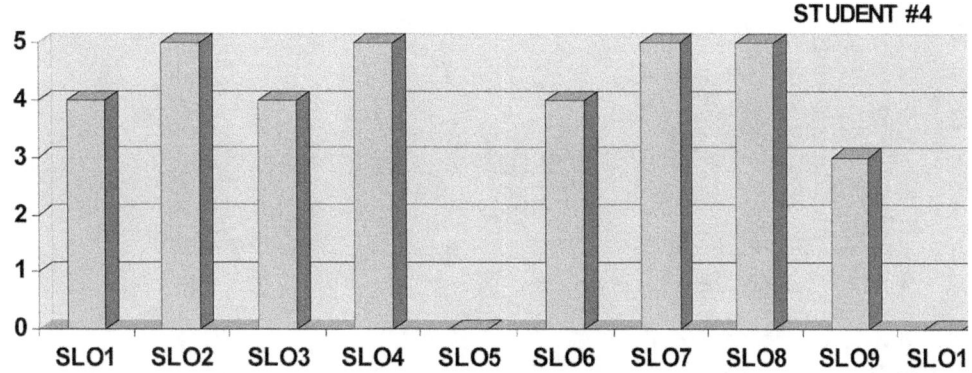

## 2. Fall 2007 portfolio evaluation: Outcomes results

1–4 found in the horizontal axis refer to student#1–#4.

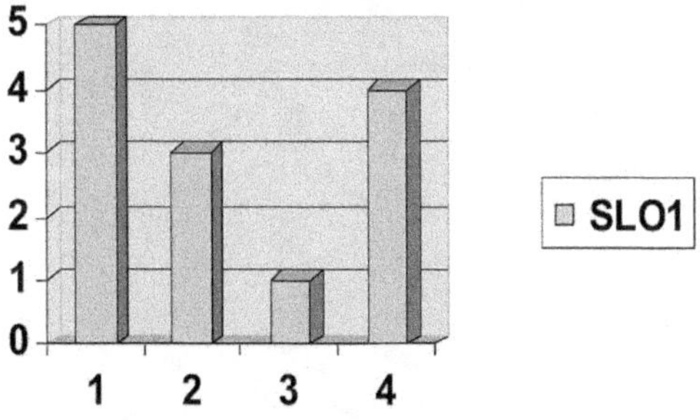

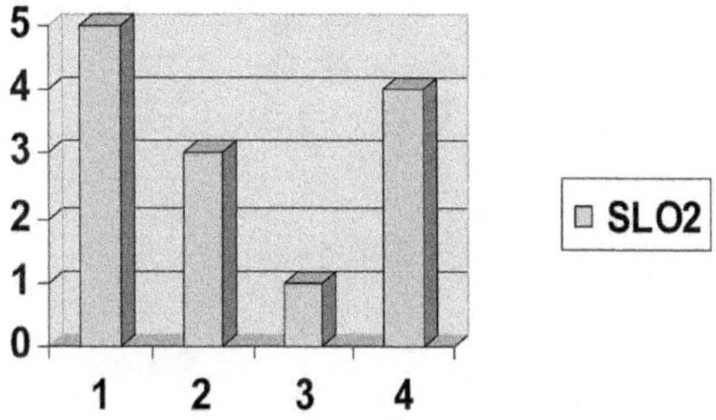

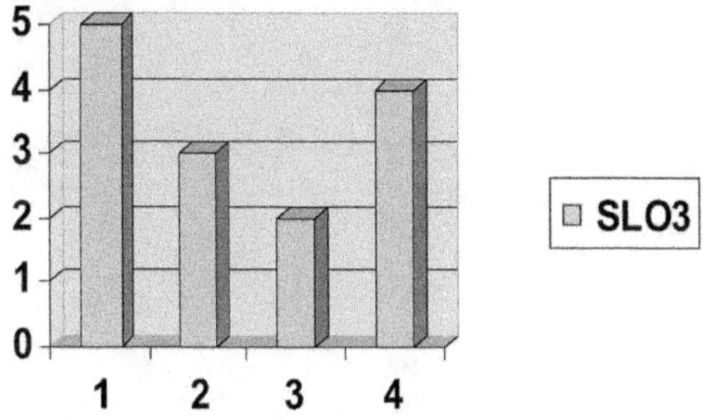

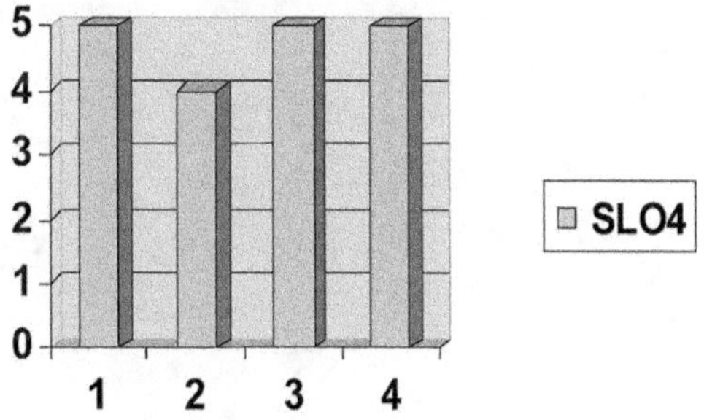

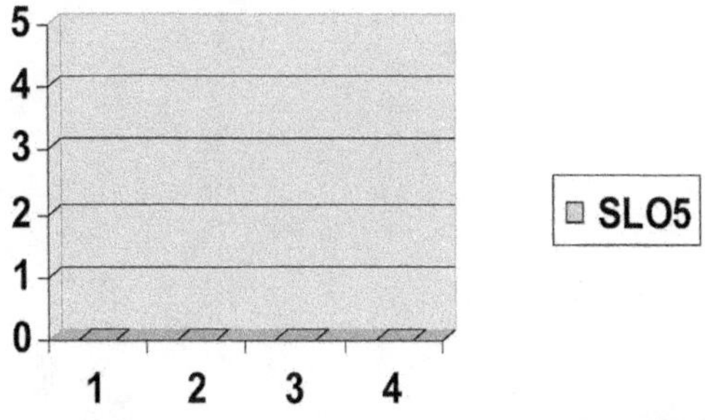

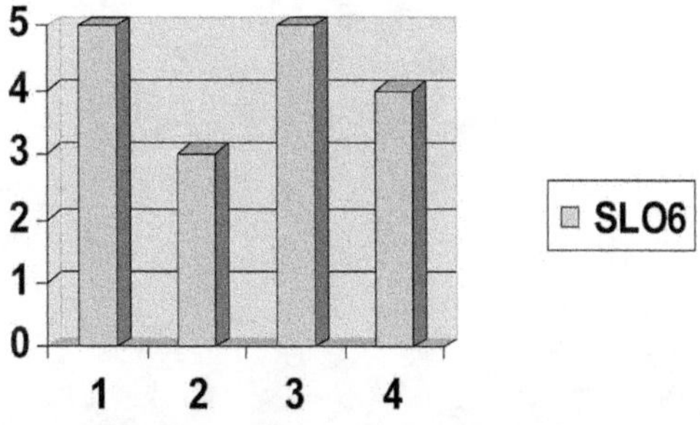

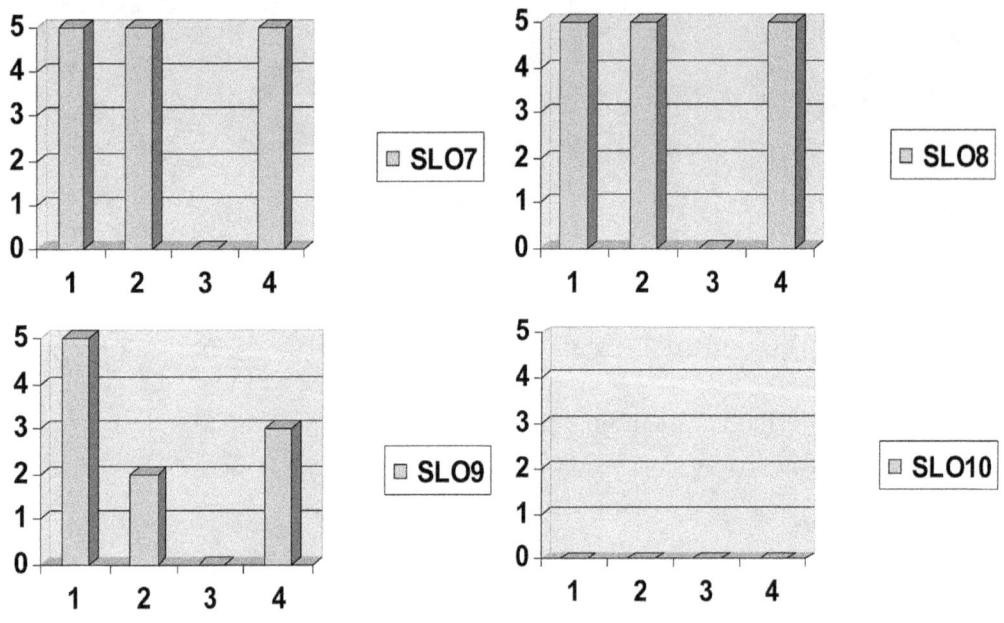

# Study Abroad and Evaluation: Critical Changes to Enhance Linguistic and Cultural Growth

Violeta Ramsay
*Linfield College, McMinnville, Oregon*

*This chapter reports on an evaluation of Spanish study abroad programs associated with the Department of Modern Languages at Linfield College that took place between December 2006 and October 2008. The project was prompted by observations of unsatisfactory student proficiency levels for returnees from study abroad sojourns in Spain. Data were collected from meetings with administrators and advisors, observations of culture and language courses abroad, interviews with student participants, and reviews of teaching materials and graded assignments. The evaluation resulted in several important changes, including cancellation of study abroad programs, stricter rules for host program selection, changes in degree requirements for minors, and a requirement that language faculty and majors stay in contact while students are abroad. This project was the first step in an ongoing process of evaluation within the Department of Modern Languages and has resulted in faculty deepening their knowledge and understanding of Linfield's study abroad programs as well as an increased capacity to meet institutional accreditation and other evaluation requirements.*

Students who live and study in a foreign country are daily exposed to the target language and the cultural and academic environments that can potentially accelerate language proficiency development and expand cultural awareness. Research on study abroad has analyzed various aspects of the experience, such as development of linguistic abilities (Brecht, Davidson, & Ginsberg, 1993; Isabelli, 2007; Freed, Segalowitz, & Dewey, 2004); the home-stay component (Rivers, 1998; Wilkinson, 1998; Schmidt-Rinehart & Knight, 2004); and social interactions and language gains (Magnan & Back, 2007; Regan, 2003). Some of these same studies acknowledge the challenges involved in doing research on study abroad due to the complex set of factors involved in the experience, and point accordingly at mixed results reported in the relevant literature (see Magnan & Back, 2007). Freed, So, and Lazar (2007) have gone a step further to indicate that the analyses of different factors may actually

---

Ramsay, V. (2009). Study abroad and evaluation: Critical changes to enhance linguistic and cultural growth. In J. M. Norris, J. McE. Davis, C. Sinicrope, & Y. Watanabe (Eds.), *Toward useful program evaluation in college foreign language education* (pp. 163–182). Honolulu: University of Hawai'i, National Foreign Language Resource Center.

be able to explain the mixed results and account for particular learning outcomes. However, it is clear that research to date has looked into programs of different lengths, used different methods for data collection, and/or focused on the interactions of different features (i.e., students' prior knowledge of the language, comparisons between home and dormitory stays, etc.). Thus, the question remains unresolved regarding which aspects of the study abroad experience create the best conditions to support linguistic and cultural learning. It should be noted that studies so far have generally not involved evaluations of the quality of host academic programs.

As with many foreign language programs in the U.S., study abroad plays an important role in the academic program of interest for the current chapter. Language faculty at Linfield College, a liberal arts institution in the state of Oregon, aim at educating globally competent students and at helping them enrich their education by expanding their exposure to the outside world. The project reported here describes initial evaluation work undertaken by the Spanish faculty there, with the objective of further understanding and improving Linfield's associated study abroad programs as an integral component of foreign language degree programs. These investigations, focused on study abroad programs and students' experiences in Spain, were the Modern Languages Department's first steps in evaluation processes and thinking, and they have served as a model for subsequent projects that have continued up to the present. Clearly, evaluation has played an important role in stimulating departmental change along the way, and the focus of this chapter will be on some of the key steps, methods, and impacts in the initial study abroad evaluations.

Beginning in approximately 2000, and over subsequent years, Spanish faculty increasingly observed disparities in language proficiency between students returning from study overseas. From those initial observations, and after many subsequent discussions and essentially anecdotal debates, in December 2006 department faculty decided to attempt to shed some empirical light on study abroad programs in order to identify issues in need of improvement and to motivate necessary changes. Further, in the summer of 2007, while informal, preliminary evaluation efforts were underway, one of the Spanish section faculty members participated in an evaluation workshop/summer institute entitled *Developing useful evaluation practices in foreign language programs* offered by the National Foreign Language Research Center at the University of Hawai'i. That workshop emphasized a utilization-focused approach to evaluation (Patton, 1997) by which processes of inquiry are conceived and implemented so as to maximize the likelihood of findings being used by decision makers. The Spanish faculty thus supplemented their early evaluation activities with lessons learned from the summer institute such that findings would be as useful as possible for intended users.

The Spanish study abroad evaluation project had three main outcomes. First, conclusions drawn from project findings at the time resulted in a number of immediate programmatic changes including the cancellation of programs, a search for replacements, stricter rules for study abroad program selection, changes in degree requirements for language minors, as well as a stipulation that advisors from Modern Languages and majors carry out an oral interview via the internet (Skype) each of the semesters students are abroad. Second, the process also gave faculty a more comprehensive knowledge and deepened understanding of the study abroad experience, as well as useful tools to continue evaluations for other overseas programs. Finally, the study abroad evaluation project occurred prior to accreditation-mandated departmental review, and it enabled faculty—in an especially effective way—to use the project's processes and findings toward the framing and completion of review requirements. The following sections elaborate this initial stage of departmental evaluation activity in the context of study abroad, and they highlight the beginnings of what has become an ongoing commitment to sustained and useful evaluation practice.

## Program context

### Foreign language programs and study abroad at Linfield

The Linfield College Department of Modern Languages includes nine full-time faculty—two in each of the French, German, and Japanese sections, and three in Spanish— in addition to one visiting scholar from China and 1–3 adjunct faculty per year. The department grants majors and minors in French, German, Japanese, and Spanish (as well as language courses in Chinese and American Sign Language), and it incorporates study abroad courses into its foreign language degree requirements. Minors must complete one semester abroad, and majors a full year (usually the junior year).

Programs abroad constitute a vital part of education at Linfield, and the college has developed its own well-regarded and innovative study-abroad programs which are administered and coordinated by the Office of International Programs (OIP), allowing roughly seventy percent of its students to benefit from academic study in a foreign country by choosing from 15 study abroad locations around the world. The three largest programs are January-term off-campus courses (3–4 week study sojourns), semester abroad, and junior-year abroad. Students who seek a language degree are required to study overseas because of the obvious benefits to language proficiency and cultural understanding (Brecht, Davidson & Ginsberg, 1993; Magnan & Back, 2007), and because of the small number of language faculty in each language section. That is, the Department of Modern Languages has neither the space nor time to offer the range of courses that a language degree requires and makes up for this deficiency by supplementing programs with study abroad credits.

Language majors complete their degree upon return and enroll in a capstone course (MLDA 483: Advanced Cross-Cultural Seminar) taught in English to all language majors by two Modern Language faculty. This seminar includes weekly meetings between majors and their respective language advisors for discussions and revisions of the senior project and for planning the oral presentation of the project each major writes during the seminar.

### Study abroad language programs

Study abroad has been a long tradition for Linfield, as academic contacts between the college and international institutions of higher education started in 1976 with the establishment of an exchange with Kanto Gakuin University in Yokohama, Japan. In 1980 the college began sending students abroad to its own programs, which through time have all changed or expanded. The college now uses several types of study abroad programs: (a) programs the college owns (e.g., in Costa Rica and Mexico), in which an onsite director and supporting staff are hired and manage the program in-country; (b) student exchange programs (e.g., Kanto Gakuin and Rikkyo Universities); and (c) 'third-party' programs (e.g., in Spain). Third-party programs are owned and managed by other US universities or private higher education organizations, and the OIP works with these entities either through consortiums or direct agreements. Though largely outside of our control, curricularly speaking, third-party programs have offered a useful option for both language minors and majors to fulfill degree requirements. Programs typically offer a range of choices for content as well as language courses, and from this selection Linfield's language faculty advise language majors on what courses to take (minors have the option of selecting whatever courses they would like to take). Language courses usually take place at a private language school outside the hosting university campus. Students are assigned an in-country academic advisor, and have a choice of either family or student residence stay.

**Impetus for evaluation**

Department faculty have increasingly seen the need to review the language education that students receive during study abroad programs. By the year 2000, faculty from all language sections noticed that students returning from study abroad language programs in fact demonstrated quite variable levels of language proficiency improvement. Some returnees had progressed well and reached a level of overall proficiency that, in the judgment of department faculty, merited participation in (and continuation of) their study abroad programs. Other students, however, returned at roughly the same proficiency level prior to leaving, generally in the Intermediate-Low or -Mid range on the ACTFL (1999, 2001) scale. Though students often spoke more fluently and had increased their vocabulary, they still produced language that was in many ways at a very basic proficiency level. Faculty were especially dismayed that some of the weaker returnees were the very foreign language majors who should have been benefitting the most from their study abroad experiences.

In particular, the Spanish faculty had observed these same phenomena occurring in their programs—some returnees showing improvement, others less so—and had been collecting information informally from various sources as part of an ad hoc evaluation effort to understand why this troubling outcome (or rather, lack of outcome!) was occurring. Our initial investigations revealed a pattern: Students returning from third-party programs in Spain were noticeably weaker compared to students returning from programs in Latin America, that is, programs Linfield College owned. We thus decided in December 2006 to begin an inquiry into the third-party programs in Spain in comparison with our programs in Latin America, in order to see what aspects of the educational experience there, if any, were contributing to students' distinct rates of improvement.

An additional project impetus had begun to emerge at the same time in relation to demands for institutional accreditation. Starting in fall 2006, the department was called upon to prepare for college re-accreditation by the Northwest Commission on Colleges and Universities, which was to take place throughout the 2007–09 academic years and which also included a self-study report. The report required, among other things, that departments and sections demonstrate evidence of an ongoing system of evaluation in which information on student learning is gathered and used toward program change. The process of evaluating study abroad programs was thus seen to meet this requirement in certain ways, especially given the relative importance of study abroad as a contributor to students' degree-level language learning outcomes. The impending accreditation and the desire to improve study abroad programs thus prompted the department to search for models, research, or methods that could assist in achieving these aims.

In early 2007, the department became aware of a summer institute entitled *Developing useful evaluation practices in foreign language programs* organized by the National Foreign Language Resource Center at the University of Hawai'i, and a Spanish faculty member (the author) was funded to participate. Upon her return from Hawai'i she shared with interested language faculty colleagues the lessons learned about utilization-focused evaluation practices (Patton, 1997), methods of data gathering, and crucial steps in evaluation projects from forming initial evaluation questions to acting on results. Subsequently, knowledge gained from the summer institute was integrated into our ongoing evaluation efforts with the hope of making our methods more effective and our findings more likely to be used by departmental and institutional decision makers.

## Participants, purposes, and uses

Because Spanish faculty would be involved in making decisions about program changes, they were considered primary intended users of evaluation findings. Further, decisions to change any of the study abroad programs required input from all department faculty, as well as administrators from the OIP, who needed to act on changes that had economic or other practical implications. As such, individuals in each of these groups were considered primary users. Intended uses for evaluation findings by these primary groups are listed in Table 1.

### Table 1: Evaluation uses

| | |
|---|---|
| 1. | Become better informed about all aspects of the study abroad experience; learn how programmatic elements interact to enhance or compromise the experience. |
| 2. | Make necessary changes or enhancements to the program. |
| 3. | Take a more active role in the education of minors and majors. |
| 4. | Establish a basis to better evaluate our own language programs. |
| 5. | Get good ideas from other programs. |

Essentially, the evaluation that was initiated in 2006 took a very exploratory approach, given the fact that we had anecdotally observed unexpected discrepancies in study abroad returnees' achievements but were uncertain what the causes might have been. As such, evaluation was to be used to shed light on the situation and to inform particular aspects of the study abroad programs and experiences in need of revision. Language faculty thought that direct observations of the components of the programs as executed would help them determine which parts of the process—family, academics, opportunities for language practice, etc.—might require changes or strengthening, such that linguistic and cultural learning outcomes would be achieved as targeted. We were ready to find out that the preparation we were giving students was not sufficient, or that achievement relied mainly on the motivation of particular students. At the same time we conjectured that programs that are too large can lose sight of the quality of their courses and selection of host families, among other aspects of program delivery. Regardless of what we would find, we planned to make adjustments on our side of the process, or to cancel agreements with programs if we deemed such steps to be necessary.

## Evaluation questions and corresponding methods

At the outset, then, it was clear that we needed to know more about study abroad experiences at the various sites Linfield students were visiting. A decision was made to investigate programs hosted in Spain first because, as noted earlier, students coming from third-party programs in that country appeared to have improved less than students coming from Linfield-owned programs in Latin America. We designed a project to respond to the following basic evaluation questions:

1. Are courses in Spanish study abroad programs at a sufficient level of academic quality to count toward Linfield foreign language degree requirements?
2. Are all aspects of the study abroad experience in Spain working effectively to facilitate language and cultural development?

In order to make judgments about acceptable levels of educational quality in study abroad programs, the department first needed to agree on what constituted an academically rigorous, high-quality study abroad experience. Faculty representatives from each language section collaborated in developing a rubric (shown in Table 2) describing the desired traits of third-party programs. The Spanish faculty also created the rubrics shown in Tables 3 and 4 below to guide the observations of evaluators visiting the programs, and another to help the evaluation team gauge the quality of teaching materials that would be collected during the visits (Table 5 below).

As shown by the "academic" criteria in Table 2, although the evaluation team was prepared to find that one single program might not satisfy all desired characteristics, or that all characteristics would not show up in one particular course, they had to ensure that majors, particularly those who advance rapidly academically, could participate in a strong and pedagogically sound academic environment that would help them achieve their highest potential. Further, programs needed to offer courses that could demonstrably help students improve their writing skills (typically their weakest skill). We also wanted to ensure that students had the opportunity to enroll in one or two non-language courses in the host institution's regular curriculum each semester of study abroad. Finally, another important requirement was the availability of effective academic advisors and peer tutors, since these two services help students during their transition to life in a foreign country. Beyond these critical academic aspects of the study abroad programs, we sought ancillary data to investigate whether non-academic aspects of the program—for example, family stay, conversation partners, chances to meet native speakers of the language—provided sufficient opportunities to practice the language of study, as shown in the second column of Table 2.

Table 2: Characteristics sought in study abroad programs

| academics | support, services, family stay |
|---|---|
| Content and language courses are effective and pedagogically sound: They address the appropriate student level and allow for ample student participation; instructors provide useful feedback to students' written work. | Academic advisors and peer tutors are easily available. |
| Teaching materials are effective and pedagogically sound. | Program offers native-speaker conversation partners or support for meeting native-speaker students. |
| Course offerings allow for choices in a two-semester stay and include extracurricular courses—community service, internships, field-studies courses, as well as courses at the regular university. | Host family integrates student into family life (single placement is most desirable). |
| | Student can change family if necessary. |

As a methodological starting point in reviewing these basic criteria, the evaluation team had available considerable information from web sites and institutional documents regarding four of the primary study abroad programs utilized by Linfield students in Spain. These programs were managed by a large American educational organization, and 39 of our students had attended them since 2002, among them the majority of our Spanish majors. Document analyses of existing data provided a starting point for the team to understand the basic design of these programs, and we also utilized pre-existing information we had gathered from student returnees as an initial basis for considering these criteria. However, much of what we wanted to find out, in terms of the academic and experiential criteria, was under-explained by conversations with returnee students or program administrators, at web sites, or in the program literature. As such, it was decided that a Spanish faculty member should visit the study abroad sites and pursue the careful collection of additional observational data in order to shed light on the range of targeted criteria.

Methods used to collect information by the faculty member during the program site visits are listed in Table 3. These included meetings with on-site administrators, class observations, interviews with Linfield and non-Linfield students, and analyses of additional documents found on-site. Also listed are specific sources of information (i.e., indicators) thought to illuminate the project's evaluation questions and foci of inquiry. Information from these sources would help the evaluation team know the degree to which a given program was meeting the desired criteria for study abroad programs (Table 2). Next to indicators are groups of individuals (i.e., key informants) the team thought could supply the needed information for a given indicator.

Table 3: On-site evaluation methods

| method | key informants | indicators |
|---|---|---|
| meetings | administrators, academic advisors | details about academic and personal support to students; information about levels of instruction |
| class observations | students and instructors | pedagogical methods, appropriateness of instructional materials, level of approach to courses, amount and quality of students' class participation |
| interviews | Linfield and non-Linfield students | students' proficiency levels and perceptions on the academic quality of courses; |
| | | information on the various aspects of the program—extracurricular courses, family life, excursions, etc.; reasons for attending a particular program |
| document analysis | provided by administrators and Linfield students | information from course materials and student work indicating the academic program quality |

## Meetings with administrators and staff

The Linfield evaluator met with administrators and staff who ran the various sites mainly to introduce herself, to ask about schedules and locations of courses to be observed, and to obtain copies of the materials programs produce for language courses. We wanted to carefully review language materials to gauge their pedagogical effectiveness, but also to supplement our observations during class visits.

## Class observations

Class visits were essential since we were interested in looking at the most basic aspects of academics: courses and instructors. We expected to find that both language and content courses offered students plenty of opportunities for active engagement with the language. In other words, we wanted to see whether students interacted with peers and instructors in more than occasional short sentences or by simply using phrases extracted from the textbook, since active and meaningful involvement are basics of effective language learning. We also hoped to find that the level of language in course materials and textbooks was appropriate to the proficiency level of the average student in each course. Class observations included 2–3 language classes and 3–5 content courses at each site, for a total of 24 class visits. Observations were documented by hand-written notes and based on a rubric created for this purpose, as shown in Table 4.

Table 4: Rubric to assess quality of courses and teaching materials

| language courses | content courses |
|---|---|
| Class goals are established in terms of student and learning: what students should be able to accomplish, advice is given for achieving goals, development of the four skills (goals are not a simple list of structural concepts). | New material is introduced or outlined (in class or in course syllabus) to help students understand what is presented throughout the class. |
| Class allows time for meaningful practice; at least some of the exercises require thinking, connecting, constructing, creating with the language. | Instructors offer students opportunities to ask questions, make comments, or discuss issues with their peers. |
| Class activities discourage the use of translation. | Instructors' use of the language can be understood by most students because they either give background information, introduce changes in topic, slow down their speech, make use of graphic material, use repetition, or make enough pauses to allow an Intermediate-Mid level student to follow. |
| Student interaction with peers or instructor amounts to language of at least two sentences (not just a phrase extracted from the book). | Students are encouraged to make connections between parts of the course, between cultures, historical periods, etc. |
| Class activities, exercises, or homework assignments support the growth of all areas of language (i.e., beyond verb phrase morphology): acquisition of useful vocabulary, the syntax of nominal, adjectival, and adverbial phrases, the dynamics of subordination and word order. | Assignments ask students to write in order to create, make comparisons or analyses, to communicate something, or to think of any of the numerous concepts of culture. They require more than summaries, restatements, repetitions of facts, or mechanical, shallow answers. |
| Vocabulary is useful: it shows up in high-frequency contexts of the target language; it is repeated, recycled, or practiced in contexts that illustrate its use. | Students receive feedback on progress or on how to make progress. |
| Students receive feedback on written assignments that helps them know how they can improve or where they need work. | |
| Grading is fair; it does not amount to exclusively giving A and B grades. | |

### Interviews with non-Linfield students

The evaluator organized interviews with 29 randomly selected US students enrolled in language or content courses. The evaluation team thought that data gathered from these interviews would tell us more about the types of students who attend these programs. If these were our students' peers, the team wanted to know more about their language proficiency, academic goals, reasons for attending a specific program, and the amount of time they dedicated to practicing Spanish. We also wanted to find out more about students' interactions with their host families since research on this aspect has opened critical questions regarding study abroad benefits (i.e., the common belief that students who have a positive experience with their host family often develop further their linguistic abilities is contested by some research studies, such as Schmidt-Rinehart & Knight, 2004; and Magnan & Back, 2007).

Students were asked whether they could meet at a public place between or after classes to talk to the evaluator, and she made appointments with those who agreed and also asked those who could not meet if they could respond to a few short questions. Thus, 11 interviews took place between class breaks, in the school halls, and they lasted 4 to 12 minutes each; the other 18 were appointments that took place at coffee houses with one or two students (three in one instance) at a time, and these lasted 25 to 40 minutes. Students were informed that the evaluator was taking notes and/or recording. Students in six of these longer interviews gave permission for audio-recording, which were later transcribed; responses in the rest were collected via hand-written notes. Depending on the willingness of the interviewees, and the detail of the responses, students were asked the following questions:

- What is your favorite course and why?
- Do you do lots of homework for courses? How long does it take you to complete assignments?
- How are your interactions with your family? Do you talk with them regularly?
- Why did you choose this program?
- Tell me about your travel routine during weekends or breaks.

### Meetings with Linfield students

The meetings with the Linfield students (three majors, six minors; one at one site; eight at another) were organized by the Linfield professor as informal chats during dinner at a quiet restaurant. The interview with the larger group lasted 2 hours 40 minutes, was conducted as a focus-group meeting, and took place primarily in English to ensure background noise would not interfere with communication and students would give as much detail as possible. The interview with one student (at a different site) was done in Spanish and lasted two hours. Data from both meetings were recorded in hand-written notes. From these interviews, the team sought to access considerable detail regarding the quality of the program and, importantly, to ask students about their interactions with their host families and their opportunities to practice Spanish in contexts beyond the classroom. The evaluator asked the same types of questions she had asked non-Linfield students (listed above), but with three important additions:

- How well do you think this program is preparing you academically?
- How much Spanish do you practice daily, and in what contexts?
- When you need an advisor, has one been provided to you? Was advising helpful?

### Document analysis

While on site visits, the evaluator asked program personnel to supply course materials in order to gauge their pedagogical effectiveness. The professor also asked students to bring copies of assignments, preferably graded, to the interviews to get an idea of the type of work students were doing at home. Students provided 11 assignments, which were analyzed at the home campus by the Spanish faculty using the rubric shown in Table 5. The rubric represents a set of principles of effective pedagogy they consider essential in language courses, and which apply in particular to the design of teaching materials and the feedback a language instructor can give to student work.

**Table 5: Rubric to assess the quality of language materials and grading of student assignments**

| At least 60% of the grammar material allows for the growth of all areas of language—acquisition of useful vocabulary, growth in the structure of noun, adjective and adverb phrase, subordination, the dynamics of word order. It is not centered on advanced verb phrase morphology (i.e., the subjunctive). | Culture is treated in at least some depth and readings and assignments require that students reflect, analyze, make informed decisions, give concrete personal comments. |
|---|---|
| Chapters include enough practice for new concepts and practice requires thinking, it invites to create with the language, describe, analyze, or compare. | Vocabulary in chapters and workbook is of high-frequency use, repeated, recycled, and contextualized to support acquisition. |
| Feedback in assignments is useful to the student—it includes advice on how to make progress or points at strong and/or weak areas. | Grading considers all aspects of language: variety of clause structure, richness of vocabulary, proficiency level (and not just on the use of advanced verb morphology). |
| Explanations are based on the idiosyncrasies of Spanish and not on translations from English. | Concepts connect to logically-connected concepts (i.e., pseudoreflexive verb phrases and the dynamics of transitivity; relative clauses and Spanish word order). |

## Findings

### Meetings with administrators and staff

Based on the meetings with administrators and staff at Spanish study abroad programs, the evaluator confirmed a number of known facts about the programs. For one, placement of students in language courses is done over the internet, and faculty do not have access to placement tests. However, the evaluator was informed that tests rely on fill-in-the-blank, multiple-choice tests of structural concepts and vocabulary, and a short personal essay. Depending on the results from the test, students are assigned to one of three language levels, though administrators were reluctant to describe those levels with reference to language proficiency. They indicated placement is done according to students' knowledge of structure and vocabulary and added that students who have studied three to four years of college Spanish usually test into the third level.

Beyond the rather vague placement procedures, the evaluator did not find any other unexpected information except that the staff at program support offices often served also as student advisors, and the director of each program had teaching functions as well. The evaluation team surmised that the heavy load of responsibilities for program personnel, in addition to hundreds of students to tend to, potentially limited their advising efforts.

### Class observations

Using the rubric formulated for this purpose (see Table 4), the evaluator made observations in content courses offered to international students and assigned points to each item in the rubric (from 1 to 10, where ten means "fully meets the criterion"). The evaluator took additional notes when something not in the rubric was observed or when hardly any of the items in the rubric could be applied to the observed course (for the most part, content courses did not meet the traits mentioned in the rubric). These notes were summarized in an oral report given to the evaluating team upon her return to the home campus. The report established that courses consisted of mainly lecturing and this factor explains why the rubric was not useful. Class interaction amounted to students infrequently asking questions, which generally received very short answers. Further, many of these exchanges were highly predictable, for example repeating something the instructor said or something from the reading material, rather than a spontaneous comment, an opinion, a reaction to the teaching material, an answer to a non-rhetorical question, or a discussion with peers. Two of the fifteen content courses observed met criteria 10, 11, and 12 with more than 7 points (see Table 4), but the rest of the courses hardly met any of the criteria.

Language courses were also evaluated using the rubric in Table 4 and each item was assigned points. However, while all courses met criterion 3 (translation is discouraged) with 9 or 10 points, and most met criterion 6 (vocabulary practice) with 6–7 points, they did not meet the rest of the items in the rubric with anything higher than a 5. The evaluator took note of other features of the courses to provide a summary of observations to the evaluation team. The report, presented at the home campus in May 2007, indicated that even though students' participation was constant throughout the class, it was noticeable that spoken exchanges were seldom longer than a sentence or two, and students used many memorized phrases. It was also noticeable that teaching style in language courses was warm and welcoming and the students generally seemed to enjoy the classes. However, the teaching focused heavily on grammar, and a large part of class time was spent on question-and-answer exchanges during which students produced many memorized sentences that included the target syntactic structure rather than a spontaneous sentence. Furthermore, instructors often conducted language classes at a level of proficiency beyond the capabilities of most students. When a meaningful exchange was encouraged, or the student was asked to create with the language, the prompt was usually presented at a level so high that responses were mostly completed by instructors themselves, with no obvious intent to help students complete the response at their own proficiency level. In other words, opportunities for meaningful exchanges were often wasted.

Another disconcerting observation in both content and language courses was the wide disparity in the difficulty level of each course: 12 of the 15 content courses were obviously challenging for most students in that the level of address and the work done in class was estimated to be at the Superior level of the ACTFL scale, while the level of students seemed to be between Novice-High and Intermediate-Mid. On the other hand, instructors in the other three courses observed used language, material, and activities of a level so basic that the course could not justifiably be called advanced or even college-level. Interactions and class activities were too basic for even the Intermediate-Low level. A course in semantics can be used to illustrate the point. The class spent 35 minutes of class reviewing an exercise students had completed as homework, which consisted of filling blanks with words selected from columns of words at the margins. Each student had to read out loud a sentence and, if correct and approved by the instructor, would prompt the next student to the right to read the following sentence. As errors were committed by 8 of the 18 students in the class (they seemed to have guessed, given their answers), the instructor gave the correct answer and, not offering any further comment, he asked the next student in line to continue. The writing style of the exercise was contrived and hard to follow because it needed to include the long list of words students were expected to use (and ideally to learn!). The instructor used the last 15 minutes of class to distribute the exercise students were going to do for the following class, indicating they needed to use the dictionary to find the distinctions between pairs of semantically-related words, giving an English translation or a short Spanish example to show the different meanings.

Another alarming feature in content courses was how lower-proficiency students brought down the level of linguistic interaction or slowed down the pace of the course. The evaluator reported a strong impression that students did not seem to have the required language proficiency to function in the content-type courses. This observation was corroborated later when students spoke with the evaluator between classes and switched languages when they became aware the evaluator could speak English.

### Meetings with non-Linfield students

The length of interviews with non-Linfield students was determined by their willingness to attend a slightly longer interview at a cafe after class, or to answer questions between classes. A total of 19 students attended the longer interviews across the four program sites, and 10 students participated in the shorter interviews.

Interviewing non-Linfield students revealed interesting new information about why they had chosen particular programs, as 17 of them chose a given site because of its location (sunny areas, next to the ocean, proximity to another country of interest). Further, many said they found their site fun because of the many American students willing to travel together, and because, above all, they wanted to visit Europe. Students made between five and eight trips during the semester, traveled with other American students, and spoke mostly English. A further discovery was that most students did not interact with their host family except on rare occasions ("a lot of what we say is just polite exchanges; not long conversations"). Family members were often busy or out of the house, and for many lodging a student was, in the words of several of the interviewees, "a source of income." Their comments on the courses they were taking were less revealing, particularly in the shorter interviews, because students had little to say. Although positive responses were common, students volunteered little detail as to why they liked a specific course more than others. The longer interviews revealed that students liked certain courses (2–3 per site were mentioned) that were recommended by their peers; they understood most of the content, were given reasonable amounts of homework, the instructor had a positive attitude, and the grading was easy. On this last issue, six of the students volunteered some disturbing information. They said they were attending study abroad at that particular site because they were sure the grades they were hoping to get would help them raise their grade point average back at home. When the evaluator pressed for details, students gave two types of responses: either the instructors were aware students were in a foreign country and they needed to be treated well, or maybe the course was meant to be easy. With regard to language courses, 23 of the students had only positive comments—instructors were fun and they taught lots of grammar ("I'm learning grammar I haven't studied before"). The other six students did not like the fact that a lot of material was presented very fast, and they felt insufficient practice was given for each concept ("I'm not sure I'm going to retain all this stuff; we review a huge new concept every week and when I'm just beginning to understand one…here comes the new one!").

### Interviews with Linfield students

Eight of the Linfield students at a single site attended a focus-group meeting organized over dinner at a restaurant. The ninth student interviewed was attending a program at a different site and consequently was interviewed by herself, over dinner as well. With one exception, all were in agreement with each other on topics that related to the educational quality of courses. Students indicated that some content courses were too difficult, because of the language level of books and the language used by instructors ("I suppose I'm learning a lot; I get good grades… but a lot I don't understand."). Students also noted that they did not ask questions during class; they felt it was inappropriate or not required since the rest of the students did not do it either. In the more challenging courses where students could hardly follow the instructor, they had to rely on the readings to get by, and they helped each other outside of class ("in my anthro class I do fine because I study sociology, but in my short-story class I struggle all the time"). Literature classes in particular, most students agreed, included difficult readings, but four of them said nobody expected them to understand everything so they did not worry ("some of the short stories I didn't understand a bit"); two others said they had to use the dictionary a lot. On the other hand, some courses were less challenging, they could easily follow ("In my history of cinema class we all understand what's going on; it's not hard"). When asked to describe the merits or faults of their best and worst courses, the focus moved to a perceived Spanish (or European) teaching style based on lectures, and on this topic opinions varied ("it's cultural; you have to adapt," "it's easier because you don't have to do anything; just take notes," "if the class is good you stay awake; if it's boring…well, you need to sit at the back"). Two of the majors, who were attending their second semester abroad, said that the problem with the lecture style of teaching is that students do not know whether they are going to retain enough material to do well in exams or papers, and that it was easier to deal with a paper because the topic was of the student's choice. The other added that the student had to be interested in the topic to be able to follow and cited the example of a history class where he missed much of what was done in class; he thought the reason was that he did not like history ("I think I can pass with a B because I'm good at memorizing"). On the issue of grading students were first uninformative, but when somebody mentioned good grades were easier to get in Spain than at Linfield similar comments followed ("my best friend said I could get good grades in these two courses," "teachers give us lots of credit"). Generally speaking, students responded positively to questions about the language courses because they were learning advanced Spanish grammar, the instructors were fun, and the courses were, in their own words, not too demanding. Students also agreed with the evaluator that the Spanish of many of their peers was poor and often unintelligible, and students noticed it particularly in language courses. Another point they agreed on was that the assignments in language courses did not require a lot of work and that in most cases, when instructors checked them, they corrected only grammar errors but gave no other feedback. The exception was one composition course two of the majors were taking, where the instructor gave them a grade and feedback, which students appreciated. When addressing the question of whether they were being adequately prepared—in language and cultural issues—three thought the education experience was going to help them in the future; the other five shrugged and said they hoped so.

With regard to comments about family-stay living arrangements, students were not in agreement, suggesting considerable variability in experiences. Six were in line with responses from non-Linfield students, reporting that families had a courteous interaction with students at meal times, but it was often the case that students and family members did not eat together. Many families were considered 'non-traditional,' for example, with no father in the family, only a mother and children, or an older mother with no child left at the house. Host family members were kind and helpful, but did not seem to have time to spend with students. Two students, however, enjoyed the exchanges and conversations they had with members of the family at meal times ("my mother asks me lots of questions about Washington" [her home state]). Further, interviews revealed an important detail about some host families in that they often lodged more than one student from different programs, and schools were unaware that students from different programs were residing in the same home.

Regarding the amount of Spanish practice available overall, all but one student remarked that they practiced with the family during the mid-day meal, in their language course, and while doing homework. Beyond those contexts—during evenings, weekends, and between classes—students mostly spoke English ("I don't know any Spanish students [from Spain] outside of my family," "I can't speak Spanish with my friend; that would feel weird"). With respect to the availability of faculty or peer advisors, five students responded they were unaware they had an advisor or had no need for one. Three said they had visited the administration office for several purposes ("I always check my e-mail in their computers"), among others to find a tutor, but while one received assistance from one of the staff members, the other two found the office busy with other students.

When asked why they had chosen their program, all respondents said their peers had recommended the site, and were also selecting courses on peer recommendations ("my Linfield advisor approved the courses I selected, but I chose them because a friend recommended them," "my roommate recommended I take courses with this Prof. and I like the course"). Students had no preference for a particular city in Spain; they only wanted to live in the country because it had many interesting regions and because they had the opportunity to travel in Europe. Linfield students were also spending many weekends traveling within Spain and, when time allowed, to other European countries ("it's so easy to travel in Europe it makes no sense to waste the opportunities"). Students planned to travel extensively in Europe when the semester ended. When asked who among them was doing any extra-curricular course or activity, all answered they were not since it made travel on the weekend difficult.

### Document analysis

In 2007, after the evaluator returned to Linfield, Spanish faculty reviewed the documents collected at site visits using the rubric shown in Table 5. They found that language course materials consisted of books and workbooks produced by the programs themselves, which included small amounts of cultural readings and large amounts of pedagogically 'old-fashioned' exercises that almost invariably centered around a list of structural, verb-related, concepts (which goes against criterion 1 in the rubric), and offered explanations that said little about the complex interactions of the various syntactic concepts of Spanish (and leaves criteria 4 and 8 unfulfilled). Vocabulary was often selected to support readings in specific chapters but was not of high frequency, and new words or phrases were not repeated, recycled, or mentioned in other parts of the materials (as criterion 6 stipulates). The most effective exercises seemed to be those that required students to write summaries of readings and to answer questions in response to readings, which partly satisfied criterion 2. We also found that cultural material was in general treated more as a set of facts; chapters seldom included questions that invited reflection or creativity (which leaves criterion 5 unfulfilled).

Spanish faculty also analyzed copies of the 11 assignments provided by Linfield students. The review revealed that grading seemed unjustifiably inflated, and we speculated that this may be due to three factors. First, oral proficiency of our students, being on average higher than those of other students, might have caused instructors to think they deserved higher grades. Second, keeping visiting students happy might be a priority for programs and higher grades might be a means to achieve this. Third, and most likely, untrained language instructors simply look for uses of the target grammatical structure but disregard the quality of the writing. In other words, a Novice-high level sample of writing that includes a (fairly advanced) grammatical structure from a given lesson receives a higher grade than a sample that includes language of higher quality but does not include the target structure. Though speculative, these interpretations helped us to conclude that the potential for learning was being decreased by the heavy emphasis on advanced grammar points treated in isolation, without an effort to connect them to related concepts and communication. We believe learning grammar concepts in isolation encourages blind memorization and prevents acquisition of essential aspects of language (i.e., syntactic connections between parts of a clause, as well as between clauses and sentences), and similarly that the treatment of culture, being shallow and disconnected, might not be conducive to an understanding of the complexities and nuances of culture.

## Conclusions and actions

In October 2007, after all data were analyzed, the Spanish faculty and the administrators at Linfield's OIP started discussions about next steps. Faculty and administrators acknowledged the positive aspects of the visited programs, found justification for some aspects of the program that were considered less-than-ideal, but on the whole considered the academic quality of the program curricula at all sites far below an acceptable standard for our students. Based on the review of data and subsequent discussions, the team formed a number of conclusions (and informed speculations) about the state of third-party study abroad programs that had been visited in Spain (elaborated below). This information was used to make a number of programmatic changes, which are listed in Table 6.

The evaluators concluded that many of the negative aspects of the programs could be explained to some extent by the type of students they seemed to attract. Programs that include a large number of students at low levels of proficiency diminish the quality of courses, create an environment where English is used frequently, and thus decrease the number of opportunities to practice Spanish. On the other hand, cultural considerations might explain why the lecture format was the preferred method of delivering education and account for certain shortcomings in language pedagogy. We agreed that being exposed to the European teaching style offered some learning opportunities, but this benefit was counterbalanced by the loss of potential contexts to develop students' language skills and it might even be counterproductive if most students could not follow what the lecturer is saying. In addition, programs publicize language and culture as their main focus and as such should offer curricula based on theories of sound language pedagogy and instructed second language acquisition. From our perspective, programs should also provide trained instructors who can deliver effective language pedagogy such that some of the problems we discovered could be avoided. At a minimum, programs should be aware that linguistic development happens more effectively when students have frequent opportunities for active communication in and out of the class, with an emphasis on meaningful, not mechanical, oral exchanges.

That said, certain traditional aspects of the language teaching (e.g., a great emphasis on advanced verbal grammar, inflated grading, heavy reliance on mechanical exercises) were not a large concern to the evaluation team for two reasons. This method of pedagogy, which in our opinion is ineffective, is well-established in many language programs in many U.S. schools, and we therefore thought it unlikely that better language instruction could be found elsewhere. Further, students seemed to have positive opinions about the traditional-style teaching and being exposed to a large number of grammatical concepts in one semester.

Nevertheless, we agreed that the teaching materials used in language courses, which focused so heavily on advanced grammar at the expense of opportunities for effective practice of new concepts and the growth of the whole sentence (not just the verb phrase), were largely unsatisfactory. As well, the treatment of culture, showing up in bits of disconnected facts, was also found to be not conducive to growth in awareness of the subtleties of culture, which in our opinion constitutes a learning area as important as language proficiency. In general, we found teaching materials inadequate for the critical role they play in the education of language students.

The evaluation revealed family-stay accommodation arrangements to be inadequate. In our Linfield-owned programs in Costa Rica and Mexico, by comparison, our students invariably consider the family stay as one of the best assets, perhaps attributable to the fact that our programs are in small cities where families are more easily found, trained, and supervised. Demanding a specific type of family for students in Spain might have improved matters, but the team realized the size of the Spanish programs and the cities where they are located would always make it difficult to find improved family situations. For example, in a city like Seville, which is the most popular site in Spain for study abroad (as program administrators stated), several educational organizations offer study abroad, each with hundreds of students. Although the city is large, it would also require a large number of program staff to find, train, and supervise families who know about the needs of international students and who are willing to spend the time required to be an effective host family. The number of staff administering these programs was clearly not sufficient to meet such demands.

Other features of the program—advising, extra opportunities for oral practice—although not optimal, would represent small shortfalls if all other aspects, especially academics, were strong, but this was not the case. In particular, with regard to academics, we decided that the observed programs fell short of fulfilling our most important expectations (refer to Tables 2, 3, and 4). The team found concerns with various academic aspects of programs: teaching methods, fluctuation in the quality of courses, perceived lack in instructors' ability to address language learners with level-appropriate language, traditional forms-focused pedagogy in language materials, and limited opportunities for active engagement in the language. We also agreed that we had the right to demand high quality courses since these study abroad programs account for the bulk of upper-division course requirements.

We had to accept the fact that the comments our students gave the evaluator would not raise, on the whole, strong concerns. However, as discussed further below, we also realized that some of our students were more concerned about traveling in Europe and improving grades rather than with the quality of the education they were getting. Their opinions were valuable to us, but often they were not based on the educational merits of the programs. We felt confident we had observed enough courses and collected enough information to know we needed to make some changes. We also pondered the possibility that we may have been asking for idealizations or expecting too much from large study abroad programs. However, at the same time, the Department of Modern Languages could not reasonably grant degrees unless students were achieving the set outcomes of our language programs, and we felt that the third-party, study abroad programs being attended in Spain did not aid students in accomplishing this aim.

As we discussed options and possible solutions, we made a list of needed changes and recommendations for further work (see Table 6 for a summary). The first, cancellation of the agreement with the programs in Spain, applied to both majors and minors. At the same time a recommendation was issued to the OIP to find two smaller, more rigorous programs in Spain that would fulfill the expectations listed in Table 2 as possibilities for Spanish majors. With regard to language minors, we decided that students would not be given the option of attending the new programs in Spain to complete their degree. We took this step for two reasons. First, many students were making the decision to study abroad in Spain based on opportunities to travel through Europe, and were not considering the academic merit of a specific site. Second, Linfield offers proprietary programs in Costa Rica and Mexico, which throughout the 2006–09 academic years have also been evaluated, with several changes being put in place to enhance their effectiveness. Students who want to complete a minor can attend those programs. Further, Linfield students could still attend a program of their choice, in Spain or any country, though with the stipulation that they could apply credits only toward general graduation requirements, but would not be awarded a language minor at Linfield.

An additional action the evaluation team decided to take was to recommend that language faculty explore methods for training students to look at the study abroad experience as a means of enriching their academic and personal lives, something beyond a merely pleasurable sojourn abroad. The department wants to emphasize that students focus on academics while overseas and on how study abroad can complement their major and their education in general. Finally, it was also decided that along with a fuller preparation of students, Linfield's language faculty advisors needed to stay in touch with them. For this purpose, we instituted an oral interview with language majors each semester they are abroad, to give faculty a chance to find out how students feel about their progress in the program, evaluate language development, offer advice on courses, and ask questions about relations with the host family.

**Table 6: Changes and recommendations to study abroad program**

| | |
|---|---|
| 1. | Cancellation of agreement between Linfield and visited third-party programs. |
| 2. | Replacement of current programs with two suitable programs in Spain for majors. |
| 3. | Changes in requirements for minors: students can still attend non-Linfield programs, but they do not earn a Spanish minor at the college. |
| 4. | Training for students to get greater benefits from the study abroad experience. |
| 5. | Mandatory communication between students and their advisors at Modern Languages. |

These changes went into effect shortly after decisions were made, and those that needed to be published appeared in the 2008–09 course catalogue. In December of 2007, following up on evaluation findings, an administrator from the OIP had visited several new programs in Spain, two of which were found suitable to our needs, and by spring of 2008 the OIP had signed agreements with them. We are sending the first cohort of majors to these new programs in fall 2009. The new, smaller programs in Spain have substantiated our hopes for establishing relationships with more academically sound programs as their more restricted curricula, rigorous programs, and higher number of staff hired to supervise all aspects of the program are the bases for our hopes. New cohorts of students and likely new evaluations will let us know if we are right.

## Further benefits, continued evaluation

The process of evaluation has given faculty in the Department of Modern Languages a lot more than just extra work. During the process we learned two critical lessons. One is that study abroad in itself does not create linguistic and cultural growth. Students need to attend programs that offer academic rigor and supervision of host families or carefully selected alternative options for living. The other is that success also depends on the motivation and the preparation of each student; it is not the case that any student who goes abroad will automatically achieve academic success. Well-thought guidance, a strong academic preparation and orientation, and the participation of advisors from the home institution can increase the probabilities of achieving desired outcomes.

We are also confident that there will be few unexpected surprises when students return from abroad and that the language degrees we grant will have been earned. Further, accreditation of the entire college ran from fall of 2007 through fall 2009, and the evaluation described here constituted a part of what the department included in its self-assessment. The extra work required by accreditation was minimal, and we are happy to say our dean thought highly of our report and wanted to take some ideas to her own department.

We have also learned more about ourselves. We confirmed the fact that we do offer an academically sound language program and that our courses and teaching methods are of high quality. We have demonstrated to ourselves and our administrators that we are caring instructors engaged in the well being of our students. In addition, we are now able to contribute to the professional growth of our field by disseminating our experience and knowledge of evaluation practices at professional conferences. So far, several groups of faculty members have done presentations at five language and study abroad conferences.

In conclusion, faculty and administrators now feel confident that the full study abroad process, from application to return, is academically sound, but at the same time we have become cognizant that things do not function flawlessly on their own, that a lot is at play, and that some other important issues remain to be evaluated. Grade inflation is an example. We have also initiated discussions on the study of culture, or rather, how to best help students increase their cultural sensitivity and how we might best assess cultural outcomes. Evaluation has been a way of assessing the academic value of our program and the opportunity to proceed on the basis of evidence rather than on idealizations or intuitions. Additionally, we have found a way of actively participating in the education of our majors and minors and of making sure we give them the best opportunities for growth during study abroad.

*Aknowledgements*
With great appreciation for the thorough work of the reviewers/editors of this book, the author thanks them for the considerable amount of feedback they have given to this chapter.

# References

American Council on the Teaching of Foreign Languages. (2001). *ACTFL proficiency guidelines: writing* (revised). Hastings-on-Hudson, NY.

American Council on the Teaching of Foreign Languages. (1999). *ACTFL proficiency guidelines: speaking* (revised). Hastings-on-Hudson, NY.

Brecht, R., Davidson, D., & Ginsberg, R. (1993). *Predictors of foreign language gain during study abroad*. ERIC document No. ED360828.

Brustein, W. (2007). The global campus: Challenges and opportunities for higher education in North America. *Journal of Studies in International Education*, 11(3/4), 382–91.

Freed, B. F., Segalowitz, N., & Dewey, D. P. (2004). Context of learning and second language fluency in French: Comparing regular classroom, study abroad, and intensive domestic immersion programs. *Studies in Second Language Acquisition*, 26(2), 275–301.

Isabelli, C. A. (2007). Development of the Spanish subjunctive by advanced learners: Study abroad followed by at-home instruction. *Foreign Language Annals*, 40(2), 330–41.

Magnan, S. S., & Back, M. (2007). Social interaction and linguistic gain during study abroad. *Foreign Language Annals*, 40(1), 43–60.

Patton, M. Q. (1997). *Utilization-focused evaluation: The new century text*. Thousand Oaks, CA: Sage.

Regan, V. (2003). Sociolinguistics and language learning in a study abroad context. *Frontiers: The Interdisciplinary Journal of Study Abroad*, 4, 61–90.

Rivers, W. (1998). Is being there enough? The effects of home stay placement on language gain during study abroad. *Foreign Language Annals, 31*, 492–500.

Schmidt-Rinehart, B., & Knight, S. (2004). The home stay component of study abroad: Three perspectives. *Foreign Language Annals, 37*(2), 254–262.

Wilkinson, S. (1998). Study abroad from the participants' perspective: A challenge to common beliefs. *Foreign Language Annals, 31*(1), 23–39.

# 8

# Curriculum, Learning, and the Identity of Majors: A Case Study of Program Outcomes Evaluation

Peter C. Pfeiffer
Heidi Byrnes
Georgetown University, Washington, DC

NFLRC
*monographs*

*This paper reports on program outcomes evaluation in the German Department at Georgetown University (GUGD) subsequent to implementation of an integrated, four-year, genre-oriented, and task-based curriculum (1997–2000). While previous assessment activities and research had indicated that the curricular reform provided a very favorable educational environment, no formal evidence existed from learners, both past and present, about the appropriateness, level of satisfaction, and perceived learning outcomes of the GUGD. The paper describes evaluation instruments developed for three learner groups (i.e., all enrolled students, German majors, and alumni), analyzes and interprets quantitative and qualitative data collected, and makes recommendations for future action.*

## Program context and impetus for evaluation

The German Department at Georgetown University (GUGD) is a comprehensive department offering B.A., M.A., and Ph.D. degrees, as well as a joint M.A. in German and European Studies (MAGES) and Ph.D. in German with the BMW Center for German and European Studies. Over a three year period, from February 1997 through the spring semester of 2000, the department embarked upon a curricular reform that resulted in an integrated, 4-year, genre-oriented, and task-based curriculum. Entitled *Developing Multiple Literacies*, the re-envisioned undergraduate curriculum sought to address a variety of academic, educational, and administrative concerns that departmental faculty had repeatedly voiced (Byrnes, 2001). One of the foundational decisions made at the time of the curricular reform was to eliminate the distinction between educational goals for majors and non-majors and to develop a unified set of educational goals for all students taking GUGD courses. This decision is reflected in the educational goals statement from the *Proposal for Curricular Revision of German Department* that guided the project:

"The German Department at Georgetown University seeks to serve all students at the University, not only the potential future majors. Such a comprehensive mission requires the creation and delivery of curricula that accomplish seemingly disparate goals. Our programs must be open, accessible, academically and personally appealing and useful to the entire university and they must reflect a clearly defined identity that will make educational sense at Georgetown University. These seemingly dichotomous demands must be creatively addressed for practical enrollment reasons, but to avoid disintegration into *service department* status in relationship to the other programs whom we are eager to serve they must be reconciled through an intellectual approach that substantiates our academic presence and contribution on its own merits" (*Developing Multiple Literacies*, 2000).

Integral to this three-year process of curriculum and materials development and re-imagined pedagogies was a complete re-thinking of assessment and evaluation practices. The terms "assessment" and "evaluation" are used here according to Norris' (2006) distinction between assessment as directed at student learning and evaluation as approaches to understanding and improving programs. While assessment-oriented reconsiderations were initially most pronounced in the area of placement testing (Norris, 2008), the curriculum project also ushered in extensive revamping of classroom-based assessment practices, fostered assessment of speaking proficiency across the curriculum (Norris & Pfeiffer, 2003), and enabled on-going research in the area of L2 writing development (Byrnes, 2002, 2009; Byrnes et al., 2005; Byrnes & Sinicrope, in preparation; Crane, 2008; Ryshina-Pankova, 2006). Indeed, it was through assessment and early informal program evaluation that all members of the department's teaching staff, faculty and graduate students, came to develop a high level of reflective understanding of the educational aims of the program, the central position of the articulated curriculum, and of their own role as practitioners in the achievement of the program's educative goals (Byrnes, 2002).

Among the findings of these initial and diverse assessment activities was that the *Developing Multiple Literacies* curriculum has provided a context in which student learning outcomes in the area of speaking proficiency appreciably outpaced benchmarks set at other institutions (Norris & Pfeiffer, 2003). Similarly, students' writing abilities compared highly favorably with those reported in one of the few other studies about collegiate German writing development (Byrnes, Maxim, & Norris, in preparation). Thus, although a lack of systematic data collection prior to 1997 precludes a straightforward comparison between pre- and post-reform student learning outcomes, these results supported initial conclusions that the reformed curriculum had created an educational environment that fosters the attainment of upper levels of ability in German across the modalities and across different student groups.

However, while these activities provided valuable information about assessed learning outcomes, we lacked formal feedback from the *learners*, both past and present, about the appropriateness, level of satisfaction, and perceived learning outcomes of the GUGD. First, we sought this feedback not only to understand whether unified learning goals were appropriate for and could be successfully implemented in a collegiate curriculum, but also because the student population that the GUGD serves is quite diverse in its academic aspirations. On the one hand, many students show a strong pre-professional orientation towards international affairs and the social sciences (in particular students of Georgetown University's School of Foreign Service), and towards the business world. On the other hand, students also have a vibrant interest in the tradition of liberal arts and humanities education as exemplified in the spread of more than 30 majors, more than 40 minors, and various certificate programs in Georgetown College, which span the full range of the humanities and the social and natural sciences.

Second, we needed student feedback on the decision to decouple the identification common in collegiate FL programs, whereby a program's educational goals are typically expressed in terms of the requirements of the major. Our curriculum reform had replaced that notion with an understanding of *program* in terms of a unified and articulated curriculum that would overcome the division between *language* courses and *content* courses and that would support all students in attaining advanced levels of ability in German. Rather, the reconfigured curriculum is defined by academic and educational goals that encompass the full range of courses that are available to all students, not just majors or minors. The extent to which such an integrated curricular approach accorded with students' actual learning experiences within the program, though, was only known in an anecdotal and ad hoc way.

A third area motivating a need for a multi-perspectival and program-wide evaluation pertained to our institutional situation. The GUGD is fortunate to exist in an institutional environment that not only permits double majors with languages but counts them in the statistics of language departments. Furthermore, the university recognizes the educational value of non-majors enrolling in upper-division classes, often accounting for as much as 50% of total enrollment in the GUGD. It is willing to read such statistics as pointing to a program's educational merit and attractiveness, because these kinds of enrollments are the result of deliberate choices in students' often highly constricted curricula. In other words, the university does not single-mindedly count majors as the only indicator of a program's quality and success. Even so, there is ample reason for assuring a sufficient pool of majors because, as a group, they constitute an academically vibrant cohort that gives weight to the presence of a separate degree program and department. For that reason, we were interested in finding out whether our reformed curricular structure was serving our majors well. Given the decoupling of educational goals from the requirements of the major, we were concerned that majors might perceive a loss of distinctiveness vis-à-vis other students in the program, and that this perception could affect the attractiveness of the German major. We used the term *identity* as a placeholder for the perceived distinctiveness, attractiveness, value, and overall satisfaction with the major.

In this context, a comment is in order. Our enrollments have generally followed the trends for German in American higher education, dropping markedly in the 1990s and then seemingly stabilizing, though on a significantly lower level. However, enrollment considerations were not the primary driving force in our interest in gathering direct feedback from our majors, much like they had not been the driving force in the original curricular reform. Study of enrollment patterns both at Georgetown and across the country had long alerted us to the fact that too many factors are at play that were neither knowable in all their diversity nor controllable by us. Also, neither at the time of the curricular reform nor in conjunction with the present evaluation effort did we have the illusion that our curricular work would readily result in higher enrollments. Then and now, we are committed to assuring the best possible programmatic context for students and doing so in a spirit of cooperation and collaboration, and with a willingness to learn in the process of curricular reform. In that effort, program evaluation came to be understood as a valuable tool, a way of analyzing, improving, and valuing what we identified as our educational goals.

Finally, because the curriculum reform had been comprehensive, encompassing the entire undergraduate program but also affecting aspects of the graduate program (e.g., particularly in graduate education toward teaching), we also wanted to determine possible differences in perceived program appropriateness, satisfaction, and outcomes between the pre- and post-curriculum reform alums, both undergraduate and graduate.

## Evaluation activities: Participants, intended uses, instruments, data collection

The evaluation project began with numerous meetings at which the previously mentioned issues were discussed. These discussions resulted in a consensus to engage in a multi-pronged evaluative inquiry, a decision that received support from an evaluation initiative directed by John Norris at the University of Hawai'i, for which the department served as a case study. They also led to a multi-staged approach, such that investigations of current students would take place during the first year of the study and alumni would be surveyed during the second year. That decision reflected both departmental work loads and activities planned under the evaluation grant. Also, in order to maximize the opportunities for faculty/graduate student professional development, all members of the department were invited to participate. Originally, three faculty members and four graduate students made up the evaluation team; a career change by one faculty member subsequently reduced the group. The group's deliberations and decisions were regularly reported at departmental meetings, including a departmental retreat that included all faculty and graduate students, and feedback was received and incorporated. The project's lead evaluators received approval for this study from Georgetown University's Institutional Review Board (IRB) for human subject research. Accordingly, the project was begun in the fall semester of 2006, and continued over two academic years; results of the project were presented to departmental faculty in the fall of 2008 and were shared with currently enrolled students at a meeting in spring of 2009.

From the initial stage-setting process, the following primary intended uses of the evaluation crystallized. The evaluation was to help us:

- understand the distinctiveness and value of the German program from the perspectives of multiple program stakeholders;
- understand the distinctiveness and value of the German major;
- identify students' perspectives on any needed changes, additions, and other adjustments in the targeted outcomes of the German program; and
- provide a basis for further curricular and other programmatic initiatives should these be needed.

Secondary intended uses of the evaluation were to:

- increase awareness and engagement among GUGD stakeholders about the nature and value of the German studies degree and the undergraduate curriculum;
- involve graduate students in work on the GUGD program in order to facilitate their understanding of and investment in the curriculum;
- provide an opportunity for teacher development through evaluation results;
- sustain evaluation practices and awareness of GUGD efforts within Georgetown University educational initiatives and within the broader national FL education context.

Accordingly, three evaluation instruments for three distinct respondent groups were developed to capture as broad a view of the program as possible: (a) all students enrolled in German courses during the spring semester 2007 were asked to complete a web-based questionnaire with Likert-scale and open-ended responses; (b) also during the spring semester 2007, two focus groups with current majors at all levels were conducted to assess holistically the attitudes and beliefs of German majors at Georgetown; and (c) an alumni questionnaire, once more with both Likert-scale and open-ended responses, was mailed to all alumni of the German Department and made available on-line in December 2007/January 2008. On-line and hard copy questionnaires were used to capture holistically the attitudes of large student groups and for ease of data collection. Focus group interviews were used for the much smaller cohort of German majors to allow for a more probing collection of data concerning majors' perceptions of program quality. (The three instruments are provided in Appendices A, B, and C).

Expertise for developing these instruments had been gained with the help of the evaluation team at the University of Hawai'i and through supplementary readings. That same team also helped to set up the online surveys using SurveyMonkey (www.surveymonkey.com). Participants submitted their responses to the two questionnaires to the team in Hawai'i, where the results were tabulated and summarized. We, as the researchers/authors, then analyzed the spring 2007 data further in conjunction with our participation in the Summer Institute on Foreign Language Program Evaluation offered at the National Foreign Language Resource Center at the University of Hawai'i.

The on-line questionnaire for all students enrolled in German classes during spring 2007 had three subcomponents that asked them to assess program delivery, learning outcomes, and their learning experience on 4-point Likert scales and with open comment sections (see Appendix A). The questionnaire concluded with four open-ended, global questions. Together with drop-down menus targeting speaking, writing, reading, listening, and cultural awareness, this resulted in a total of 32 items in addition to the options for comments. The questionnaires were piloted with three current German students in order to identify any potential misunderstandings or miscues. Some adjustments were made in phrasing, the questionnaire was finalized, and all students were asked in an e-mail message from the chair to complete it. Students completed the questionnaire outside of class. Several reminders were sent through the departmental listserve that includes all students. 76 respondents, approximately 30% of that semester's enrolled students, completed the questionnaire.

For the focus group interviews, all German majors were invited by the chair of the department via e-mail to participate in the sessions and meet afterwards for a pizza dinner. About 50% of the majors responded and agreed to participate. These students were divided into two groups small enough to allow for ample time for each student to speak to the items raised by the moderator. One professor from the research group served as moderator, using guiding questions that had been developed by the research group (see Appendix B). The other professor took notes. A previous pilot study had indicated that students preferred faculty members over outsiders as moderators because they were very familiar with them and took the focus groups as an opportunity to talk about their academic experiences in the department. An assistant from the university's learning center served as second notetaker. The focus group sessions were audio-recorded, which allowed reviewing of taped evidence if critical differences occurred in the two separate sets of notes. However, no such differences occurred.

Finally, the alumni questionnaire was sent to all past German majors for which the department had current records—a total of 526 former students dating back to the late 1950's (see Appendix C). In recent years, alumni had been kept apprised of happenings in the department through annual letters from the department chair. A response rate of 143 completed questionnaires (both hard copy and on-line) was at the high end of expectations (> 27%). This instrument, too, had closed-ended and open-ended items. In addition to personal background information on the degree earned at GU, year of graduation, further degrees and careers pursued, the directed items asked alumni to evaluate their learning experience in the GUGD from the perspectives of their professional and personal life, by rating the language abilities and the cultural/literary knowledge they had developed in the program, as well as their overall educational experience. Six of the seven items provided a 4-point Likert scale and a comment section for open-ended responses. The concluding item requested input on how the program might have been better able to serve them in both their personal and their professional lives.

## Data analysis and findings

The overall tenor of quantitative and qualitative responses in all three data collection instruments showed a high to very high level of satisfaction on the part of students and alumni with their educational experiences, the learning environment, and the effectiveness of teaching in the GUGD. In particular, students recognized the high level of commitment on the part of faculty to their education and development. Furthermore, high levels of expectations on the part of the faculty were seen as positive and served to create a sense of identity and identification with the department.

### The on-line questionnaire for students taking German classes

Results of the on-line questionnaire for all students enrolled in the spring of 2007 were disaggregated along a variety of categories that the evaluation team had identified as potential indicators of different student perspectives on the educational experience in the department. Responses were grouped according to:

- students' majors (three groups: German majors; majors in the liberal arts-oriented Georgetown College; majors in the social science/policy-oriented School of Foreign Service, including a few business school students);
- study abroad experience of at least four weeks (with or without) (Abr/Nabr);
- starting curricular level for first enrollment in the GUGD (e.g., SL1, SL2);
- length of experience in the GUGD by curricular level (e.g., EL1/EL2);
- first language (English or other).

Analysis of the average responses to the closed questions showed that disaggregation according to the above criteria resulted in no sizeable differentiation among any of the groups (see Table 1). Similarly, analysis of themes identified in the open-ended responses from the sub-groups supported the major finding that no demonstrable or sustained difference between the themes emerged from any of the subgroups. Responses varied somewhat in the intensity of students' judgments but were very much alike in overall outlook (see below for further discussion). These results supported the interpretation that students of spring 2007 in general perceived their educational needs and goals regarding language learning as very similar, despite their varying courses of study and somewhat varying background and experiences.

Another way of analyzing the quantitative data was through closer scrutiny of responses in the lower ranges ($\leq 3$ on the Likert scale), looking for possible patterns (see shaded areas in Table 1).

Table 1: Current students questionnaire

| item | Ger | Col | SFS | abr | nabr | sl1 | sl2 | sl3 | sl4+ | el1 | el2 | el3 | el4 | Eng | other |
|---|---|---|---|---|---|---|---|---|---|---|---|---|---|---|---|
| 1 | 3.40 | 3.08 | 3.25 | 3.15 | 3.24 | 3.20 | 2.78 | 3.25 | 3.31 | 3.09 | 3.27 | 3.17 | 2.67 | 3.31 | 3.21 |
| 2 | 3.67 | 3.18 | 3.33 | 3.20 | 3.40 | 3.30 | 2.89 | 3.42 | 3.42 | 3.13 | 3.43 | 3.67 | 3.17 | 3.42 | 3.33 |
| 3 | 3.27 | 3.10 | 3.40 | 2.96 | 3.26 | 3.12 | 2.90 | 3.17 | 3.15 | 3.04 | 3.10 | 3.50 | 3.33 | 3.15 | 3.10 |
| 4 | 3.47 | 3.27 | 3.40 | 3.16 | 3.42 | 3.36 | 3.10 | 3.50 | 3.08 | 3.13 | 3.24 | 3.50 | 4.00 | 3.08 | 3.28 |
| 5 | 3.53 | 3.17 | 3.53 | 3.28 | 3.24 | 3.28 | 3.00 | 3.50 | 3.08 | 3.04 | 3.29 | 3.67 | 3.50 | 3.08 | 3.26 |
| 6 | 2.80 | 2.52 | 2.60 | 2.60 | 2.58 | 2.48 | 2.70 | 2.33 | 2.77 | 2.48 | 2.52 | 2.83 | 2.83 | 2.77 | 2.60 |
| 7 | 3.00 | 2.79 | 2.60 | 2.88 | 2.82 | 2.80 | 2.80 | 2.83 | 2.85 | 2.65 | 3.05 | 2.83 | 2.33 | 2.85 | 2.84 |
| 8 | 3.20 | 2.98 | 2.80 | 3.08 | 3.00 | 3.00 | 3.00 | 3.17 | 2.85 | 2.91 | 2.90 | 3.67 | 2.83 | 2.85 | 3.00 |
| 9 | 3.60 | 3.31 | 3.60 | 3.44 | 3.34 | 3.60 | 2.70 | 3.67 | 3.15 | 3.09 | 3.43 | 3.67 | 3.83 | 3.15 | 3.44 |
| 10 | 3.53 | 3.19 | 3.40 | 3.20 | 3.32 | 3.16 | 3.20 | 3.50 | 3.23 | 3.00 | 3.24 | 3.83 | 3.83 | 3.23 | 3.20 |
| 11 | 3.00 | 2.89 | 3.07 | 2.83 | 2.97 | 3.00 | 2.70 | 2.92 | 2.83 | 2.86 | 2.95 | 3.00 | 3.00 | 2.83 | 2.92 |
| 12 | 3.50 | 3.26 | 3.60 | 3.00 | 3.47 | 3.47 | 2.75 | 2.67 | 3.50 | 3.00 | 3.45 | 3.00 | 3.60 | 3.50 | 3.33 |
| 13 | 3.57 | 3.40 | 4.00 | 3.64 | 2.67 | 3.00 | 3.40 | 4.00 | 3.50 | 3.00 | 3.25 | 3.75 | 3.33 | 3.50 | 3.47 |
| 14 | 2.73 | 3.05 | 3.14 | 3.00 | 2.97 | 3.29 | 2.38 | 3.00 | 2.82 | 3.00 | 2.94 | 3.00 | 3.17 | 2.82 | 3.02 |
| 15 | 3.87 | 3.48 | 3.67 | 3.56 | 3.58 | 3.68 | 3.20 | 3.75 | 3.46 | 3.43 | 3.57 | 3.67 | 4.00 | 3.46 | 3.56 |
| 16 | 2.93 | 3.09 | 3.33 | 2.92 | 3.14 | 3.08 | 2.70 | 3.42 | 2.77 | 2.95 | 2.90 | 3.17 | 3.67 | 2.77 | 3.02 |
| 17 | 3.60 | 3.30 | 3.33 | 3.40 | 3.35 | 3.29 | 3.20 | 3.67 | 3.38 | 3.23 | 3.38 | 3.67 | 3.50 | 3.38 | 3.38 |
| 18 | 3.53 | 3.34 | 3.33 | 3.36 | 3.41 | 3.38 | 3.20 | 3.33 | 3.62 | 3.23 | 3.43 | 3.83 | 3.50 | 3.62 | 3.42 |
| 19 | 3.20 | 3.17 | 3.33 | 3.08 | 3.24 | 3.21 | 2.90 | 3.33 | 3.08 | 3.14 | 3.05 | 3.17 | 3.33 | 3.08 | 3.16 |
| 20 | 2.60 | 2.60 | 2.73 | 2.56 | 2.62 | 2.67 | 2.60 | 2.50 | 2.54 | 2.64 | 2.29 | 3.33 | 3.17 | 2.54 | 2.60 |
| 21 | 3.53 | 3.26 | 3.60 | 3.20 | 3.41 | 3.29 | 3.10 | 3.67 | 3.23 | 3.23 | 3.29 | 3.67 | 3.50 | 3.23 | 3.36 |
| 22 | 3.93 | 3.47 | 3.60 | 3.44 | 3.68 | 3.50 | 3.30 | 3.67 | 3.92 | 3.50 | 3.71 | 3.83 | 3.67 | 3.92 | 3.62 |
| 23 | 2.67 | 2.47 | 2.60 | 2.56 | 2.49 | 2.46 | 2.80 | 2.42 | 2.46 | 2.41 | 2.38 | 2.83 | 2.83 | 2.46 | 2.46 |
| 24 | 3.20 | 3.09 | 3.33 | 3.12 | 3.11 | 3.25 | 2.60 | 3.50 | 2.92 | 3.05 | 3.19 | 3.17 | 3.17 | 2.92 | 3.14 |
| 25 | 3.27 | 3.04 | 3.13 | 3.16 | 3.05 | 2.96 | 3.10 | 3.50 | 2.92 | 2.77 | 3.14 | 3.50 | 3.67 | 2.92 | 3.10 |
| 26 | 3.17 | 2.57 | 2.67 | 2.88 | 2.45 | 2.33 | 2.57 | 3.33 | 2.80 | 1.83 | 2.70 | 3.40 | 2.67 | 2.80 | 2.68 |
| 27 | 3.53 | 2.98 | 3.07 | 3.16 | 3.08 | 2.96 | 2.90 | 3.50 | 3.15 | 2.86 | 3.19 | 3.50 | 3.33 | 3.15 | 3.10 |
| 28 | 3.53 | 3.15 | 3.27 | 3.32 | 3.19 | 3.29 | 2.80 | 3.25 | 3.46 | 2.95 | 3.38 | 3.50 | 3.67 | 3.46 | 3.28 |
| 29 | 3.47 | 3.21 | 3.33 | 3.28 | 3.27 | 3.08 | 3.00 | 3.50 | 3.62 | 3.32 | 3.29 | 3.50 | 2.67 | 3.62 | 3.28 |
| 30 | 3.80 | 3.13 | 3.20 | 3.32 | 3.27 | 3.13 | 3.00 | 3.67 | 3.38 | 2.91 | 3.48 | 3.83 | 3.17 | 3.38 | 3.30 |
| 31 | 3.80 | 3.34 | 3.53 | 3.40 | 3.49 | 3.63 | 2.90 | 3.50 | 3.62 | 3.32 | 3.57 | 3.67 | 3.33 | 3.62 | 3.50 |
| 32 | 3.40 | 2.79 | 2.87 | 3.00 | 2.89 | 2.83 | 2.80 | 3.17 | 3.08 | 2.59 | 3.14 | 3.50 | 4.00 | 3.08 | 2.94 |

key: Ger=German major; Col=other major in Georgetown College; SFS=student in the School of Foreign Service; abr=study abroad of at least 4 weeks; nabr=no study abroad; sl1–4=starting curricular level; EL1–4=length of experience in the program by curricular level; Eng=native English speaker; other=native speaker of a language other than English

It is important to note that the scores in and of themselves are not necessarily direct indicators of positive or negative evaluations. For example, the outlier in the dataset, a score of 1.83 for question 26 by students with the experience of one curricular level, is easily explained: Question 26 asked to what degree the current course prepared students to be ready for direct matriculation in study abroad at a German-language university. Students' responses are quite accurate in that the particular course they were currently enrolled in did not, in all likelihood, prepare them for such an undertaking.

Nevertheless, potentially important patterns did emerge. Scores of ≤ 3 suggested closer analysis for one of the disaggregated student groups (SL2: students who began their studies at the second level of the curriculum) and for 9 items within the 32 item questionnaire: questions #6, 7, 8, 11 (all connected with the use of technology in curriculum delivery), #14 (extra-curricular activities), #16 (content focus of curriculum and speaking abilities), #20 and 23 (focus on writing in the curriculum), and #26 (preparation for direct matriculation at a German university). Closer analysis of these items was also motivated by the fact that responses generated large standard deviations (SD), often approaching 1.0, thereby indicating considerable disparity across students in their responses.

To that end, we analyzed the corresponding open-ended responses in all three areas—curriculum delivery, learning experience, and learning outcomes—in order to uncover themes and possible patterns in students' answers to these items. Individual comments varied considerably and may have contributed to an overall lower score, yet two identifiable themes emerged from multiple responses. First, students noted a relatively low use of learning technology in classes, often arriving at that judgment by comparing their experience with other select German classes, for example:

> "We could have used more computer-based learning in the course. In the first course I took in German—Business in Germany—, we had a lot of exercises using computers and investing in the stock exchange game."

> "Use of films or television in class would have been nice, or a project or paper related to cultural topics. The only class I strongly remember using technology is the Hörspiele course."

> "Very few of my German courses made significant use of technology, with the exception of films."

> "There is not enough audiovisual components after *Text in Context* level."

Second, students experienced German classes as having good connections to other courses in other departments, as reflected in these comments:

> "I have found connections between German classes and my other classes here, i.e., the discussion of the EU in *Text in Context* has made me more aware when the EU is discussed in other classes."

> "I felt well informed enough to write my term paper for *European Civilization*, an assignment which strongly discouraged use of outside sources, on Germany's significant changes in its national self-perception after the two World Wars."

> "Being an Art History major, I greatly enjoyed learning to talk about art in German [in a presentation on a Gustav Klimt painting]."

No particular themes emerged concerning extra-curricular activities or the balance between speaking and writing in students' learning. Students commented on German Club and other extra-curricular activities and made some suggestions. Some students perceived their speaking abilities as having developed less rapidly than their writing abilities.

Likewise, no particular theme emerged for students who had started at the second curricular level (SL2). Since the second curricular level concludes the language requirement in Georgetown College, responses may have been tilted in a particular direction; also, standard deviations are relatively high in these responses (.5 ≤), indicating a greater dispersion of student reactions.

Therefore, no clear answers presented themselves explaining the lower scores in the items indicated above with the exception of the relatively low use of technology in curriculum delivery, where the open-ended responses highlighted the relatively low use of technology in some German courses.

The same technique of identifying themes was used for an analysis of responses to the four open-ended questions, asking students to comment on the name of the GUGD's curriculum, on the genre- and task-based approach, on any perceived differences to previous language learning experiences, and on the most memorable experience of their studies in the German Department.

First, students were not generally aware of the curriculum's name *Developing Multiple Literacies* and the formal aspects of the teaching approach used. However, that did not keep them from sharing insights based on their concrete learning experience, using a broad, rather than a purely instrumental, interpretation of the nature of language learning. Their comments made reference to all modalities, cultural awareness, literature, history, and political and intellectual traditions, as exemplified here:

> "*Developing Multiple Literacies* suggests the capacity to understand the world in multiple ways, insomuch as each language redefines and linguistically portions out the world in its own way."

> "When learning another language, one learns not only the words and the grammar but also the culture and meaning behind them. In order to be literate in German, it is not enough to simply understand each word. One must also be able to understand concepts and ideas."

> "To me, [*Developing Multiple Literacies*] means expanding my language abilities to acquire knowledge of another language, the culture that goes with it, and the skills of communication with a new set of people."

One student was particularly articulate: "The concept of developing multiple literacies recognizes the variety of uses to which language may be put and the importance of context, both at the macro-level of culture and at the lower levels of field and situations, then stresses learner awareness of these aspects of language use, and attempts to allow the learner, particularly at an advanced level, to focus his efforts in areas of particular interest to him."

Second, student comments showed a high level of programmatic meta-awareness and reflective learning. They experienced the program's emphasis on broad cultural content areas, as addressed in the curriculum through the construct of genre, as an attractive intellectual engagement that was couched in terms of educational experience. In that context it is noteworthy that they responded to the program *not*, or at least not primarily, in terms of language learning as a separate factor. In fact, for some students the program did not meet the usual expectations with regard to *language learning*, which tend to focus heavily on grammar, vocabulary lists, and quotidian language. At the same time, the complexities of acquiring advanced levels of ability were differentially understood. In any case, students displayed ambivalence with regard to what they wanted from the program: On the one hand, they demanded social, everyday language use; on the other hand, they desired high levels of sophistication and academic abilities, that is, language to be used, as one student put it, "from a bar to a board room." Other comments reflected this range of perspectives:

> "The approach has really helped me as a beginner in German by teaching me an aspect of the language and then making sure I understand/remember it by making me perform tasks that enhance my understanding."

> "Genre-based study addresses my need to be intellectually stimulated and connected to the culture about which I am learning; task-based study provides a foundation, so I can comprehend what I am supposed to be learning about that culture."

> "I would actually prefer less of a topic-based learning approach and a more disciplined, grammar-intensive (with more homework practice) curriculum."

> "[…] we should be given more lists of vocabulary to learn […]"

> "I would have benefitted from more vocabulary lists. I love the linkage between language and content, but it does not need to exclude beneficial memorization in my opinion."

Third, students' comments on perceived differences to other language learning experiences were varied and generally very positive toward the GUGD, focusing on the demanding, fast-paced intensity of instruction, the strong organization and structure of the courses, and the emphasis "on gaining insights to the culture right away." In the words of one student: "[The German classes] have focused more on culture, speaking, and writing rather than solely on grammar and vocabulary." The learner-focused approach was seen as forcing "the student to become more active in the education process." Students also noted the heavy emphasis on writing, at times stating that their speaking had not improved as much. Students were ambivalent about the use of materials packets rather than textbooks, particularly in the lower curricular levels. On the one hand, it was seen positively ("never do any busywork"); on the other hand, the quality of the packets was viewed as "not as good as the possibilities textbook learning presents" and "They are out of date […]."

A number of students pointed to the comparatively greater intellectual engagement in German classes and the connections to their overall education: "The language studies in the German Department not only teach students the language, but how to think in general about how meaning is conveyed, whether it be in speaking or writing, skills which have proved extremely useful in other classes, regardless of the subject matter."

Finally, student responses to the concluding question—about a memorable experience in the program—highlighted three themes. First, and most prominently, students praised their extraordinary study abroad experiences as defining moments in their lives and studies. These included all Georgetown-sponsored programs: the five-week summer program in Trier and the semester or year abroad programs in Berlin, Munich, Tübingen, and Vienna. The second prominent theme was the students' pride in specific academic accomplishments. These included substantial speaking performances, such as fifteen-minute formal presentations, active participation in substantive, well prepared round-table discussions, as well as the completion of major research papers and final essays written in German. In these comments, students indicated their appreciation of the time, intellectual stimulation, and care they received from instructors.

## The focus groups for majors

The focus groups for majors were conducted to collect data regarding any issues specific to the German majors' educational experiences in the department. We compared the two sets of notes from the focus groups generated by the note takers and identified themes in majors' responses. Overall, satisfaction with the program, relationships with professors, and the education received were judged to be excellent to very good.

Two themes in particular arose in the focus group responses: (a) the importance of the study abroad experience in any of the adopted versions (summer program; semester- or year-long direct matriculation), with a particular emphasis on the department's Trier summer program; and (b) the centrality of the educational experience in the signature course of the curriculum, *Text in Context: Reading Germany*. The latter is a Level IV, 4-credit-hour course targeting advanced levels of formal and public language with a heavy emphasis on writing. It is the highest course into which students can place when they arrive at Georgetown University. In the curricular sequence, it follows any combination of three- or six-credit courses for Levels I–III, with a total of 255, 50-minute periods of instruction.

While these two themes were not unexpected, the unanimity and forcefulness of the students' statements was striking. Upon further probing, students stated that a more explicit integration of study abroad (both prior to the stay and upon students' return) would add to the benefits of the experience and to learning outcomes, and they unanimously referred to the centrality of the learning experience in *Text in Context* [TiC] as strongly marking their identity as German majors. Students raised questions about the work-load and characterized their course experience in a broad variety of ways—from excellent to strenuous. Yet, all acknowledged the importance of the course for their learning of German and for their identity as majors: if you made it through *TiC*, you could make it anywhere. A sub-theme arose when a number of students questioned the advisability of taking *TiC* as the first course for incoming first year students. At the same time, give-and-take in the groups attributed the perceived high demands of the course for incoming students both to the course itself and to the demands students face while adjusting to a new and competitive environment. Representative comments are:

> "*TiC* is a catch 22. If you are a freshman placed into it, it is very difficult. It was difficult in my case, and I took it my sophomore year. I had figured out a lot more."

> "*TiC*, you can complain about it, but it really was needed to move you up to that next level."

> "But if we didn't take it [*TiC*] we would never be as far along, have as high quality work and classes as it is right now."

> "*TiC* is a really good example of how it all ties together."

> "*TiC* was like brain surgery."

## The alumni questionnaire

Responses to the alumni questionnaire, too, were tabulated and submitted to initial analysis by our partner evaluators at the University of Hawai'i, to ensure anonymity of responses. We received responses from 143 alumni who had graduated between 1957 and 2007. Of these, 109 respondents had gained undergraduate degrees, 9 undergraduate and graduate degrees, and 21 M.A. and/or Ph.D. degrees (4 respondents did not volunteer degree information).

As a first step, respondents' background information was analyzed. GUGD alums pursued a variety of additional degrees after graduation, especially MBAs (N=17), advanced degrees in academic fields such as German, psychology, linguistics, theology, economics, philosophy, political science, and Russian (N=15), and a broad range of more professionally-oriented degrees in fields such as law, international affairs/international relations, medicine, journalism, marketing, public administration, human resources, archaeology, and security studies (N=34).

Among the 140 respondents, 32 indicated that they use or used German for their career, some of them in a German-speaking country. Frequently mentioned career paths (multiple responses possible) related to the business world, such as marketing, management, and finance (N=63), to K–16 education and educational administration (N=59), to translation (N=24), and to positions in local or federal government (N=21). But the breadth of career paths was captured best by 72 alums who identified a great variety of careers, from services, publishing, advocacy work, law, telecommunications, media, and journalism to medicine and veterinary medicine; from real estate and law enforcement to social work, religion, international development, library work, advertising, and writing to a career as an artist.

For a more precise analysis of the closed-ended items, responses were first disaggregated by the degree alumni had received, that is, either undergraduate or graduate. The current analysis focuses on those students who received undergraduate degrees only, because the curricular reform primarily targeted the undergraduate curriculum. We intend to return to responses by graduate degree holders at a future date. Students who completed multiple degrees were not included in the undergraduate data.

Responses of undergraduates were further disaggregated by their graduation date. Because we introduced the "Developing Multiple Literacies" curriculum in the fall semester of 1997, we selected students with a graduation date of 1999 as the first cohort to have potentially been exposed to a significantly different learning experience. Therefore, the data were disaggregated by graduation date, pre-1999 vs. post-1999. Furthermore, analyses were based on respondents who provided ratings for each question; respondents who did not answer all questions were eliminated from analysis. Table 2 below provides an overview of the responses to how satisfied alums were with the learning experience in the GUGD. The rating scale ranged from 1 (not satisfied) to 4 (very satisfied).

Table 2: Alumni satisfaction with educational experiences

| Q5: Looking back on your learning experiences in the Georgetown German program, how satisfied are you with... | undergraduate (N=99) | | | |
|---|---|---|---|---|
| | pre99 (N=77) | | post99 (N=22) | |
| | M | SD | M | SD |
| German language abilities | 3.51 | 0.70 | **3.59** | 0.59 |
| cultural and literary knowledge and appreciation | 3.42 | 0.77 | **3.77** | 0.43 |
| overall educational experience | 3.48 | 0.80 | **3.91** | 0.29 |

On average, ratings of post-1999 alums for all three categories—language abilities, cultural and literary knowledge, and overall educational experience—indicated higher satisfaction levels than for students who completed their terminal degree in 1998 or earlier (see bolded average values). In addition, students were more in agreement regarding their satisfaction levels as indicated by the lower standard deviation values. The greatest difference in values occurred in the rating of the overall educational experience, with an extraordinarily high value of 3.91 on a 4-point scale and a low standard deviation figure.

These results were closely mirrored by answers to the second closed-ended question regarding the benefits of areas of learning, presented in Table 3. These were also rated on a four-point scale from 1 (not at all) to 4 (very much).

**Table 3: Benefits of learning to professional and personal life**

| Q6: To what extent have the following three areas of learning in the German Department benefited you in your professional and personal life?... | | undergraduate (N=99) | | | |
|---|---|---|---|---|---|
| | | pre99 (N=77) | | post99 (N=22) | |
| | | M | SD | M | SD |
| German language abilities | professional | 2.84 | 1.00 | 2.86 | 1.13 |
| | personal | 3.27 | 0.84 | 3.55 | 0.67 |
| cultural and literary knowledge and appreciation | professional | 2.69 | 1.05 | 2.86 | 1.04 |
| | personal | 3.36 | 0.78 | 3.59 | 0.67 |
| overall educational experience | professional | 2.94 | 0.96 | 3.27 | 0.88 |
| | personal | 3.27 | 0.88 | 3.73 | 0.63 |

On average, ratings from students on the benefits of the three areas of learning ranged from *some* to *very much* with the exception of ratings of professional benefits from language abilities and cultural/literary knowledge. Again, alums from the post-1999 group rated all three categories higher on average than students who completed their terminal degree in 1998 or earlier. Personal benefits of the three categories were rated much higher than the professional benefits. Responses to the personal benefits of the three areas of learning had consistently lower standard deviations, meaning that students' responses were more similar. The higher standard deviations in students' responses regarding the benefits of the three areas of learning for their professional lives point towards the broad range of students' professional aspirations and activities. German naturally plays very different roles in the professional life of a dentist when compared to a translator. The high standard deviations thus reflect the wide scope of career paths that alumni have chosen, which may or may not include a German component.

GUGD alumni consistently rated their educational experience and the benefit of that education very highly. On average, post-1999 alumni responded more favorably and with greater consistency in that favorable rating. To get a finer-grained understanding of the data, we looked closely at how alums elaborated on their responses in the open-ended parts of the questions. Overall, students' comments echoed the very positive evaluation of their experiences at GUGD. Taken together, pre-1999 alums voiced more negative comments than did post-1999 respondents, even after the results were adjusted for the greater number of respondents in the former group.

With regard to *language abilities*, almost twice the percentage of post-1999 alumni (45%) commented on their highly competent use of language than did pre-1999 alumni (23%):

"Still speak nearly fluent German" (pre-1999);

"The curriculum really focused on how to speak academically, not just how to speak" (post-1999).

Concerning the *literary and cultural knowledge* students acquired in the program, some pre-1999 graduates saw a lack of articulation between literature, culture, linguistics, and language. Similar concerns were voiced by two students in the post-1999 group, suggesting the need for better contextualization of literature courses. "I'd give greater context to the Lit" (post-1999).

The satisfaction level of the *educational experience* was consistently very high for both groups. Both groups remarked on the challenging and intensive nature of instruction. Alums viewed these challenges positively as a motivating factor to foster their German competence. Both pre- and post 1999 groups commented very positively on the extensive care and personal attention by the faculty:

> "The faculty cared for me on both a professional and personal level and I owe what I am today largely to their efforts" (pre-1999).

> "I felt that the expectations were set high for us as majors, and we were taken seriously as students" (post-1999).

Alums' comments about the *personal and professional benefit of their language abilities* were almost entirely positive. The few concerns in responses addressed a lack of career guidance and the possible need for more job- or subject-specific language learning, but they were minimal in comparison to comments such as:

> "Learning the German language and culture allowed me to meet people who had a great impact on my emotional life" (pre-1999).

> "Despite the fact that my German colleagues spoke very good English, it was often helpful to feel part of the team outside of the formal professional context or to act as a messenger between my American/British co-workers and my German co-workers" (pre-1999).

> "The experience I had at Georgetown only served to strengthen that interest in the language and culture, which has influenced my career choice as well as cultivated friendships and connections abroad" (post-1999).

> "The skills that I learned in learning a new language are applicable in many different types of learning" (post-1999).

> "My ability to communicate proficiently in German has been essential to my professional life" (post-1999).

Comments on the *personal and professional benefits of cultural and literary knowledge* were also nearly all positive, with little evidence that would allow a clear distinction between pre- and post-1999 groups. The few negative comments came from both groups in terms of a perceived lack in the utility of literature courses. However, there were voices that highlighted the attractiveness of delving into (non-utilitarian) literature. Most frequent comments in both groups concerned the personal enrichment, enjoyment, and appreciation of literature, culture, and the arts, garnered from or inspired by the German program. Cross-cultural knowledge and awareness was mentioned frequently.

> "Having any specific knowledge of another culture helps in all aspects of dealing with people—both professionally and personally" (pre-1999).

> "In terms of my personal life, the literature I read at Georgetown has opened up an entire world of new literature for me, and I am quickly developing quite a library of German works" (post-1999).

The *personal and professional benefits of the educational experience* in GUGD were consistently rated very high. The reputation of a Georgetown degree was mentioned frequently. Students in both groups valued the discipline required to complete the challenging courses and the confidence that was inspired by those challenges:

> "Overall, I struggled in every German class I took at Georgetown. This was a humbling experience, but also a wonderful challenge. I went from not knowing ja or nein to writing 20 page papers in German and living in Austria. This is a testament to how well the department and intensive classes work" (pre-1999).

> "The German program was hard. It gave me lots of discipline" (post-1999).

> "Professionally speaking, knowing that I succeeded at Georgetown and the constant reminder of the motivation I received from my professors has made me a much more confident person" (post-1999).

Suggestions for improvement from alums were very similar for the pre- and post-1999 groups. The most frequent suggestion from both groups was to offer more special purpose courses, especially those related to business German. Better internship opportunities coupled with enhanced career guidance were also proposed. Numerous responses commented on the value of study abroad, with specific comments pointing to a need for better coordination of study abroad with on-campus academic life.

## Discussion, recommendations, and uses

The initial impulse for reforming the curriculum in the German Department at Georgetown University was energized by the idea that the department would best be able to assert an intellectual presence in the university, best contribute educational value to all students' undergraduate education, and best fulfill its own educational goals by developing a programmatic profile and curricular structure that would integrate the acquisition of literary-cultural knowledge and language learning throughout the entire undergraduate sequence. The envisioned sequence would need to be conceptualized in a way that could offer, to all students who would avail themselves of this opportunity, the possibility of attaining advanced levels of literary-cultural and linguistic competence. At the time, our own reflections were very much driven by observing and having close contact with our own students, whose interests and ambitions were increasingly becoming more diverse and more pronounced in a globalized environment where they see themselves as actors, even leaders, on the international stage. Since then, as exemplified by the recent MLA report on the future of foreign languages in higher education (MLA, 2007), the profession has arrived at similar conclusions about the need to integrate and articulate curricula carefully, and to face the dual challenge of both affirming the old liberal arts tradition of foreign language education and recognizing the valid, though often competing demands and opportunities, of globalization.

The responses from current students, current majors, and alums of the German Department at Georgetown University provided broad evidence for their strong overall sense of being associated with a very high quality program. More important for this particular evaluation project, current students and post-1999 graduates supported the appropriateness of the department's fundamental decision to eliminate the bifurcation between language and content courses and between service courses for non-majors and majors courses. The information gathered consistently projects essentially no differences between the educational outlook and aspirations among the various student groups at Georgetown University who take courses in the GUGD. The data also suggest that students' own educational goals are very well served by an approach that integrates socially, culturally, and politically relevant topics with a strong focus on developing advanced language abilities, even when those goals range from more traditionally humanities-oriented interests to those with a strong pre-professional slant.

Returning to our central query about the identity of our majors within this integrated program, one might initially interpret such findings as compromising any notion of a separate identity for our majors. However, a closer look at the data reveals a stance on their part that nonetheless has its own forms of distinctiveness. That distinctiveness seems to lie less in separate goals and aspirations; rather, it appears to be located in the *intensity* and *depth* with which they pursue those goals and are willing to engage in assuring that they attain them to the greatest extent possible. Their focus on the study abroad experience and their insistent and complex discussion of the *Text in Context* course are lively testimony to that form of identity construction. From the programmatic standpoint, such findings are reassuring in that they allow the department to continue investing in various ways of improving the existing integrated curriculum that serves all Georgetown students. At the same time, they point to particular ways in which we might seek to create better opportunities to deepen and broaden the major's central educational experiences. Because a broad range of students participate in both study abroad and in the department's upper level courses, most especially *Text in Context*, the program has the special opportunity to make itself intellectually attractive to Georgetown undergraduates in general while further refining its own curricular offerings. In the end, that strategy may be the best way to support a strong and attractive German major program at Georgetown University.

On the basis of these findings, then, the evaluation team recommended the following:

1. Enable all students to participate in a study abroad experience. The value of study abroad was voiced universally by all respondent groups. The department should work to eliminate all practical hindrances (such as high program costs) that would keep students from going abroad.

2. Develop a better understanding of needs and models of pre- and post-study abroad integration into current classes and departmental activities, potentially with a research component. The respondents' desire for specific purpose courses, practical language classes and career guidance could be linked within the study abroad context. The increasing occurrence of spring semester only study abroad opens up the possibility of using the January to March period for diverse formats, particularly an internship program that would address all three issues. A more formalized collaboration with a partner in Germany, such as the *Steuben-Schurz Gesellschaft* (a civic organization in Frankfurt am Main supported by the state of Hesse and the US consul general with the aim of fostering German-US understanding and exchange), may be a way to organize such a program. This would call for careful attention to integrating study abroad with the overall learning experience both before and after study abroad along the lines recommended by Kinginger (2008) in her comprehensive investigation of study abroad. We may also wish to consider the recommendations made in Streitwieser and Leephaibul (2007) for linking undergraduate research opportunities in a variety of disciplinary areas with study abroad in the German context, a direction that would connect well with diverse Georgetown initiatives and its self-identification as a student-centered research university.

3. Review the intensity and educational delivery of the *Text in Context* course while retaining, to the extent possible, its high educational goals. Even as *Text in Context* is central to German majors' educational experience, its intensity and workload may need adjustment. Depending on enrollments, one possible solution would be to dedicate one section of the course offered during the fall semester to freshman students to enable instructors to consider adjustment needs. The extent to which such a 'separatist' solution might at the same time undermine what entering students clearly understood as strong signals for putting shoulders to the wheels is difficult to judge.

4. Assure purposeful use of educational technology as part of the curriculum and review its delivery modes regularly. While the somewhat sparing use of technology was, in part, a conscious decision because much of what is advocated does not directly support the department's dual educational goals of language learning *and* content learning (for example, blogging is not well suited to developing advanced formal writing abilities, and simply consulting web sites does not challenge students to acquire a range of genres and registers), there is a need to evaluate continuously how technology can contribute to effective delivery of the curriculum. Such considerations would include the explicit incorporation of themes pertaining to media and technology and the use of media in currently taught and yet to be developed courses.

In the process of gathering and analyzing the data as described above, the evaluation group already made several presentations to the members of the GUGD on preliminary findings, and some of these recommendations have already been taken up by the department as action items. As of the writing of this report, the following steps have been taken based on the evaluation:

- The GUGD has dedicated an additional named fellowship to support majors in participating in the Trier Summer Program, thereby enabling additional students with insufficient resources to participate.
- The department has established a committee to review and potentially redesign the *Text in Context* course as part of revisiting all level IV course offerings.
- A departmental conversation has been initiated about how to enhance students' study abroad experience and how to integrate it better with on-campus learning.
- The GUGD has intensified the business internship component of its Trier Summer Program through closer collaboration with the *Vereinigung Trierer Unternehmer*, a local organization of entrepreneurs.

The results of the evaluation project will continue to be used by the GUGD faculty and graduate students to shape long-term responses to the suggestions made by students, including those made by graduate student alums. A report on the entire evaluation project will be made available to relevant university administration as an example of GUGD's ongoing evaluation practices and as a basis for programmatic development. Results will also be communicated to current students as a follow-up to their participation in the evaluation project and to increase awareness of the nature and value of the study of German in general and a German studies degree in particular, and they will be posted on the departmental webpage. All alums will be made aware of the availability of the report as a way of recognizing their participation and feedback in the evaluation project.

Above, we have described the measurable results and insights we as a department have gained from the three aspects of this evaluation project. But the significance and effects of such an evaluation project go far beyond measurable results. At the broadest level, this project further grounded insights the department had gradually gained over the now more than ten years since the inception of the curriculum reform project and its subsequent iterative adjustments, namely an awareness of the interconnectedness between educational values, curriculum, pedagogy, and assessment. It also further substantiated the faculty's experience that collaboratively developed assessment and evaluation can become the kind of benevolent 'task-master' any educational project needs in order to achieve the degree of precision in goal setting, in educational praxes, and in evidence-based knowledge that it must attain to hold up to external public scrutiny and to demonstrate internal credibility and substance. Only in this way can we garner both internal and external benevolence and support. Assessment and evaluation can serve in that important function because they require a careful spelling out of the values that are at the heart of responsible educative action; in turn, that level of precision fosters greater understanding of precisely those values and allows them to become a reality in the educative practices of a program. This realization is in direct contradiction to notions that frequently deem such values to be beyond the reach of evaluation and assessment or even in opposition to them. But as we have learned, it is the demand for articulated precision—in the several meanings of that wording—which facilitated the building of consensus in our group of educators, which enabled our knowing what we believed in and valued, and, finally, which helped shape our plans for further educative action. Seen from the outside, the view of educational policy and administration, assessment and evaluation can create and sustain the kind of departmental culture of reflective and actionable conversation about educational goals and praxes that is so much in demand in contemporary education. Seen from the inside, the perspective of the educational practitioners themselves, assessment and evaluation can nurture the most sought-after commodity of university life, intellectual community.

### Acknowledgements

We would like to thank John Norris and the National Foreign Language Resource Center at the University of Hawai'i, the Georgetown University German Department, the Dean of Georgetown College, the Center for New Designs in Learning & Scholarship (CNDLS), and the Associate Provost for Academic Affairs for their financial and material support.

## References

Developing multiple literacies: A curriculum renewal project of the German Department at Georgetown University, 1997–2000. (2000). Electronic document, available at http://www1.georgetown.edu/departments/german/programs/undergraduate/curriculum/

Byrnes, H. (2001). Reconsidering graduate students' education as teachers: It takes a department! *Modern Language Journal, 85*, 512–530.

Byrnes, H. (2002). The role of task and task-based assessment in a content-oriented collegiate FL curriculum. *Language Testing, 19*, 419–437.

Byrnes, H. (2009). Emergent L2 German writing ability in a curricular context: A longitudinal study of grammatical metaphor. *Linguistics and Education, 20*, 50–66.

Byrnes, H., Maxim, H. H., Norris, J. M., & Ryshina-Pankova, M. (2005). Revisiting writing development: A curriculum-based study of syntactic complexity. Symposium presented at the 14th World Congress of Applied Linguistics (AILA). Madison, WI.

Byrnes, H., Maxim, H. H., & Norris, J. M. (forthcoming). Realizing advanced L2 writing development in collegiate FL education: Curricular design, pedagogy, and assessment. *Modern Language Journal, 94* (Monograph Issue).

Byrnes, H., & Sinicrope, C. (in preparation). Emergent life as a noun in L2 writing development: A curriculum-based longitudinal study.

Crane, C. (2008). *Evaluative choice in advanced L2 writing of German: A genre perspective.* Unpublished doctoral dissertation, Georgetown University, Washington, DC.

Kinginger, C. (2008). *Language learning in study abroad: Case studies of Americans in France. Modern Language Journal, 93.* (Monograph Issue).

MLA Ad Hoc Committee on Foreign Languages. (2007). Foreign languages and higher education: New structures for a changed world. *Profession 2007,* 234–245.

Norris, J. M. (2006). The why (and how) of assessing student learning outcomes in college foreign language programs. *Modern Language Journal, 90,* 576–583.

Norris, J. M. (2008). *Validity evaluation in foreign language assessment.* Frankfurt/Main: Peter Lang.

Norris, J. M., & Pfeiffer, P. C. (2003). Exploring the use and usefulness of ACTFL oral proficiency ratings and standards in college foreign language departments. *Foreign Language Annals, 36,* 572–581.

Ryshina-Pankova, M. (2006). Creating textual worlds in advanced learner writing: The role of complex theme. In H. Byrnes (Ed.), *Advanced language learning: The contribution of Halliday and Vygotsky* (pp. 164–183). London: Continuum.

Streitwieser, B., & Leephaibul, R. (2007). Enhancing the study abroad experience through independent research in Germany. *Die Unterrichtspraxis, 40,* 164–170.

## Appendix A

Questionnaire administered to all Georgetown undergraduate students enrolled in German classes, spring 2007

The Georgetown University German department is seeking information on the effectiveness of its undergraduate program. The information you provide on this questionnaire will help us better understand the effectiveness of the curriculum and identify possible areas that might be enhanced for the benefit of current and future students in the program.

The questionnaire has five components:

It begins with a brief set of questions that elicit information about your course of study and your background in German.

The next three sections ask you to indicate the degree to which you agree with statements in three areas of the program:

- your experience with how the German program was delivered;
- your learning outcomes within the program
- your experience as a learner and user of German.

At the end of each of the four sections, you will have a chance to clarify any of your answers or to add other comments on that particular subtopic. To help you with that you will be able to glance back at the questions in each section.

The final section consists of three open-ended questions about the program. We invite you to provide us with as much information as you find useful so that we might be able to get a full picture of your experience in the program.

We thank you for participating in this survey about the German department's undergraduate curriculum.

### Background information

a) How old are you?
b) What is your expected year of graduation?
c) What is/are your major(s) at GU?
d) What is/are your minor(s) at GU?
e) What was your first German course taken at GU?
f) How many German courses have you taken at GU, including courses taken in Trier and during this semester?
g) How many years of high school German did you have?
h) What is your native language?
i) Which other language(s) do you know? Indicate language and estimated level of ability near-native, very high, high, intermediate, low [pull-down menu]
j) List the three most significant experiences you have had in the German-speaking world. Indicate (1) age when there; (2) length of stay (in weeks); and (3) nature of experience (e.g., 16–17 years old; 40 weeks; high school year in Germany)

**Please tell us how you have experienced the German program at Georgetown.**

1. When I first entered the program, I was placed into a course appropriate for my ability.
   ☐ strongly disagree ☐ disagree ☐ agree ☐ strongly agree ☐ n/a

2. In terms of what was expected of me, I have experienced a smooth transition from one course to the next.
   ☐ strongly disagree ☐ disagree ☐ agree ☐ strongly agree ☐ n/a

3. The topics of my courses have been interesting.
   ☐ strongly disagree ☐ disagree ☐ agree ☐ strongly agree ☐ n/a

4. The topics of my courses fit well with their language-learning goals.
   ☐ strongly disagree ☐ disagree ☐ agree ☐ strongly agree ☐ n/a

5. The topics of my courses were presented through a good variety of media.
   ☐ strongly disagree ☐ disagree ☐ agree ☐ strongly agree ☐ n/a

6. The *use* of technologies (e.g., audiovisual materials, computer-, and web-based activities, Blackboard) enhanced my abilities in the following areas:
   speaking, writing, reading, listening, cultural awareness [pull-down menus]
   ☐ strongly disagree ☐ disagree ☐ agree ☐ strongly agree ☐ n/a

7. The *amount* of technology-based instruction was appropriate for improving my German in...
   speaking, writing, reading, listening, cultural awareness [pull-down menus]
   ☐ strongly disagree ☐ disagree ☐ agree ☐ strongly agree ☐ n/a

8. Changing from a textbook to a course packet, from level I to level II, was not a problem for me.
   ☐ strongly disagree ☐ disagree ☐ agree ☐ strongly agree ☐ n/a

9. Study abroad was well-integrated into my studies.
   ☐ strongly disagree ☐ disagree ☐ agree ☐ strongly agree ☐ n/a

10. The German department offers an appropriate number of extra-curricular activities.
    ☐ strongly disagree ☐ disagree ☐ agree ☐ strongly agree ☐ n/a

11. My German teachers are readily available for consultation.
    ☐ strongly disagree ☐ disagree ☐ agree ☐ strongly agree ☐ n/a

Please feel free to clarify any of your previous responses and/or add further comments about how the German program is delivered.

**Please assess your learning outcomes**

12. The department's approach to teaching links language and content. I feel that this approach has enhanced...
    my ability to speak, my ability to read, my ability to write, my aural comprehension [pull-down menus]
    ☐ strongly disagree ☐ disagree ☐ agree ☐ strongly agree ☐ n/a

13. The department has a strong focus on writing. I feel that this focus has enhanced...
    my ability to speak, my ability to read, my ability to write, my aural comprehension [pull-down menus]
    ☐ strongly disagree ☐ disagree ☐ agree ☐ strongly agree ☐ n/a

14. My courses prepared me for direct matriculation at a German-speaking university.
    ☐ strongly disagree ☐ disagree ☐ agree ☐ strongly agree ☐ n/a

15. My learning of German was enhanced because grammar *and* vocabulary were integrated into the topics of each course.
    ☐ strongly disagree  ☐ disagree  ☐ agree  ☐ strongly agree  ☐ n/a

16. I feel well informed about the German-speaking world because of the German courses I have taken at Georgetown.
    ☐ strongly disagree  ☐ disagree  ☐ agree  ☐ strongly agree  ☐ n/a

17. Courses in the German department have enabled me to make connections to my other studies.
    ☐ strongly disagree  ☐ disagree  ☐ agree  ☐ strongly agree  ☐ n/a

Please feel free to clarify any of your previous responses and/or add further comments about the outcomes of your learning of German at Georgetown.

**Please reflect on your experience as a learner and user of several languages**

18. The courses I have taken make it clear that the German program aims to develop advanced levels of ability in German for formal and professional use.
    ☐ strongly disagree  ☐ disagree  ☐ agree  ☐ strongly agree  ☐ n/a

19. Developing advanced levels of ability in German for formal and professional use matches my goals as a language learner.
    ☐ strongly disagree  ☐ disagree  ☐ agree  ☐ strongly agree  ☐ n/a

20. Learning German at Georgetown has made me appreciate how choices in language affect what meaning is conveyed.
    ☐ strongly disagree  ☐ disagree  ☐ agree  ☐ strongly agree  ☐ n/a

21. Learning German at Georgetown has made me aware of my strengths and weaknesses as a user of German.
    ☐ strongly disagree  ☐ disagree  ☐ agree  ☐ strongly agree  ☐ n/a

22. Learning German at Georgetown has taught me how to improve my German on my own.
    ☐ strongly disagree  ☐ disagree  ☐ agree  ☐ strongly agree  ☐ n/a

Please feel free to clarify any of your previous responses and/or add further comments about your experience as a learner in the Georgetown German program.

**Open questions**

23. The German department's curriculum is entitled "Developing Multiple Literacies." What does that mean to you?
    _____
    _____

24. The German department's curriculum is genre- and task-based. Please comment on what this means to you and how you have experienced this approach to learning German.
    _____
    _____

25. How have your language studies in the German department differed from other language learning experiences that you have had?
    _____
    _____

26. Please describe your most memorable experience inside *or* outside of class that is related to the study of German at Georgetown.
    _____
    _____

## Appendix B: Guiding questions for the focus group meetings with German majors

What led you to major in German at Georgetown University?

What would you say to a prospective student regarding majoring in German at GU? Potential issues to raise/explore:

- being a double major
- language development
- content and language acquisition
- being in an integrated curriculum
- study abroad— preparation for, experience during, integration after
- shared experiences with other majors

Please tell us about a significant experience connected with majoring in German at GU.

What might we do to enhance the experience of majors?

Anything else that you would like add?

## Appendix C: Alumni questionnaire

As a component of its regular program review, the German department is contacting all its alums to respond to a few questions. This will help us evaluate aspects of our program and guide us as we work to improve the education we offer.

The following questionnaire has two sections. The first asks for some background information that will help us to contextualize your responses. The second section elicits your perspectives on the education you received in the German department.

The questionnaire is completely anonymous. It should not take more than about ten to fifteen minutes of your time to complete. In particular, we want to encourage you to respond to the open-ended questions.

There are two ways to complete the survey. You can *complete this survey on-line* by going to the German department's website at http://www1.georgetown.edu/departments/german/ and click on the button that indicates "Questionnaire for Alums."

Alternatively, you can *complete the paper form enclosed in this letter* and send it back to us in the enclosed postage paid envelope. The paper surveys will be forwarded, unopened, to our partner in this evaluation project at the National Foreign Language Resource Center at the University of Hawai'i who will tabulate the findings and communicate them to us anonymously.

We ask that you complete the questionnaire within *two weeks* of receipt of this letter and that you complete the questionnaire only once— either on-line or as hard copy.

Thank you very much for your help.

Viele Grüße vom Hill Top.

Ihre

Friederike Eigler

Professor of German and Chair

## Background Information

1. What is your gender?    male    female    (circle one)
2. Which degree programs did you complete in the German department?
   a) undergraduate degree
   b) Master's degree
   c) Ph.D. degree
3. In what year(s) did you graduate from the above program(s)?
4. What career(s) have you pursued since graduating from Georgetown? Include additional studies as well as employment.

## Evaluation of your learning experience in the German department at Georgetown University

5. Looking back on your learning experiences in the Georgetown German Program, how satisfied are you with…(circle one each)

   a) the language abilities you developed in the program?

   | 1 | 2 | 3 | 4 |
   |---|---|---|---|
   | not satisfied | somewhat satisfied | satisfied | very satisfied |

   Please comment/clarify. _____
   _____

   b) …the cultural and literary knowledge and appreciation you developed?

   | 1 | 2 | 3 | 4 |
   |---|---|---|---|
   | not satisfied | somewhat satisfied | satisfied | very satisfied |

   Please comment/clarify. _____
   _____

   c) …the overall educational experience in the department's program?

   | 1 | 2 | 3 | 4 |
   |---|---|---|---|
   | not satisfied | somewhat satisfied | satisfied | very satisfied |

   Please comment/clarify. _____
   _____

6. To what extent have the following three areas of learning in the German department benefitted you in your professional and personal life? (circle one each)

   a) language abilities

   professional life

   | 1 | 2 | 3 | 4 |
   |---|---|---|---|
   | not benefited at all | benefited somewhat | benefited | benefited very much |

   personal life

   | 1 | 2 | 3 | 4 |
   |---|---|---|---|
   | not benefited at all | benefited somewhat | benefited | benefited very much |

   Please comment/clarify. _____
   _____

   b) cultural and literary knowledge and appreciation

professional life

| 1 | 2 | 3 | 4 |
|---|---|---|---|
| not benefited at all | benefited somewhat | benefited | benefited very much |

personal life

| 1 | 2 | 3 | 4 |
|---|---|---|---|
| not benefited at all | benefited somewhat | benefited | benefited very much |

Please comment/clarify. _____

_____

c) overall educational experience in the department's program

professional life

| 1 | 2 | 3 | 4 |
|---|---|---|---|
| not benefited at all | benefited somewhat | benefited | benefited very much |

personal life

| 1 | 2 | 3 | 4 |
|---|---|---|---|
| not benefited at all | benefited somewhat | benefited | benefited very much |

Please comment/clarify. _____

_____

7. Given what you now know about your personal and professional life, please suggest other educational experiences that would have been beneficial to your education in the German department.

_____
_____
_____
_____
_____
_____

# College Foreign Language Program Evaluation: Current Practice, Future Directions

John McE. Davis
*University of Hawai'i at Mānoa*

Castle Sinicrope
*Berkeley Policy Associates, California*

Yukiko Watanabe
*University of Hawai'i at Mānoa*

*This chapter draws on lessons learned from evaluation practices observed in the seven case studies collected in this volume and suggests ways to respond to evaluation demands unique in college foreign language (FL) programs. As positive practice, we highlight three main features of useful evaluations (i.e., those that lead to use of information for understanding and improving programs): (a) ownership of evaluation among local educators who adopt a proactive approach; (b) cyclical and sustained inquiry, through careful prioritization processes and adaptation of evaluation design to contextual constraints; and (c) development of organizational capacity and a culture of evaluation. To guide future directions toward more useful evaluations in FL education, we then target practical strategies for balancing internal and external evaluation impetuses, the adoption of a use-driven approach to student learning outcomes assessment, and consider ways to build professional identity and expertise as evaluators in college FL education communities and programs.*

In this final chapter we reflect on the seven program evaluation projects from the volume, highlight important aspects of how each was undertaken, and comment on some implications for doing evaluation work in contemporary and future tertiary FL education. Our aim is twofold. First, as one purpose of this volume is heuristic—to show examples of useful FL program evaluation practice for those looking to undertake similar projects elsewhere—we highlight key project elements that suggest positive and productive ways of undertaking FL evaluation within what might generally be termed a utilization-focused framework. Projects on the whole achieved successful results, and we analyze what we think accounts for the effectiveness of FL evaluation work as represented here. Second, after noting the positive directions in which FL program evaluation has developed, we further discuss where we think FL evaluation probably needs to go, noting challenges for FL program evaluation to contribute maximally to understanding and improving FL education. In response to these challenges, we propose an agenda for future FL program evaluation practice and strategies that might effectively push that agenda ahead.

We begin by pointing out that projects in this volume are arguably unique within contemporary FL program evaluation. Though the seven cases emerged from different impetuses and aimed to accomplish different things, they are similar in that each was to one degree or another influenced by a utilization-focused evaluation approach (Patton 1997, 2008). Utilization-focused evaluation begins with the premise that validity of evaluation be judged by "utility and actual use" and thus works to make evaluation outcomes and processes as beneficial and effectively usable for intended users as possible (Patton, 2005, p. 429). All of the FL evaluators in these cases were exposed to this evaluation paradigm, either via participation in the 2007 National Foreign Language Resource Center Summer Institute or through consultation with staff from the Foreign Language Program Evaluation Project (FLPEP). Though dealing with many of the same accountability-related external pressures prevalent throughout contemporary higher education, projects nevertheless managed to display certain use-focused characteristics that arguably distinguish them from other modes of language program evaluation. For example, evaluation was initiated by program insiders and driven by local concerns; evaluation activities were undertaken by program-internal evaluation teams; projects involved collaboration with diverse stakeholders; use of project findings was determined by program insiders and put toward program-local as well as external purposes; and, in most cases, evaluation seemed to develop into an ongoing cyclical activity, becoming an integral part of program functioning. As such, these projects represent an important iteration within the microcosm of FL education, reflective of an evolution that has been occurring gradually in the broader field of contemporary language program evaluation, and they can be added to the ranks of what Norris (2009) calls a "small cadre" of language programs doing evaluation that "serve[s] internal as well as external interests, can inform formative as well as summative purposes, can empower language teachers and learners as well as ensure adherence to standards or outcomes...and can transform the value as well as the effectiveness of language education in society" (p. 469).[1]

In order to understand the extent of this contribution, our task here is to highlight aspects of projects that are reflective of this use-focused evolution in contemporary FL evaluation work, and, by so doing, add to an important re-specification of what we and others think evaluation should fundamentally mean within tertiary FL education contexts (Byrnes, 2008; Norris, 2006c, 2008, 2009). Such a reconceptualization follows on from Norris's descriptions of evaluation above; that is, conceiving of evaluation as a locally initiated, sustained, and cyclical mode of program inquiry that focuses on usefulness of evaluation findings, energetically builds evaluation capacity, and integrates evaluation practice and thinking into the functioning of FL programs. The first half of our chapter thus highlights aspects of projects that exemplify this particular type of FL evaluation paradigm, focusing in particular on how local stakeholders took ownership of evaluation, learned from evaluation processes, and worked toward maintaining continued cycles of evaluation and program inquiry.

---

1  For recent examples of utilization-focused evaluation in the broad domain of language education, see the 2009 special issue of *Language Teaching Research* (volume 13, 1) edited by John Norris.

However, we further envision a mode of evaluation that simultaneously and strategically equips FL evaluators to meet not only internal needs but also the contemporary demands of educational accountability. On this point, it is perhaps less clear how projects in this volume are addressing the various and at times conflicting impetuses of evaluation that can issue from internal and external demands. We therefore comment on how evaluators might effectively balance such demands, and we single out the important role of student learning outcomes assessment within that effort. Furthermore, these challenges arguably derive from the fact that only recently has attention been paid to ideas like utilization-focused (or any kind of) evaluation within FL education. As such, FL educators will need to know more about how best to evaluate their programs, given the current exigencies of delivering FL education, and we suggest that advances in evaluation knowledge and practice could most productively come from a transformed conception of FL professionalism itself, one that involves a commitment to developing evaluation expertise and contributing thereby to a heightened discourse of FL educational research and practice.

## Positive evaluation practices

We start by discussing particular aspects of projects that most strongly account for the direct usefulness of findings, efficacy of actions, and likely continuance of evaluation practice in the future. Positive practices included program insiders (a) taking ownership of evaluation in various ways, (b) conceiving of and implementing evaluation as a long term, cyclical enterprise, and (c) productively using the evaluation process itself to achieve various aims. These achievements, we believe, represent a timely showcase of intentionally useful evaluation practice and bode well for the future of FL program evaluation and FL education in general.

### Ownership: Internally motivated evaluation and self-determined uses

Fundamentally, it is worth emphasizing that the completed evaluation projects in this volume represent successful evaluations in that findings were actually used by people to do something constructive. Such successes are no accident. Certainly, many of the projects came about in concert with the influence of utilization-focused evaluation ideas, as articulated above. However, to ensure that projects lead to desired actions, a utilization-focused approach recommends doing evaluation in a specific way. A number of elements are needed, but perhaps the key component is the active engagement of locally invested parties (i.e., intended users and stakeholders) in all facets of evaluation activities (Norris, 2006c, 2009). When program-related individuals participate in evaluation together, investment in the evaluation increases, understanding about the program increases, and so too does the probability of findings being put to desired ends (Norris, 2009; Patton, 2008). Therefore, we argue that an optimal approach to conducting evaluation is characterized by local "ownership" of the undertaking; that is, evaluation done by and for people within programs (Byrnes, 2008). In the projects described herein, we see ownership prevalent in the ways local groups of stakeholders are (a) initiating evaluation, (b) determining for themselves how findings are to be used, and (c) involving a variety of stakeholders in evaluation activities.

First, encouraging in these cases is how evaluation was motivated by individuals within programs rather than mandated by outside forces, even when the projects themselves may have responded to such forces in effective ways. Many of the projects commendably buck the trend of simply reacting to accountability and accreditation-type impetuses, engaging instead in internally-motivated evaluation that was conceived, planned, and implemented by FL faculty in accordance with specific identified needs and empirical questions. The a-typicality of projects coming about in such a way is worth emphasizing. In each instance, evaluation was proactively undertaken by autonomous actors who shaped projects in the interests of their programs, and as such, worked within an evaluation paradigm that led to findings really being used in specific and intended ways.

Further, many cases show how ownership of evaluation starts with those who have the most to gain (and lose) initiating evaluation on their own terms, but doing so in ways that intentionally address program-relevant purposes. Perhaps the most disempowering aspect of educational accountability or accreditation-type evaluation impetuses is that the use of project outcomes and findings, never mind "measures" that are employed, are often controlled by entities beyond a department or program. Projects in this volume were thus notable in how the uses of findings were determined by program-internal personnel, explicitly articulated to meet a range of specific needs, and designed methodologically to do so.

Ownership of use is further indicated by the diverse applications of evaluation findings beyond the immediate goals of program improvement and development. Within programs, for example, evaluators used (or planned to use) evaluation findings to have positive effects on stakeholders involved in evaluation activities or associated with their programs. Evaluation processes were used to raise awareness (e.g., Georgetown), enhance understanding of program elements by students, teachers, and administrators (e.g., Evansville, Georgetown, New Mexico, Linfield), increase investment in programs by involving people in evaluation activities (e.g., Georgetown, Linfield), and promote engagement and consensus among various groups of local stakeholders such as colleagues, students, and faculty in other departments (e.g., Duke, Evansville, Georgetown, Johns Hopkins). Other important benefits included engendering a "culture" of evaluation (e.g., California State University, Monterey Bay [CSUMB], New Mexico), developing individual evaluation capacity (e.g., New Mexico), and sustaining current and future evaluation practice (e.g., CSUMB, Georgetown, New Mexico). Beyond internal program concerns, faculty used evidence of successful program practice (e.g., developing learning outcomes assessment, implementing program improvements, the process of evaluation itself, etc.) for strategic promotion of programs, showcasing the good work of educators and students, and thereby demonstrating the value of programs and the people within them (e.g., Duke, Evansville, Linfield, New Mexico). Importantly, findings also were used to promote FL program evaluation practice itself at the national level, facilitate FL program evaluation research, and demonstrate the value of FL education generally (e.g., Duke). In each instance, self-determined uses crucially reflected the common goals and shared vision of a department or program, and from the outset were more likely to be realized since the individuals who devised them had a vested interest in applying relevant evaluation findings toward a wide array of purposes that directly impacted their professional lives.

Paramount among the various features of ownership, then, is local-stakeholder participation. Successful application of evaluation findings derives from the involvement of a diversity of stakeholders throughout evaluation processes; evaluators who planned and implemented projects with stakeholder input set the stage for use since they responded to democratically agreed upon and realized sets of program priorities. Participation of relevant FL program stakeholders in all aspects of evaluation, then, might be understood as a powerful predictor of the degree to which findings and processes will actually be used (Norris, 2006c). Indeed, authors of these cases describe how their projects were notable for their unprecedented participation and collaboration, involving adjunct faculty, junior tenure-track faculty, tenured faculty, contract staff, FL language colleagues from other institutions, students, prospective students and their parents, assessment professionals, and employers. The University of Evansville evaluators capture well just how increased self-determination, investment, and a sense of shared destiny result when evaluation involves program-local actors: "the entire group experienced an enhanced *can-do* attitude, a positive feeling of team work, a sense of collective ownership of the project, and a better understanding of our identity and goals as a department" (this volume).

## Evaluation as an on-going and cyclical activity

Although evaluation can be conceptualized as on-going and cyclical in many ways, we focus here on three aspects of the evaluation projects in this volume that we believe provide particularly important lessons for the college FL education audience: (a) evaluators actively prioritizing and reprioritizing their focus with specific uses in mind; (b) evaluators considering and reconsidering feasibility of implementation at different points; and (c) evaluators using findings to make programmatic decisions and take action, often leading to new cycles of evaluation activity. An overarching point to be made here is that evaluation work that takes these three aspects into consideration greatly increases the likelihood of uncovering meaningful findings and leading to evaluation use. In different ways, the evaluation cases in this volume show how evaluators can prioritize and reprioritize the focus of their work based on the intended uses of the evaluation and how these priorities can evolve over time. The evaluators in these cases refocused their work in response to changes and growth within their programs, evolving local contexts surrounding their programs, and developments in their own evaluation projects that led them to prioritize different evaluation methods and approaches.

The Georgetown University German Department project shows how keeping evaluation use in mind can help programs prioritize the focus of their evaluations at different points. At Georgetown, previous cycles of evaluation work had examined student learning and achievement of outcomes but had not drawn on formal feedback from the learners' perspectives. For this reason, the evaluation cycle reported in this volume built on the previous evaluation cycles and focused on eliciting feedback from current students and alumni.

Considering and reconsidering priorities with use in mind, however, is not limited to the scope of program changes or the participants in programs, but can also include evaluation approaches and methods. Within their planned multi-year project, the Duke evaluation team prioritized piloting and implementing of only external direct measures in the initial stages, delaying the development of internal measures until later stages. By resisting the "temptation to do everything at once" and planning for future stages, the Duke evaluators laid the groundwork for a cyclical process of evaluation:

> It is important to emphasize that effective evaluation is a cyclical process that involves continual phases of prioritization, data collection, and use, which in turn engender new prioritization with new foci...We conceived the project from the outset as a multi-year, ongoing process to be accomplished in stages. (this volume)

A final note on prioritizing and reprioritizing evaluation is worth emphasizing: changing priorities is not always a matter of choice or design for program evaluators, as many programs are constrained by their contexts, politics, and environments. When a senior administrator at CSUMB rejected the request for a degree name change, the CSUMB evaluation team responded by shifting their focus to requesting permission to plan a new, stand-alone pilot program. This shift in focus allowed the evaluators at CSUMB to move forward and use their evaluation findings, despite the unexpected constraints of the institutional landscape. At Johns Hopkins University, when the academic council review committee mandated a FL teacher training course, the evaluation shifted from exploring whether a teacher training course should be developed to investigating what kind of teacher training course would be most useful. As in both of these cases, in order for FL evaluators to generate useful findings and take action on that basis, they must be responsive to the realities of program contexts and take new priorities into account as situations unfold.

The second characteristic, the importance of maintaining feasibility throughout the evaluation process, is linked with prioritization. *The Program Evaluation Standards* (Joint Committee on Standards for Educational Evaluation, 1994) highlight the importance of feasibility and provide program evaluators guiding standards for ensuring evaluations are "realistic, prudent, diplomatic, and frugal" (p. 63). To be feasible, evaluation work must take into account (a) practical procedures, (b) political viability, and (c) cost effectiveness. Within FL departments, often, a lack of prioritization leads to unfeasible evaluations, in which faculty are overwhelmed with creating instruments that measure everything possible, collecting, analyzing, and interpreting data, and taking action on the basis of findings, all generally within an annually repeated cycle that is required by the university administration for accreditation purposes.

Turning again to the evaluation projects, as the Duke evaluator points out, evaluation goals and expectations must be measured against available financial, institutional, and human resources. In Duke's evaluation, the high cost of maintaining a cadre of trained SOPI raters challenged the evaluators to invest in mapping their own internal instruments to external instruments, such as the SOPI, and thereby reduce and replace costly assessments with course-embedded assessments at later stages. Despite their explicit prioritization of particular evaluation methods and uses and their planning for future evaluation work, however, the Duke evaluators found themselves overextended mid-way through the project and admitted that their timeline was "overly ambitious" (this volume). Such realizations mid-way through evaluation projects are not uncommon, and they offer key moments for evaluation teams to re-examine the feasibility of their work and re-prioritize their evaluation focus and intended uses.

The third interrelated characteristic of cyclical and on-going evaluation is the use of evaluation findings to make program-level decisions and changes, which, in turn, creates the opportunity for continued evaluation. Across the different cases, evaluation use led to program-level decision-making and action, not only at different stages of the evaluation process, but also at different developmental stages of the programs themselves. Program action, in turn, can lead to new program stages and open doors to new cycles of evaluation. This kind of organic, developmental evaluation is itself a growing emphasis within the field (Patton, 2008) and offers a practical alternative to the traditional outcomes- or effectiveness-oriented approaches, both for programs that are in the process of defining, creating, and shaping themselves (e.g., CSUMB, New Mexico, and Johns Hopkins) and for well-established programs (e.g., Georgetown). Patton (2008) describes how program change is a key component of developmental evaluation:

> Developmental evaluation supports program and organizational development to guide adaptation to emergent and dynamic realities from a complex systems perspective. Developmental evaluation differs from typical program improvement evaluation (making a program better) in that it involves changing the program model itself as part of innovation and response to changed conditions and understandings. (p. 278)

At Evansville, then, the results of an initial strength and weakness analysis led to the decision to develop a student learning outcomes (SLOs) assessment framework, which in turn led to mapping the curriculum to the SLOs and piloting a portfolio assessment.

Findings from the piloted assessment revealed adjustments and changes needed for subsequent data collection on the achievement of SLOs, such as making the portfolio a stand alone assessment rather than a course-embedded one. These changes, in turn, will lead to new evaluation cycles. Similarly, the New Mexico case features the second evaluation cycle of an on-going project. The first cycle consisted of learner needs analysis that resulted in (a) changing student recruitment and placement strategies and (b) convincing administrators to accept the creation of new, experimental Portuguese courses for Spanish and non-Spanish speaking students. Based on the results from the first evaluation cycle, the second evaluation cycle focused on accuracy of learner placement, effectiveness of program advertisement, and effectiveness of fulfilling students' expectations and learning needs. Looking forward, a third cycle of evaluation might examine experimental graduate-level Portuguese courses, the training of teachers, or the use of specialized materials, if the program chooses to develop and implement these steps.

Finally, both Georgetown and CSUMB conclude their chapters by taking or proposing action on the basis of their findings, and anticipating new cycles of evaluation that will emerge as their programs develop. If the proposal for the pilot program is accepted at CSUMB, the evaluation team will begin a new cycle of developmental evaluation to examine the program's effectiveness in attracting new students. At Georgetown, program actions included (a) dedicating additional support for study abroad and increasing collaboration with local internship providers, and (b) reconsidering the intensiveness and educational delivery of their *Text in Context* course, such as creating a separate advanced-level course for entering freshmen. On the basis of these actions, future evaluation cycles at Georgetown might examine the effect of such programmatic changes on students' study abroad and overall experiences within the German department.

What these diverse case studies demonstrate, then, is that putting evaluation findings to use can lead to programmatic decisions and new cycles of evaluation and change. If we view these three interrelated characteristics together, the case studies reveal the important conceptualization of evaluation as an on-going and cyclical process, with prioritization and feasibility considerations embedded in every stage, including focusing the evaluation, selecting methods, acting on findings, and beginning new cycles of evaluation. This approach, we believe, stands a much better chance (compared with static summative evaluations) of helping FL educators deal with the realities of ever-changing students, institutions, and social/political values that persistently pressure language educators to better understand themselves and adapt their programs in order to survive, if not thrive.

## Building evaluation culture and capacity through evaluation processes

As highlighted above, evaluators not only used evaluation findings to make desired program changes (known in evaluation literature as "findings use"); they also used the *process* of evaluation itself to achieve various transformative aims, known as "process use." Patton (2008) defines process use as "individual changes in thinking, attitudes, and behavior, and program or organizational changes in procedures and culture that occur among those involved in evaluation as a result of the learning that occurs during the evaluation process" (p. 155). Recall that some evaluators in the cases in this volume were intentionally using the evaluation to achieve precisely these kinds of aims, including building evaluation culture (e.g., CSUMB) and facilitating program understanding and investment (e.g., Georgetown). Even when such goals were not explicitly part of project planning, many evaluators showed that simply engaging in evaluation engendered valuable transformations in communication, thinking, awareness, knowledge, and professional relationships. In this section we discuss a number of important instances of process use, in which by doing evaluation stakeholders: (a) increased their awareness of the value of evaluation generally; (b) made important gains in evaluation skills and knowledge; (c) increased capability for and valuing of "evaluative thinking"; and (d) increased communication, enlightenment, and program understanding between various stakeholders. We further argue that these instances of process use enabled evaluators to undertake useful organizational changes and develop evaluation capacity in important ways.

First, participating in evaluation processes can make stakeholders aware of the importance of evaluation in engendering program change, which can lead to concrete steps toward increasing evaluation capacity. Such realizations can bring about important changes in program procedures. For example, at Johns Hopkins, the project caused the department to obtain institutional funding for a post-doctoral fellowship position, the purpose of which was to assist in developing a teacher training program, but also to "conduct evaluation activities to assess participants' learning and use this data to improve future training" (A. Zannirato, personal communication, January 22, 2009). Here the evaluation process resulted in faculty and administrators seeing the need to hire personnel with evaluation expertise, and was an important step toward developing and sustaining evaluation capacity.

Another effective use of evaluation processes was the way in which FL evaluators increased their evaluation competency by simply doing evaluation. Indeed, evidence from participatory evaluation research suggests that by engaging in evaluation participants gain evaluation knowledge and skills (Cousins & Earl, 1995; Mackay, Wellesley & Bazergan, 1995), thereby increasing the likelihood of sustaining future evaluation efforts. In a number of projects, educators in managerial positions (e.g., chairs, deans, etc.) proactively initiated or supported program evaluation in a way that resulted in local stakeholders being involved in and learning from evaluation activities. Internal evaluation committees, for example, intentionally involved a range of stakeholders in evaluation processes, including teaching staff and graduate students (e.g., Georgetown and New Mexico), by which teachers and graduate students were acculturated into evaluation practice.

Further, we see evidence in some case studies for evaluators developing and recognizing the value of "evaluative thinking" as a result of being involved in evaluation processes. Evaluative thinking is a logical mode of thought informed by systematic, rational, and purposeful information gathering. The application of evaluative thinking results in organizational decision-making being driven by reasoned choices based on empirical evidence. CSUMB's desire to avoid making program decisions based on "personal anecdotes, assumptions, politics, and individual preferences" (this volume) led them to welcome an evaluation process that valued evidence-based decision making. At Duke University, where evaluators had a history of proactive evidence-based self-improvement, external intervention by FLPEP staff still enhanced evaluative thinking in productive ways. FLPEP staff persistently asked Duke evaluators to clarify the rationale for each step in their evaluation process. In turn, evaluators became more conscientious in designing and implementing aspects of their evaluation project. Process use, then, can result in important conceptual transformations about how to bring about program change, whether a program is new to evaluation, in which evaluative thinking creates an evidence-based decision making culture (e.g., CSUMB), or experienced in evaluation, in which evaluative thinking strengthens an already reflexive evaluative practice (e.g., Duke).

Finally, evaluators also noted how close collaboration and communication within and between programs resulted in stakeholder enlightenment and deepened program understanding. At Duke University, for example, evaluation provided an opportunity for departments to communicate with one another about common assessment challenges, thereby increasing cooperation in seeking solutions. Further, evaluation projects triggered communication flow not only laterally but also vertically between institutional administration and department faculty. At CSUMB, the department chair made an effort to continually communicate with the college dean to "make informed decisions about the program change [request]" (this volume). Finally, sharing and communicating understandings about a program and its evaluation projects is likely to generate a common language and a shared conceptual framework to tackle future program issues. At Evansville, faculty collaborated across different language tracks to create a common set of student learning outcomes for majors, resulting in deeper understanding about faculty perceptions, curricular coherence, and the value of FL education.

By using evaluation processes—intentionally or otherwise—language programs have the potential to realize a wide range of organizational improvements. From these case studies, we see process use resulting in awareness of the importance of evaluation in bringing about program change; we see increased evaluation knowledge and skills leading to collective appreciation of evidence-based program change; and we see increased collaboration, communication, and deepened program knowledge. Process use, then, brings an added value to FL programs in that it enables program change beyond the immediate focus of explicit evaluation goals.

## Directions for future evaluation practice

Having highlighted what we view as key positive evaluation practices in the case studies, we turn now to three challenges that we believe must come to the fore and be addressed if evaluation is to achieve a sustained contributory role in FL education, particularly at the college level. These three challenges are: (a) balancing internal and external impetuses, (b) balancing local and global assessments, and (c) cultivating evaluation on a professional level. In response to these challenges, and to indicate likely future directions, we suggest concrete steps, tips, and strategies for FL educators who aspire to make evaluations that are useful and used a core component of FL educational practice.

### Balancing internal and external impetuses

We are reminded by the FLPEP needs analysis data from chapter one that FL program evaluation is often the result of top-down directives such as accreditation mandates, institutional program review, or dictates from college-level or university upper administration. Though many projects in this volume were, again, internally motivated and inwardly focused, some were explicitly the result of external impetuses (e.g., Duke), or they used (or planned to use) evaluation to meet external, mainly accreditation-related demands (e.g., Linfield). The contemporary reality of FL evaluation, then, often involves responding to such demands, and in an environment where the pressures of accountability and shrinking budgets are ever present, it is important to consider how FL departments and programs might undertake evaluation that negotiates potentially conflicting impetuses of accountability requirements and program-internal concerns. In this section we speculate about how FL evaluators faced with a variety of impetuses and needs might most effectively undertake evaluation, arguing that proactive, local, ongoing evaluation practice will serve FL educators best when attempting to balance program-internal and -external demands.

Tertiary FL educators are no doubt aware of how accountability-mandated evaluation often results in processes and outcomes that work against the best interests of faculty and students, or fail to assist them in realizing positive educational experiences to the extent that they might. External evaluation demands can be inconveniently timed, asking faculty to gather data quickly and hastily report findings. FL departments are often asked to collect and analyze information, make changes, and report findings to university administrators on an annual basis, ostensibly for the purposes of institution-wide self study in accreditation frameworks. In such top-down initiatives, the usefulness of evaluation findings can often become de-emphasized and geared more toward data extraction (often for compliance-related purposes). Furthermore, outside audiences may not understand the long-term nature of language learning and expect instructional programs to show unrealistically quick effects. As we know, language learning is multi-dimensional, and to form a sufficiently comprehensive view of student learning requires time and use of multiple methods.

Some projects in this volume are responding to these same impetuses, and, on the face of things, in constructive ways such that programs are effectively meeting their accountability requirements and at the same time realizing locally useful evaluation outcomes (e.g., Evansville, Linfield). However, all of the evaluators could arguably benefit from a more nuanced consideration of how their evaluation practices might best balance internally and externally driven evaluation impetuses. For projects motivated by accreditation demands, with impetuses deriving from the upper administration (e.g., Duke), one might question if evaluation will expand beyond the arguably narrow foci of accountability-related uses (e.g., learning outcomes assessment) and transform into a more sustained, ongoing, and internally motivated mode of evaluation that works toward a variety of program-internal aims (i.e., not necessarily focused on outcomes per se). Conversely, for program evaluations that are for the most part internally focused on local concerns (e.g., CSUMB, New Mexico, Johns Hopkins), it is worth asking whether evaluators in those contexts are pursuing evaluation in a way that is sufficiently mindful of and prepared for accountability-mandated demands that will ask for specific kinds of evidence.

Some of the cases reported here are suggestive of how such potentially conflicting impetuses might be managed. In the first instance, where evaluation impetuses come from beyond programs or departments, Duke shows how institutionally mandated evaluation initiatives might be taken up in locally productive ways. Their reaccreditation impetus notwithstanding, the college dean wanted evaluation and outcomes assessment to do more than just meet institutional accreditation requirements. The project was to be the start of ongoing educational improvement and to do so, the dean involved program insiders, "those who would be in the best position to establish this culture and to effect curricular improvements in language teaching at Duke" (this volume). Thus, it would seem that when evaluation is motivated from the outside, it can nevertheless be initiated in such a way that promotes inclusiveness and participation by local stakeholders, and allows for a certain control and ownership of evaluation processes and outcomes. By contrast, for projects that were motivated largely from within programs and more focused on program-internal issues in the first instance, Linfield shows how findings from locally initiated evaluation outcomes might also be used tactically to meet accreditation requirements. Internally motivated evaluation stood Linfield educators in good stead when asked to supply a self-report for accreditation purposes: "The extra work required by accreditation was minimal..." (this volume).

Of the two scenarios, we think the second delineates the more effective option, that is, using established in-house evaluation capacity to deal with external demands when they arise (Norris, 2006c). The implication is that program-internal actors should be initiating evaluation for themselves on a cyclical basis, addressing internal concerns as they arise, though with an eye toward using findings for meeting a range of needs, both program-internal and -external. We return, then, to the notion of ownership. Strong, locally owned evaluation can empower FL educators to meet external demands in proactive ways. A dedicated committee of program-internal evaluators who focus intently on program needs and work with local stakeholders can generate rich, relevant, and useful data leading to deeper understandings of program functioning and outcomes. Sustained and cyclical evaluation practice of this kind allows stakeholders to put findings toward a myriad of uses, and on soundly evidentiary bases. By so doing, effective language programs and the FL professionals that run them can mount cogent, empirical responses to outside forces that may want to hold programs and individuals to account.

Such an established local evaluation practice might resolve some of the difficulties posed by external demands in several ways. With systematic and reliable data gathering occurring regularly within an established evaluation system (e.g., consistently solicited and analyzed faculty, student, and alumni feedback; data from various outcomes assessments), sudden requests for data can be met either by drawing on existing repositories of information, or by making use of existing evaluation capacity to gather new data (e.g., modifying faculty, student, alumni surveys, or interview and focus group protocols). In situations where external audiences expect learning to occur in excessively short periods of time, multi-faceted outcomes assessment, along with consistently gathered and analyzed assessment data, allows faculty to show evidence of longitudinal language learning and persuasively argue for accurate understandings about language learning compared with learning in other disciplines (e.g., Byrnes, Maxim, & Norris, forthcoming; Norris & Pfeiffer, 2003).

It is also in FL educators' interests to be strategically aware of where internal evaluation needs and institutionally mandated pressures overlap–in particular, in the typical form of accreditation-mandated student learning outcomes assessment. U.S. institutional accreditation practices require evidence of ongoing program improvement based on periodic review of learning outcomes assessment data, and educators are often unaware of the parity between such requirements and the kinds of evaluation-type activities conscientious FL professionals are likely to undertake anyway (Norris, 2006a). The evaluative actions that we see in most cases in this volume—improvements in program functioning, curricular innovation, teacher development, development of learning outcomes and outcomes assessment—are precisely what some external audiences are interested in seeing. The Western Association of Schools and Colleges (2008), for example, requires that programs have "a fully-articulated, sustainable, multi-year assessment plan that describes when and how each outcome will be assessed and how improvements based on findings will be implemented" (p. 1). Accreditation-driven outcomes assessment thus operationalizes institutional evaluation capacity (the cyclical collection and analysis of student assessment data) as well as evaluation use (ongoing program change based on SLOs data) in a way that FL educators can well take advantage of. Indeed, such a mandate coincides with voices advocating for the proactive ownership, and "transformative potential," of outcomes assessment in FL evaluation and FL education more generally (c.f. Byrnes, 2008; Norris, 2006a). In this volume, for example, Evansville shows a way forward in that they undertook evaluation that put SLO assessment data to a number of internal and external uses, including enabling the dean to meet accreditation requirements. Focusing internal evaluation efforts on outcomes assessment, then, can go a long way toward strategically helping FL educators realize formative, as well as summative aims, a topic we take up in detail in the following section.

Finally, and more speculatively, though external requirements may emphasize extraction of information and de-emphasize usefulness, internal capacity dedicated to useful findings and internal concerns might enable FL educators to transform the demands themselves into useful evaluation practice. The CSUMB case is suggestive in this respect. Evaluators there noted how their "recently gained [evaluation] expertise" would "help make [upcoming WASC accreditation] as meaningful and useful a process as possible" (this volume). We regard this delineation of the transformative potential of locally owned evaluation a worthy aim, and in our own evaluation work we have seen programs with established use-focused evaluation systems marshal external pressures to their own purposes and translate external demands into locally useful outcomes. However, specifically how established local evaluation capacity and useful evaluation practice can transform external mandates into internally beneficial uses is as yet an open question. We see this lacking information, then, as one of a number of issues FL educators will need to know more about in order to effectively manage internal and external evaluation demands. Practical strategies from published examples of successful projects (e.g., additional instantiations of volumes such as this one) would help educators maximize their evaluation efforts and suggests the need for more research on evaluation in FL programs.

**Table 1: Strategies for balancing internal and external evaluation impetuses**

- Establish strong in-house evaluation capacity dedicated to internal uses, while strategically keeping an eye out for ways to effectively meet external needs.
- Consider focusing evaluation on student learning outcomes assessment so as to effectively meet internal as well as external (e.g., accreditation-related) demands.
- If faced with externally mandated evaluation, aim for project "ownership," or implement projects so that as many stakeholders as possible are involved in project planning and implementation.

### Balancing local and global assessment

We have noted above how outcomes assessment[2] can be a key strategy in helping FL educators meet various evaluation demands; however, we see a number of potential issues that arise should FL educators embark on evaluation projects that focus on assessment or use assessment as an evaluation methodology (mainly the generation of useless and unused assessment data). Our overall argument in this section is that an optimal approach to implementing effective student learning assessments is analogous to implementing use-focused evaluation. That is, careful thinking is needed from the outset about specifically how assessment will be used and by whom. Assessment planning that keeps use firmly in mind will help to ensure that assessment will provide meaningful, reliable, valid, and ultimately useful data for stakeholders to use in the various ways they desire.

A key concern in outcomes assessment practice is the mismatch between the assessment method and relevance of data to programs, resulting in non-useful assessment findings. In general, there is a tendency toward over-reliance on easy-to-administer and popular global assessments (e.g., proficiency testing related to the American Council on the Teaching of Foreign Languages [ACTFL] Guidelines, or commercially available inter-cultural

---

2 Note that there are many varieties of assessment uses in educational programs, including assessment for individual-level decision making such as placement and admission; for classroom-level decision making, such as using assessment for diagnosing learner needs; and for program-level decision making, like revising curricula (Norris, 2006a). Outcomes assessment may play a role at all of these levels, but we generally conceive of it as programmatic in nature, being used for taking actions at the curricular or program level. Thus, in this section, assessment refers to a systematic information gathering about SLOs that informs program-level and course-level decision making.

development instruments) along with program-external standards being adopted as program-specific outcomes. This practice becomes problematic when there is little concern for the extent to which the global assessment and/or standards align with the diverse types of learning that happen in a program or the values faculty believe the program should be about. In order not to misrepresent or devalue what learners are accomplishing in a program, while illuminating program outcomes in ways interpretable to external audiences, a balancing of local, program-dependent assessment and program-independent global assessment should be considered (Norris & Pfeiffer, 2003). To choose appropriate assessment methods for a variety of SLOs assessment purposes, the intended uses of assessment should drive methods decisions, not vice versa (Norris, 2006c, 2008).

Before jumping into the selection of assessment instruments, a utilization-focused approach seeks to clarify and prioritize the purpose and use of assessments in order to make sure that use is built in from the outset and not only considered once the data are in. Various purposes and uses of SLOs assessments may exist. In this volume, they included: to demonstrate the effectiveness of a program (summative purpose; e.g., Duke, Evansville); to understand merit, value, and distinctiveness of a program (illuminative purpose; e.g., Georgetown); to make adjustments in the target outcomes (formative purpose; e.g., Evansville, Georgetown); and to provide an opportunity for teacher development (enlightenment purposes; e.g., Duke, Georgetown). The realities of such distinct uses will affect the type of information to be collected and the ways in which it is analyzed and reported. Thus, a prioritization process should be embedded from the beginning of assessment development to acknowledge the diverse potential uses advocated by intended users, and to focus on what is most necessary.

The prioritization process also extends to deciding on which outcomes, what questions, and what information are most immediately relevant. By focusing attention on high priority outcomes, the assessment process should become feasible, practical, and meaningful to the primary intended users of assessment. The end product of this process will be a series of questions to answer, and these questions guide in turn the type of evidence needed to answer the question. As questions themselves may require multiple types of evidence to ensure confidence in the findings, it is clear that different assessment methods will be called upon to provide distinct ways of eliciting, analyzing, and reporting data (i.e., offering distinct perspectives on the story of students' knowledge, abilities, or dispositions). Primary intended users need to make an informed decision—based on the intended uses of an assessment—about which methodology is most appropriate, feasible, cost-effective, credible, and realistic for getting the information they need.

By way of example, in the Evansville case, evaluators sought a more "objective" standardized measure because they were concerned with biases inherent in locally created portfolio and oral interview assessments. Options included a simulated oral proficiency interview and the web-based DIALANG assessments. The DIALANG, a diagnostic language test, was chosen due to its no-cost availability and the fact that it is based on the Common European Framework of Reference (Council of Europe, 2001). However, evaluators found from pilot-test results that DIALANG was insufficiently informative, and thus had to seek an alternative standardized test. The point here is that use of curriculum–independent standardized tests, such as DIALANG, can serve evaluation purposes, but only when the design of the test aligns with the program-specific intended uses. Moreover, personal views and biases towards certain assessment methodologies may come into play when deciding on methods; hence, which methodology can reveal a believable and accurate picture of the language learning occurring within a program should be discussed among primary intended users of assessment. A single instrument may not be enough to provide a full picture of language and cultural learning. Thus, triangulation of data is recommended, whenever possible.

In addition, the feasibility of developing and implementing assessment instruments also constrains which methods will be appropriate. In general, faculty may prefer to use locally tailored criterion-referenced assessment tools (Brown & Hudson, 2002) that can provide directly relevant feedback on how students learn. Locally crafted assessment that is carefully aligned with intended uses and produces sufficiently trustworthy and credible results encourages faculty to use assessment findings. However, when developing a local assessment tool, FL educators need to bear in mind not to underestimate the time and resources required for developing, piloting, and revising assessment instruments. Duke evaluators, for example, initially adopted standardized intercultural competence measures, so they could take the needed time to develop course-embedded assessments over the long term. Further, using course-embedded assessment tools may constrain the interpretation of assessment data to local contexts; results often cannot be compared or transferred to contexts elsewhere. Such a limitation may not be a concern for stakeholders and users of assessment findings with strictly local needs in mind. However, should the need arise to make claims about performance to outside audiences, norm-referenced, standardized assessments (Brown, 2005) may be necessary.

The main point regarding a way forward, then, is that assessment decisions should start not from whatever is commercially or otherwise available, but instead from a careful consideration of intended use that clarifies "who will use the assessment information, to make what kinds of interpretations about learners, in order to inform what kinds of decisions or actions, to result in what consequences for whom" (Norris, 2006b). A key first issue for FL evaluators to resolve is why distinct audiences, internal as well as external, want to know about what particular kinds of learner outcomes. After all, it is the intended users who will make informed decisions based on assessment data, and unless their voices are reflected initially, data gathering will be wasted in all likelihood. We know too well that assessment that does not get used can result in negative consequences and can be detrimental for programs wanting to continue outcomes assessment and evaluation activities. To avoid such negative washback, user-focused evaluative thinking should drive assessment choices.

**Table 2: Strategies for balancing local and global assessments**

- Clarify and prioritize the purpose and use of assessment to make sure that use is built in from the outset and not only considered once the data are generated (i.e., assessment led by intended use).

- Identify distinct audiences, internal as well as external, who want to know about particular kinds of learning outcomes, and consider these needs when selecting assessment methods.

- Focus attention on high priority outcomes, so that assessment processes are feasible, practical, and meaningful to users of assessment data.

- Triangulate assessment data to reveal an accurate picture of the language learning occurring within a program.

### Becoming program evaluators: Cultivating evaluation on a professional level

Looking forward, we see that a final challenge on the future agenda is to continue cultivating evaluation on a professional level within FL programs. In many tertiary FL contexts today, evaluation is still considered a peripheral activity and not a core component of program functioning in the same way as teaching and research, nor even a common "service" element associated with faculty duties. As suggested by case studies in this volume, a key aspect of cultivating evaluation is transforming our professional identities by developing and adding a program evaluation dimension. This kind of transformation is clearly illustrated in the CSUMB, Georgetown, and New Mexico cases, where evaluators explicitly acknowledged the growing culture of evaluation in their departments. Engaging in the evaluation process and transforming professional identities toward being FL evaluators achieved a number of successes, some unanticipated. As FL educators became educator-evaluators, they took ownership of their evaluation projects, laid the foundation for communities of evaluation practice, and disseminated a culture of evaluation within their programs, departments, institutions, and beyond.

Moving forward, the push for FL educators to continue transforming their professional identities toward including program evaluation must occur on both local and national levels, with local and national trends reinforcing each other. On the local level—in FL departments and on college and university campuses—integrating evaluation into the core responsibilities of FL educators will continue to raise awareness about the wide range of evaluation uses and the importance of programmatic thinking. As evaluation takes on a more central role in FL language programs and as the benefits of useful evaluation work gain visibility on campuses, institutions will be more likely to allocate funding and release time for staff to receive training, engage in internal evaluation, and bring in outside evaluation experts to provide guidance.

Examples of local strategies for enhancing engagement in evaluation activities might include requiring participation in department evaluation projects, recognizing and rewarding faculty involvement and leadership in evaluation, or demonstrating use of evaluation in one's academic work as part of tenure and promotion review. Although the cases in this volume acknowledge the importance of evaluation as part of their intellectual agendas and on-going scholarship, few seem to promote evaluation as a core activity for all faculty. Further, to date, only a handful of published examples in FL education show evaluation promoting useful evaluative thinking, as opposed to local evaluators perfunctorily discharging duties mandated by accreditation-types of evaluation (Dassier & Powell, 2001; Mathews & Hansen, 2004).

Within departments and programs, FL educators can contribute to evaluative thinking in FL education by actually using evaluations and by acculturating new faculty into the evaluation culture early on. By leading through doing, FL educators can send a powerful message within departments, to peers, and to other institutions. Examples of leading through doing can include initiating and making visible small evaluation projects and modeling evaluative thinking and use within FL programs.

In turn, the demand for professional development and training will raise awareness and encourage the spread of FL-specific evaluation investment and attention on the national level. Increased interest in evaluation in the field of FL education will raise the demand for professional development opportunities like the summer institute that provided the foundation for many of the case studies featured in this volume. Large conferences, such as the annual ACTFL conference, as well as smaller events, such as the Association of Departments of Foreign Languages summer seminars, are among several national venues that might feature increased evaluation workshops and related professional development opportunities. Another approach to increasing support at the national level would be for FL teacher training and certification programs to add an evaluation competency component. Such commitment from professional organizations on a national level would encourage, even require, institutions and departments to invest in evaluation resources and capacity building on the local level.

However, to have a lasting impact and move the agenda forward, the handful of currently active evaluators in FL education would do well to committing themselves to awareness-raising about FL evaluation, not only in familiar local circles but also in larger evaluation contexts like the American Evaluation Association (AEA) and American Educational Research Association (AERA). Of the over forty topical interest groups (TIGs) in the AEA, not one is devoted to program evaluators in language education. Similarly, none of the fifteen special interest groups (SIGs) in ACTFL currently address issues of evaluation in FL education. Such strategies should bring together a greater variety of people involved in FL program evaluation in a space dedicated to exchanging ideas, building resources, and developing peer support. In our increasingly connected world, raising the profile of FL evaluation will necessarily include greater networking and communication through list-serves, on-line communities, and topical and special interest groups in national organizations like the AEA, AERA, and ACTFL. By taking many small local steps at our own institutions and contributing to the national evaluation and education agenda, FL educators can work together to increase recognition of the importance of FL evaluation and its critical role in understanding and improving FL education.

**Table 3: Strategies for cultivating evaluation on a professional level**

- Make evaluation a core component of program functioning.

- Push for FL communities to include evaluation on national and local levels.

- Focus attention on high priority outcomes, so that assessment processes are feasible, practical, and meaningful to users of assessment data.

- Raise awareness about FL evaluation in the larger evaluation community.

*Acknowledgements*
We would like to thank Dr. John Norris for his helpful suggestions, constructive comments, and encouragement throughout the writing of this chapter.

# References

Brown, J. D. (2005). *Testing in language programs: A comprehensive guide to English language assessment* (2nd ed.). New York: McGraw-Hill.

Brown, J. D., & Hudson, T. (2002). *Criterion-referenced language testing.* New York: Cambridge University Press.

Byrnes, H. (2008). Owning up to ownership of foreign language program outcomes assessment. *ADFL Bulletin, 39*(2–3), 28–30.

Byrnes, H., Maxim, H., & Norris, J. M. (forthcoming). Realizing advanced FL writing development in collegiate education: Curricular design, pedagogy, assessment. *Modern Language Journal*, Monograph. Cambridge: Blackwell.

Council of Europe (2001). *Common European framework of reference for languages: Learning, teaching, assessment.* Strasbourg: Author.

Cousins, J. B., & Earl, L. M. (1995). The case for participatory evaluation. *Educational Evaluation and Policy Analysis, 14*(4), 397–418.

Dassier, J. P., & Powell, W. (2001). Formative foreign language program evaluation: Dare to find out how good you really are. *Dimension 2001: The odyssey continues. Selected proceedings of the 2001 Conference of the Southern Conference on Language Teaching,* Birmingham, AL, 15–30.

Mackay, R., Wellesley, S., & Bazergan, E. (1995). Participatory evaluation. *ELT Journal, 49*(4), 308–317.

Mathews, T., J., & Hansen, C., M. (2004). Ongoing assessment of a university foreign language program. *Foreign Language Annals, 37*(4), 630–640.

Norris, J. M. (2006a). Assessing foreign language learning and learners: From measurement constructs to educational uses. In H. Byrnes, H. Weger-Guntharp & K. Sprang (Eds.), *GURT 2005: Educating for advanced foreign language capacities: Constructs, curriculum, instruction, assessment* (pp. 167–187). Washington, DC: Georgetown University Press.

Norris, J. M. (2006b, November). *The transformative potential of assessment in college foreign language education.* Paper presented at the American Association of Teachers of German/American Council on the Teacher of Foreign Languages annual meeting, Nashville, TN.

Norris, J. M. (2006c). The why (and how) of student learning outcomes assessment in college FL education. *Modern Language Journal, 90*(4), 576–583.

Norris, J. M. (2008). *Validity evaluation in language assessment.* New York: Peter Lang.

Norris, J. M. (2009). Understanding and improving language education through program evaluation: Introduction to the special issue. *Language Teaching Research, 13*(1), 469–475.

Norris, J. M., & Pfeiffer, P. (2003). Exploring the uses and usefulness of ACTFL oral proficiency ratings and standards in college foreign language departments. *Foreign Language Annals, 36*(4), 572–581.

Patton, M. Q. (1997). *Utilization-focused evaluation: The new century text* (3rd ed.). Thousand Oaks, CA: Sage.

Patton, M. Q. (2005). Utilization-focused evaluation. In S. Mathison (Ed.), *Encyclopedia of evaluation* (pp. 429–432). Thousand Oaks, CA: Sage.

Patton, M. Q. (2008). *Utilization-focused evaluation* (4th ed.). Thousand Oaks, CA: Sage.

The Joint Committee on Standards for Educational Evaluation. (1994). *The program evaluation standards: How to assess evaluations of educational programs* (2nd ed.). Thousand Oaks, CA: Sage.

Western Association of Schools and Colleges (2008). *Program learning outcomes: Rubric for assessing the quality of academic program learning outcomes.* Retrieved from http://www.wascsenior.org/findit/files/forms/Program_Learning_Outcome_Rubric__080430_.pdf

Zannirato, A. (2008, January 22). Postdoctoral fellowship opportunity. Message posted to the Foreign Language Program Evaluation Discussion list, progeval-l@hawaii.edu.

# About the Contributors

## Editors

**John McE. Davis** is a Ph.D. student in the Department of Second Language Studies at the University of Hawai'i at Mānoa and a research assistant with the Foreign Language Program Evaluation Project. His research interests are in language program evaluation and multilingualism and identity. He has published research on second language pragmatics and resistance in study abroad contexts.

**John M. Norris** is an associate professor in the Department of Second Language Studies at the University of Hawai'i at Mānoa. His research focuses on assessment, evaluation, and pedagogy in second and foreign language programs and in higher education. His recent books explore the topics of task-based language teaching (*Task-based language teaching: A reader*, 2009) validation (*Validity evaluation in language assessment*, 2008), and research synthesis (*Synthesizing research on language learning and teaching*, 2006).

**Castle Sinicrope** is a research analyst at Berkeley Policy Associates in Oakland, CA, and a graduate of the Master's program in the Department of Second Language Studies at the University of Hawai'i at Mānoa. She currently works in research and evaluation in education, focusing on program implementation and outcomes.

**Yukiko Watanabe** is a Ph.D. student in the Second Language Studies Department at the University of Hawai'i at Mānoa. She has extensive experience coordinating, facilitating, and conducting utilization-focused program evaluation in various educational contexts including Japanese high school EFL programs, Japanese college information literacy programs, and U.S. college foreign language programs. Her dissertation research highlights the impact of program evaluation (in particular, student learning outcomes assessment) on organizational learning and student learning in college foreign language education.

## Authors

**Heidi Byrnes** is George M. Roth Distinguished Professor of German at Georgetown University. Recent co-edited and edited volumes addressing her interest in advanced levels of ability in a foreign language are *Educating for advanced foreign language capacities: Constructs, curriculum, instruction, assessment* (2006); *Advanced language learning: The contribution of Halliday and Vygotsky* (2006); and *The longitudinal study of advanced L2 capacities* (2008).

**Rafael Gómez** is a professor of Spanish at California State University, Monterey Bay and the resident director of international programs in Spain. His research focuses on language pedagogy, study abroad, and Latin American Culture. He is a co-author of Rumbos (2009), an intermediate-level Spanish textbook and the author of *Mexican immigration and the question of identity in the United States* (2007) and *El trabajador inmigrante mexicano en el mercado laboral de los Estados Unidos* (2007).

**Marta González-Lloret** is an assistant professor in the Spanish Division at the University of Hawai'i at Mānoa. Her areas of interest include development and evaluation of foreign language programs, especially task-based language programs, and the application of new technologies to pedagogy and assessment. Her recent publications have explored online and hybridized course delivery in foreign language education.

**Antonio Grau Sempere** is an assistant professor of Spanish at the University of Evansville. His research focuses on Ibero-Romance prosodic morphology. His articles explore the topic of conflicting quantity patterns in Portuguese (*(In)sensibilidad a la cantidad silábica en la prosodia portuguesa*, 2006) and Catalan (*Conflicting quantity patterns in Valencian Catalan prosody*, 2008).

**Frauke Loewensen** (M.A., M.B.A.) is a Spanish instructor at the School of World Languages & Cultures at California State University, Monterey Bay. She has taught foreign languages (including Spanish, French, German, and ESL/EFL) at various institutions, among them Amherst College, Indiana University, Leeward and Kapiolani Community Colleges, the University of Hawai'i, the Alliance Française, and the Monterey Institute of International Studies. Her professional interests include foreign language pedagogy and online learning.

**Margo Milleret** is associate professor of Portuguese and Spanish at the University of New Mexico. She has dual scholarly and teaching interests in Latin American theater, and pedagogy/foreign language program development. She has published *Latin American Women On/In Stages* (2004) and articles on Brazilian theater, teaching speech acts, and Brazilian culture, and on Portuguese program development and evaluation.

**M. Chris Mohn** is an assistant professor of Spanish at the University of Evansville, where she teaches all levels of language and literature. Her research focuses on 20th and 21st century peninsular narrative, in particular the works of the contemporary Spanish author Álvaro Pombo.

**Peter C. Pfeiffer** is professor and former chair of the German Department at Georgetown University. He has published on Robert Musil, Thomas Mann, and Theodor Fontane, among others. His latest book is *Marie von Ebner-Eschenbach: Tragödie, Erzählung, Heimatfilm* (2008). He has worked extensively and published on projects in academic administration, especially graduate education, curriculum, and assessment.

**Roger Pieroni** is associate professor of French and chair of the Department of Foreign Languages at the University of Evansville. His current research interests include the poetic novel and the Vietnamese colonial novel written in French. He has published articles on francophone writers Andrée Chedid and Sony Labou Tansi, and he is an English>French ATA certified translator.

**Violeta Ramsay** is associate professor of Spanish and former chair of the Department of Modern Languages at Linfield College. Her research centers on learning, second language acquisition, and the teaching of culture. Her latest articles are critiques on the design of foreign language textbooks.

**Loreto Sánchez-Serrano**, Ph.D., is director of the Spanish Language Program in the Department of German and Romance Languages and Literatures at Johns Hopkins University. She specializes in foreign language teaching with a particular focus on CALL materials and online teaching and learning. She also serves as content expert at University of Maryland University College where she develops online Spanish language courses. She was awarded the Peterson's Award in Innovative Distance Education and an E-Learning Design Honorable Mention for Excellence in Online Instructional Design.

**Agripino S. Silveira's** research focuses on language change, subjectivity, and usage-based linguistics as seen in his latest article on the subjectification of discourse markers. He is currently working on his Ph.D. dissertation s. He has also worked as a supervisor for the Portuguese program at the University of New Mexico and an ESL and Portuguese instructor at UNM and other institutions.

**Ingeborg C. Walther** is associate professor of the practice and former chair of the German Department at Duke University, where she currently serves as associate dean of the college. Her research interests include German theater, second language acquisition, and foreign language pedagogy. She has published a monograph on the theater of Franz Xaver Kroetz, and articles on curriculum development, theories of language acquisition, and approaches to teaching German language, culture, and literature at the college level.

**Alessandro Zannirato** is a senior lecturer and director of the Italian Language Program in the Department of German and Romance Languages and Literatures at the Johns Hopkins University. His publications and research interests reflect his background in both applied linguistics and conference interpreting. He has worked as a foreign language instructor, teacher trainer, technical translator, and conference interpreter for various institutions in Africa, Europe, and North America.

# NATIONAL FOREIGN LANGUAGE RESOURCE CENTER
University of Hawai'i at Mānoa

*ordering information at nflrc.hawaii.edu*

## Pragmatics & Interaction
*Gabriele Kasper, series editor*

Pragmatics & Interaction ("P&I"), a refereed series sponsored by the University of Hawai'i National Foreign Language Resource Center, publishes research on topics in pragmatics and discourse as social interaction from a wide variety of theoretical and methodological perspectives. P&I welcomes particularly studies on languages spoken in the Asian-Pacific region.

### TALK-IN-INTERACTION: MULTILINGUAL PERSPECTIVES
KATHLEEN BARDOVI-HARLIG, CÉSAR FÉLIX-BRASDEFER, & ALWIYA S. OMAR (EDITORS), 2006

This volume offers original studies of interaction in a range of languages and language varieties, including Chinese, English, Japanese, Korean, Spanish, Swahili, Thai, and Vietnamese; monolingual and bilingual interactions, and activities designed for second or foreign language learning. Conducted from the perspectives of conversation analysis and membership categorization analysis, the chapters examine ordinary conversation and institutional activities in face-to-face, telephone, and computer-mediated environments..

430 pp., ISBN(10): 0–8248–3137–3, ISBN(13): 978–0–8248–3137–0      $30.

## Pragmatics & Language Learning
*Gabriele Kasper, series editor*

Pragmatics & Language Learning ("PLL"), a refereed series sponsored by the National Foreign Language Resource Center, publishes selected papers from the biannual International Pragmatics & Language Learning conference under the editorship of the conference hosts and the series editor. Check the NFLRC website for upcoming PLL conferences and PLL volumes.

### PRAGMATICS AND LANGUAGE LEARNING VOLUME 11
KATHLEEN BARDOVI-HARLIG, CÉSAR FÉLIX-BRASDEFER, & ALWIYA S. OMAR (EDITORS), 2006

This volume features cutting-edge theoretical and empirical research on pragmatics and language learning among a wide-variety of learners in diverse learning contexts from a variety of language backgrounds (English, German, Japanese, Persian, and Spanish) and target languages (English, German, Japanese, Kiswahili, and Spanish). This collection of papers from researchers around the world includes critical appraisals on the role of formulas in interlanguage pragmatics and speech-act research from a conversation-analytic perspective. Empirical studies examine learner data using innovative methods of analysis and investigate issues in pragmatic development and the instruction of pragmatics.

430 pp., ISBN(10): 0–8248–3137–3, ISBN(13): 978–0–8248–3137–0     $30.

# NFLRC Monographs
*Richard Schmidt, series editor*

Monographs of the National Foreign Language Resource Center present the findings of recent work in applied linguistics that is of relevance to language teaching and learning (with a focus on the less commonly-taught languages of Asia and the Pacific) and are of particular interest to foreign language educators, applied linguists, and researchers. Prior to 2006, these monographs were published as "SLTCC Technical Reports."

### SECOND LANGUAGE TEACHING AND LEARNING IN THE NET GENERATION
RAQUEL OXFORD & JEFFREY OXFORD (EDITORS), 2009

Today's young people—the Net Generation—have grown up with technology all around them. However, teachers cannot assume that students' familiarity with technology in general transfers successfully to pedagogical settings. This volume examines various technologies and offers concrete advice on how each can be successfully implemented in the second language curriculum.

240pp., ISBN 978–0–9800459–2–5     $30.

### CASE STUDIES IN FOREIGN LANGUAGE PLACEMENT: PRACTICES AND POSSIBILITIES
THOM HUDSON & MARTYN CLARK (EDITORS), 2008

Although most language programs make placement decisions on the basis of placement tests, there is surprisingly little published about different contexts and systems of placement testing. The present volume contains case studies of placement programs in foreign language programs at the tertiary level across the United States. The different programs span the spectrum from large programs servicing hundreds of students annually to small language programs with very few students. The contributions to this volume address such issues as how the size of the program, presence or absence of heritage learners, and population changes affect language placement decisions.

201pp., ISBN 978–0–9800459–0–1     $40.

### CHINESE AS A HERITAGE LANGUAGE: FOSTERING ROOTED WORLD CITIZENRY
AGNES WEIYUN HE & YUN XIAO (EDITORS), 2008

Thirty-two scholars examine the socio-cultural, cognitive-linguistic, and educational-institutional trajectories along which Chinese as a Heritage Language may be acquired, maintained and developed. They draw upon developmental psychology, functional linguistics, linguistic and cultural anthropology, discourse analysis, orthography analysis, reading research, second language acquisition, and bilingualism. This volume aims to lay a foundation for theories, models, and master scripts to be discussed, debated, and developed, and to stimulate research and enhance teaching both within and beyond Chinese language education.

280pp., ISBN 978–08248–3286–5     $40.

## PERSPECTIVES ON TEACHING CONNECTED SPEECH TO SECOND LANGUAGE SPEAKERS
JAMES DEAN BROWN & KIMI KONDO-BROWN (EDITORS), 2006

This book is a collection of fourteen articles on connected speech of interest to teachers, researchers, and materials developers in both ESL/EFL (ten chapters focus on connected speech in English) and Japanese (four chapters focus on Japanese connected speech). The fourteen chapters are divided up into five sections:

- What do we know so far about teaching connected speech?
- Does connected speech instruction work?
- How should connected speech be taught in English?
- How should connected speech be taught in Japanese?
- How should connected speech be tested?

290 pp., ISBN(10) 0–8248–3136–5, ISBN(13) 978–0–8248–3136–3 $38.

## CORPUS LINGUISTICS FOR KOREAN LANGUAGE LEARNING AND TEACHING
ROBERT BLEY-VROMAN & HYUNSOOK KO (EDITORS), 2006

Dramatic advances in personal-computer technology have given language teachers access to vast quantities of machine-readable text, which can be analyzed with a view toward improving the basis of language instruction. Corpus linguistics provides analytic techniques and practical tools for studying language in use. This volume provides both an introductory framework for the use of corpus linguistics for language teaching and examples of its application for Korean teaching and learning. The collected papers cover topics in Korean syntax, lexicon, and discourse, and second language acquisition research, always with a focus on application in the classroom. An overview of Korean corpus linguistics tools and available Korean corpora are also included.

265 pp., ISBN 0–8248–3062–8 $25.

## NEW TECHNOLOGIES AND LANGUAGE LEARNING: CASES IN THE LESS COMMONLY TAUGHT LANGUAGES
CAROL ANNE SPREEN (EDITOR), 2002

In recent years, the National Security Education Program (NSEP) has supported an increasing number of programs for teaching languages using different technological media. This compilation of case study initiatives funded through the NSEP Institutional Grants Program presents a range of technology-based options for language programming that will help universities make more informed decisions about teaching less commonly taught languages. The eight chapters describe how different types of technologies are used to support language programs (i.e., Web, ITV, and audio- or video-based materials), discuss identifiable trends in elanguage learning, and explore how technology addresses issues of equity, diversity, and opportunity. This book offers many lessons learned and decisions made as technology changes and learning needs become more complex.

188 pp., ISBN 0–8248–2634–5 $25.

## AN INVESTIGATION OF SECOND LANGUAGE TASK-BASED PERFORMANCE ASSESSMENTS
JAMES DEAN BROWN, THOM HUDSON, JOHN M. NORRIS, & WILLIAM BONK, 2002

This volume describes the creation of performance assessment instruments and their validation (based on work started in a previous monograph). It begins by explaining the test and rating scale development processes and the administration of the resulting three seven-task tests to 90 university level EFL and ESL students. The results are examined in terms of (a) the effects of test revision; (b) comparisons among the task-dependent, task-independent, and self-rating scales; and (c) reliability and validity issues.

240 pp., ISBN 0–8248–2633–7 $25.

## MOTIVATION AND SECOND LANGUAGE ACQUISITION
Zoltán Dörnyei & Richard Schmidt (Editors), 2001

This volume—the second in this series concerned with motivation and foreign language learning—includes papers presented in a state-of-the-art colloquium on L2 motivation at the American Association for Applied Linguistics (Vancouver, 2000) and a number of specially commissioned studies. The 20 chapters, written by some of the best known researchers in the field, cover a wide range of theoretical and research methodological issues, and also offer empirical results (both qualitative and quantitative) concerning the learning of many different languages (Arabic, Chinese, English, Filipino, French, German, Hindi, Italian, Japanese, Russian, and Spanish) in a broad range of learning contexts (Bahrain, Brazil, Canada, Egypt, Finland, Hungary, Ireland, Israel, Japan, Spain, and the US).

520 pp., ISBN 0–8248–2458–X $25.

## A FOCUS ON LANGUAGE TEST DEVELOPMENT: EXPANDING THE LANGUAGE PROFICIENCY CONSTRUCT ACROSS A VARIETY OF TESTS
Thom Hudson & James Dean Brown (Editors), 2001

This volume presents eight research studies that introduce a variety of novel, non-traditional forms of second and foreign language assessment. To the extent possible, the studies also show the entire test development process, warts and all. These language testing projects not only demonstrate many of the types of problems that test developers run into in the real world but also afford the reader unique insights into the language test development process.

230 pp., ISBN 0–8248–2351–6 $20.

## STUDIES ON KOREAN IN COMMUNITY SCHOOLS
Dong-Jae Lee, Sookeun Cho, Miseon Lee, Minsun Song, & William O'Grady (Editors), 2000

The papers in this volume focus on language teaching and learning in Korean community schools. Drawing on innovative experimental work and research in linguistics, education, and psychology, the contributors address issues of importance to teachers, administrators, and parents. Topics covered include childhood bilingualism, Korean grammar, language acquisition, children's literature, and language teaching methodology. [in Korean]

256 pp., ISBN 0–8248–2352–4 $20.

## A COMMUNICATIVE FRAMEWORK FOR INTRODUCTORY JAPANESE LANGUAGE CURRICULA
Washington State Japanese Language Curriculum Guidelines Committee, 2000

In recent years the number of schools offering Japanese nationwide has increased dramatically. Because of the tremendous popularity of the Japanese language and the shortage of teachers, quite a few untrained, non-native and native teachers are in the classrooms and are expected to teach several levels of Japanese. These guidelines are intended to assist individual teachers and professional associations throughout the United States in designing Japanese language curricula. They are meant to serve as a framework from which language teaching can be expanded and are intended to allow teachers to enhance and strengthen the quality of Japanese language instruction.

168 pp., ISBN 0–8248–2350–8 $20.

## FOREIGN LANGUAGE TEACHING AND MINORITY LANGUAGE EDUCATION
Kathryn A. Davis (Editor), 1999

This volume seeks to examine the potential for building relationships among foreign language, bilingual, and ESL programs towards fostering bilingualism. Part I of the volume examines the sociopolitical contexts for language partnerships, including:

- obstacles to developing bilingualism
- implications of acculturation, identity, and language issues for linguistic minorities.
- the potential for developing partnerships across primary, secondary, and tertiary institutions

Part II of the volume provides research findings on the Foreign language partnership project designed to capitalize on the resources of immigrant students to enhance foreign language learning.

152 pp., ISBN 0–8248–2067–3 $20.

## DESIGNING SECOND LANGUAGE PERFORMANCE ASSESSMENTS
John M. Norris, James Dean Brown, Thom Hudson, & Jim Yoshioka, 1998, 2000

This technical report focuses on the decision-making potential provided by second language performance assessments. The authors first situate performance assessment within a broader discussion of alternatives in language assessment and in educational assessment in general. They then discuss issues in performance assessment design, implementation, reliability, and validity. Finally, they present a prototype framework for second language performance assessment based on the integration of theoretical underpinnings and research findings from the task-based language teaching literature, the language testing literature, and the educational measurement literature. The authors outline test and item specifications, and they present numerous examples of prototypical language tasks. They also propose a research agenda focusing on the operationalization of second language performance assessments.

248 pp., ISBN 0–8248–2109–2 $20.

## SECOND LANGUAGE DEVELOPMENT IN WRITING: MEASURES OF FLUENCY, ACCURACY, AND COMPLEXITY
Kate Wolfe-Quintero, Shunji Inagaki, & Hae-Young Kim, 1998, 2002

In this book, the authors analyze and compare the ways that fluency, accuracy, grammatical complexity, and lexical complexity have been measured in studies of language development in second language writing. More than 100 developmental measures are examined, with detailed comparisons of the results across the studies that have used each measure. The authors discuss the theoretical foundations for each type of developmental measure, and they consider the relationship between developmental measures and various types of proficiency measures. They also examine criteria for determining which developmental measures are the most successful and suggest which measures are the most promising for continuing work on language development.

208 pp., ISBN 0–8248–2069–X $20.

## THE DEVELOPMENT OF A LEXICAL TONE PHONOLOGY IN AMERICAN ADULT LEARNERS OF STANDARD MANDARIN CHINESE
Sylvia Henel Sun, 1998

The study reported is based on an assessment of three decades of research on the SLA of Mandarin tone. It investigates whether differences in learners' tone perception and production are related to differences in the effects of certain linguistic, task, and learner factors. The learners of focus are American students of Mandarin in Beijing, China. Their performances on two perception and three production tasks are analyzed through a host of variables and methods of quantification.

328 pp., ISBN 0–8248–2068–1 $20.

## NEW TRENDS AND ISSUES IN TEACHING JAPANESE LANGUAGE AND CULTURE
HARUKO M. COOK, KYOKO HIJIRIDA, & MILDRED TAHARA (EDITORS), 1997

In recent years, Japanese has become the fourth most commonly taught foreign language at the college level in the United States. As the number of students who study Japanese has increased, the teaching of Japanese as a foreign language has been established as an important academic field of study. This technical report includes nine contributions to the advancement of this field, encompassing the following five important issues:

- Literature and literature teaching
- Technology in the language classroom
- Orthography
- Testing
- Grammatical versus pragmatic approaches to language teaching

164 pp., ISBN 0–8248–2067–3 $20.

## SIX MEASURES OF JSL PRAGMATICS
SAYOKO OKADA YAMASHITA, 1996

This book investigates differences among tests that can be used to measure the cross-cultural pragmatic ability of English-speaking learners of Japanese. Building on the work of Hudson, Detmer, and Brown (Technical Reports #2 and #7 in this series), the author modified six test types that she used to gather data from North American learners of Japanese. She found numerous problems with the multiple-choice discourse completion test but reported that the other five tests all proved highly reliable and reasonably valid. Practical issues involved in creating and using such language tests are discussed from a variety of perspectives.

213 pp., ISBN 0–8248–1914–4 $15.

## LANGUAGE LEARNING STRATEGIES AROUND THE WORLD: CROSS-CULTURAL PERSPECTIVES
REBECCA L. OXFORD (EDITOR), 1996, 1997, 2002

Language learning strategies are the specific steps students take to improve their progress in learning a second or foreign language. Optimizing learning strategies improves language performance. This groundbreaking book presents new information about cultural influences on the use of language learning strategies. It also shows innovative ways to assess students' strategy use and remarkable techniques for helping students improve their choice of strategies, with the goal of peak language learning.

166 pp., ISBN 0–8248–1910–1 $20.

## TELECOLLABORATION IN FOREIGN LANGUAGE LEARNING: PROCEEDINGS OF THE HAWAI'I SYMPOSIUM
MARK WARSCHAUER (EDITOR), 1996

The Symposium on Local & Global Electronic Networking in Foreign Language Learning & Research, part of the National Foreign Language Resource Center's 1995 Summer Institute on Technology & the Human Factor in Foreign Language Education, included presentations of papers and hands-on workshops conducted by Symposium participants to facilitate the sharing of resources, ideas, and information about all aspects of electronic networking for foreign language teaching and research, including electronic discussion and conferencing, international cultural exchanges, real-time communication and simulations, research and resource retrieval via the Internet, and research using networks. This collection presents a sampling of those presentations.

252 pp., ISBN 0–8248–1867–9 $20.

## LANGUAGE LEARNING MOTIVATION: PATHWAYS TO THE NEW CENTURY
REBECCA L. OXFORD (EDITOR), 1996

This volume chronicles a revolution in our thinking about what makes students want to learn languages and what causes them to persist in that difficult and rewarding adventure. Topics in this book include the internal structures of and external connections with foreign language motivation; exploring adult language learning motivation, self-efficacy, and anxiety; comparing the motivations and learning strategies of students of Japanese and Spanish; and enhancing the theory of language learning motivation from many psychological and social perspectives.

218 pp., ISBN 0–8248–1849–0 $20.

## LINGUISTICS & LANGUAGE TEACHING: PROCEEDINGS OF THE SIXTH JOINT LSH-HATESL CONFERENCE
CYNTHIA REVES, CAROLINE STEELE, & CATHY S. P. WONG (EDITORS), 1996

Technical Report #10 contains 18 articles revolving around the following three topics:

- Linguistic issues—These six papers discuss various linguistic issues: ideophones, syllabic nasals, linguistic areas, computation, tonal melody classification, and wh-words.
- Sociolinguistics—Sociolinguistic phenomena in Swahili, signing, Hawaiian, and Japanese are discussed in four of the papers.
- Language teaching and learning—These eight papers cover prosodic modification, note taking, planning in oral production, oral testing, language policy, L2 essay organization, access to dative alternation rules, and child noun phrase structure development.

364 pp., ISBN 0–8248–1851–2 $20.

## ATTENTION & AWARENESS IN FOREIGN LANGUAGE LEARNING
RICHARD SCHMIDT (EDITOR), 1996

Issues related to the role of attention and awareness in learning lie at the heart of many theoretical and practical controversies in the foreign language field. This collection of papers presents research into the learning of Spanish, Japanese, Finnish, Hawaiian, and English as a second language (with additional comments and examples from French, German, and miniature artificial languages) that bear on these crucial questions for foreign language pedagogy.

394 pp., ISBN 0–8248–1794–X $20.

## VIRTUAL CONNECTIONS: ONLINE ACTIVITIES AND PROJECTS FOR NETWORKING LANGUAGE LEARNERS
MARK WARSCHAUER (EDITOR), 1995, 1996

Computer networking has created dramatic new possibilities for connecting language learners in a single classroom or across the globe. This collection of activities and projects makes use of email, the internet, computer conferencing, and other forms of computer-mediated communication for the foreign and second language classroom at any level of instruction. Teachers from around the world submitted the activities compiled in this volume—activities that they have used successfully in their own classrooms.

417 pp., ISBN 0–8248–1793–1 $30.

## DEVELOPING PROTOTYPIC MEASURES OF CROSS-CULTURAL PRAGMATICS
THOM HUDSON, EMILY DETMER, & J. D. BROWN, 1995

Although the study of cross-cultural pragmatics has gained importance in applied linguistics, there are no standard forms of assessment that might make research comparable across studies and languages. The present volume describes the process through which six forms of cross-cultural assessment were developed for second language learners of English. The models may be used for second language learners of other languages. The six forms of assessment involve two forms each of indirect discourse completion tests, oral language production, and self-assessment. The procedures involve the assessment of requests, apologies, and refusals.

198 pp., ISBN 0-8248-1763-X                $15.

## THE ROLE OF PHONOLOGICAL CODING IN READING KANJI
SACHIKO MATSUNAGA, 1995

In this technical report, the author reports the results of a study that she conducted on phonological coding in reading kanji using an eye-movement monitor and draws some pedagogical implications. In addition, she reviews current literature on the different schools of thought regarding instruction in reading kanji and its role in the teaching of non-alphabetic written languages like Japanese.

64 pp., ISBN 0-8248-1734-6                $10.

## PRAGMATICS OF CHINESE AS NATIVE AND TARGET LANGUAGE
GABRIELE KASPER (EDITOR), 1995

This technical report includes six contributions to the study of the pragmatics of Mandarin Chinese:

- A report of an interview study conducted with nonnative speakers of Chinese; and
- Five data-based studies on the performance of different speech acts by native speakers of Mandarin—requesting, refusing, complaining, giving bad news, disagreeing, and complimenting.

312 pp., ISBN 0-8248-1733-8                $15.

## A BIBLIOGRAPHY OF PEDAGOGY AND RESEARCH IN INTERPRETATION AND TRANSLATION
ETILVIA ARJONA, 1993

This technical report includes four types of bibliographic information on translation and interpretation studies:

- Research efforts across disciplinary boundaries—cognitive psychology, neurolinguistics, psycholinguistics, sociolinguistics, computational linguistics, measurement, aptitude testing, language policy, decision-making, theses, dissertations;
- Training information covering program design, curriculum studies, instruction, school administration;
- Instruction information detailing course syllabi, methodology, models, available textbooks; and
- Testing information about aptitude, selection, diagnostic tests.

115 pp., ISBN 0-8248-1572-6                $10.

## PRAGMATICS OF JAPANESE AS NATIVE AND TARGET LANGUAGE
Gabriele Kasper (Editor), 1992, 1996

This technical report includes three contributions to the study of the pragmatics of Japanese:
- A bibliography on speech act performance, discourse management, and other pragmatic and sociolinguistic features of Japanese;
- A study on introspective methods in examining Japanese learners' performance of refusals; and
- A longitudinal investigation of the acquisition of the particle ne by nonnative speakers of Japanese.

125 pp., ISBN 0–8248–1462–2 $10.

## A FRAMEWORK FOR TESTING CROSS-CULTURAL PRAGMATICS
Thom Hudson, Emily Detmer, & J. D. Brown, 1992

This technical report presents a framework for developing methods that assess cross-cultural pragmatic ability. Although the framework has been designed for Japanese and American cross-cultural contrasts, it can serve as a generic approach that can be applied to other language contrasts. The focus is on the variables of social distance, relative power, and the degree of imposition within the speech acts of requests, refusals, and apologies. Evaluation of performance is based on recognition of the speech act, amount of speech, forms or formulæ used, directness, formality, and politeness.

51 pp., ISBN 0–8248–1463–0 $10.

## RESEARCH METHODS IN INTERLANGUAGE PRAGMATICS
Gabriele Kasper & Merete Dahl, 1991

This technical report reviews the methods of data collection employed in 39 studies of interlanguage pragmatics, defined narrowly as the investigation of nonnative speakers' comprehension and production of speech acts, and the acquisition of L2-related speech act knowledge. Data collection instruments are distinguished according to the degree to which they constrain informants' responses, and whether they tap speech act perception/comprehension or production. A main focus of discussion is the validity of different types of data, in particular their adequacy to approximate authentic performance of linguistic action.

51 pp., ISBN 0–8248–1419–3 $10.

www.ingramcontent.com/pod-product-compliance
Lightning Source LLC
Chambersburg PA
CBHW080547230426
43663CB00015B/2745